Reference Sources on the Internet: Off the Shelf and Onto the Web

Forthcoming topics in *The Reference Librarian* series:

• Business Reference Services and Sources: How End Users and Librarians Work Together, Number 58

Published:

Reference Services in the 1980s, Numbers 1/2
Reference Services Administration and Management, Number 3
Ethics and Reference Services, Number 4
Video to Online: Reference Services and the New Technology, Numbers 5/6
Reference Services for Children and Young Adults, Numbers 7/8
Reference Services and Technical Services: Interactions in Library Practice, Number 9
Library Instruction and Reference Services, Number 10
Evaluation of Reference Services, Number 11
Conflicts in Reference Services, Number 12
Reference Services in Archives, Number 13
Personnel Issues in Reference Services, Number 14
The Publishing and Review of Reference Sources, Number 15
Reference Services Today: From Interview to Burnout, Number 16
International Aspects of Reference and Information Services, Number 17
Current Trends in Information: Research and Theory, Number 18
Finance, Budget, and Management for Reference Services, Number 19
Reference Services and Public Policy, Number 20
Information and Referral in Reference Services, Number 21
Information Brokers and Reference Services, Number 22
Expert Systems in Reference Services, Number 23
Integrating Library Use Skills into the General Education Curriculum, Number 24
Rothstein on Reference . . . with some help from friends, Numbers 25/26
Serials and Reference Services, Numbers 27/28
Weeding and Maintenance of Reference Collections, Number 29
Continuing Education of Reference Librarians, Number 30
The Reference Library User: Problems and Solutions, Number 31
Government Documents and Reference Services, Number 32
Opportunities for Reference Services: The Bright Side of Reference Services in the 1990's, Number 33
Access Services: The Convergence of Reference and Technical Services, Number 34
In the Spirit of 1992: Access to Western European Libraries and Literature, Number 35
Library Services for Career Planning, Job Searching, and Employment Opportunities, Number 36
The Reference Librarian and Implications of Mediation, Number 37
Assessment and Accountability in Reference Work, Number 38
Modern Library Technology and Reference Services, Number 39
Reference Service Expertise, Number 40

Librarians on the Internet: Impact on Reference Services, Numbers 41/42

References Services Planning in the 90s, Number 43

School Library Reference Services in the 90s: Where We Are,
    Where We're Heading, Number 44

Racial and Ethnic Diversity in Academic Libraries: Multicultural Issues, Numbers 45/46

Reference Services in the Humanities, Number 47

Social Science Reference Services, Number 48

Library Users and Reference Services, Numbers 49/50

Library Instruction Revisited: Bibliographic Instruction Comes of Age,
    Numbers 51/52

Reference Services for the Unserved, Number 53

The Roles of Reference Librarians: Today and Tomorrow, Number 54

Career Planning and Job Searching in the Information Age, Number 55

Reference Services for Archives and Manuscripts, Number 56

Reference Sources on the Internet: Off the Shelf and Onto the Web, Number 57

References Sources on the Internet: Off the Shelf and Onto the Web has been co-published simultaneously as *The Reference Librarian*, Number 57 1997.

Cover design by Thomas J. Mayshock Jr.

The Haworth Press, Inc., 10 Alice Street, Binghamton, NY 13904-1580 USA

Library of Congress Cataloging-in-Publication Data

Reference sources on the Internet : off the shelf and onto the Web / Karen R. Diaz, editor.
    p. cm.
    Includes bibliographical references (p.) and index.
    ISBN 0-7890-0358-9
    1. Web sites. 2. Electronic reference sources. I. Diaz, Karen R.
ZA4226.R44 1997
025.04–dc21   97-28052
                                                                    CIP

Reference Sources on the Internet: Off the Shelf and Onto the Web

Karen R. Diaz
Editor

The Haworth Press, Inc.
New York • London

INDEXING & ABSTRACTING

Contributions to this publication are selectively indexed or abstracted in print, electronic, online, or CD-ROM version(s) of the reference tools and information services listed below. This list is current as of the copyright date of this publication. See the end of this section for additional notes.

- *Academic Abstracts/CD-ROM,* EBSCO Publishing Editorial Department, P.O. Box 590, Ipswich, MA 01938-0590

- *Academic Search: data base of 2,000 selected academic serials, updated monthly:* EBSCO Publishing, 83 Pine Street, Peabody, MA 01960

- *CNPIEC Reference Guide: Chinese National Directory of Foreign Periodicals,* P.O. Box 88, Beijing, People's Republic of China

- *Current Awareness Abstracts,* Association for Information Management, Information House, 20-24 Old Street, London EC1V 9AP, England

- *Current Index to Journals in Education,* Syracuse University, 4-194 Center for Science and Technology, Syracuse, NY 13244-4100

- *Educational Administration Abstracts (EAA),* Sage Publications, Inc., 2455 Teller Road, Newbury Park, CA 91320

- *IBZ International Bibliography of Periodical Literature,* Zeller Verlag GmbH & Co., P.O.B. 1949, d-49009 Osnabruck, Germany

- *Index to Periodical Articles Related to Law,* University of Texas, 727 East 26th Street, Austin, TX 78705

- *Information Science Abstracts,* Plenum Publishing Company, 233 Spring Street, New York, NY 10013-1578

- *Informed Librarian, The,* Infosources Publishing, 140 Norma Road, Teaneck, NJ 07666

- *INSPEC Information Services,* Institution of Electrical Engineers, Michael Faraday House, Six Hills Way, Stevenage, Herts SG1 2AY, England

(continued)

3 1460 00075 0397

- *INTERNET ACCESS (& additional networks) Bulletin Board for Libraries ("BUBL"), coverage of information resources on INTERNET, JANET, and other networks.*
  - JANET X.29: UK.AC.BATH.BUBL or 00006012101300
  - TELNET: BUBL.BATH.AC.UK or 138.38.32.45 login 'bubl'
  - Gopher: BUBL.BATH.AC.UK (138.32.32.45). Port 7070
  - World Wide Web: http: / / www.bubl.bath.ac.uk./BUBL/ home.html
  - NISSWAIS: telnetniss.ac.uk (for the NISS gateway) The Andersonian Library, Curran Building, 101 St. James Road, Glasgow G4 ONS, Scotland

- *Journal of Academic Librarianship: Guide to Professional Literature, The*, Grad School of Library & Information Science/Simmons College, 300 The Fenway, Boston, MA 02115-5898

- *Konyvtari Figyelo-Library Review,* National Szechenyi Library, Centre for Library and Information Science, H-1827 Budapest, Hungary

- *Library & Information Science Abstracts (LISA),* Bowker-Saur Limited, Maypole House, Maypole Road, East Grinstead, West Sussex, RH19 1HH England

- *Library Literature,* The H.W. Wilson Company, 950 University Avenue, Bronx, NY 10452

- *MasterFILE: updated database from EBSCO Publishing,* EBSCO Publishing, 83 Pine Street, Peabody, MA 01960

- *Newsletter of Library and Information Services,* China Sci-Tech Book Review, Library of Academia Sinica, 8 Kexueyuan Nanlu, Zhongguancun, Beijing 100080, People's Republic of China

- *OT BibSys,* American Occupational Therapy Foundation, P.O. Box 31220, Bethesda, MD 20824-1220

- *Referativnyi Zhurnal (Abstracts Journal of the Institute of Scientific Information of the Republic of Russia),* The Institute of Scientific Information, Baltijskaja ul., 14, Moscow A-219, Republic of Russia

- *Sage Public Administration Abstracts (SPAA),* Sage Publications, Inc., 2455 Teller Road, Newbury Park, CA 91320

(continued)

SPECIAL BIBLIOGRAPHIC NOTES

related to special journal issues (separates)
and indexing/abstracting

☐ indexing/abstracting services in this list will also cover material in any "separate" that is co-published simultaneously with Haworth's special thematic journal issue or DocuSerial. Indexing/abstracting usually covers material at the article/chapter level.

☐ monographic co-editions are intended for either non-subscribers or libraries which intend to purchase a second copy for their circulating collections.

☐ monographic co-editions are reported to all jobbers/wholesalers/approval plans. The source journal is listed as the "series" to assist the prevention of duplicate purchasing in the same manner utilized for books-in-series.

☐ to facilitate user/access services all indexing/abstracting services are encouraged to utilize the co-indexing entry note indicated at the bottom of the first page of each article/chapter/contribution.

☐ this is intended to assist a library user of any reference tool (whether print, electronic, online, or CD-ROM) to locate the monographic version if the library has purchased this version but not a subscription to the source journal.

☐ individual articles/chapters in any Haworth publication are also available through the Haworth Document Delivery Services (HDDS).

Reference Sources on the Internet: Off the Shelf and Onto the Web

CONTENTS

Introduction: Doing Reference "Off the Shelf"   1
Karen R. Diaz

GENERAL

WWW Search Tools in Reference Services   5
Stacey Kimmel

Career and Employment Resources on the Internet   21
Rachel F. Fenske

A Virtual Government Documents Reference Collection   31
Deborah R. Hollis

Patent Resources on the Internet: A Reference Librarian's
Guide   45
Lisa Pillow

BUSINESS AND SOCIAL SCIENCES

Reference Sources on the Internet: Geography
and International Studies   51
Susan E. Clark

Education Resources   55
Margaret M. Jobe

Reference Sources on the Internet: Psychology   63
Lorrie A. Knight

Social Problems and Human Services/Social Sciences
  Solutions on the Internet   69
  Gary McMillan

Internet Resources for Reference: Finance and Investment   77
  Brent Alan Mai

Internet Resources for Reference: General Business
  and Company Information   85
  Brent Alan Mai

Internet Resources for Reference: International Trade   93
  Brent Alan Mai

Selected Ethnic and Gender Studies Internet Sources
  for Reference Use   97
  Lisa Pillow

Politics by Other Media: A Guide to National Political
  Information Resources on the Internet   111
  Robert Richards

Economics Internet Sites for Reference Librarians   127
  Miles Yoshimura

HUMANITIES

Internet Reference Sources in the Performing Arts   139
  Richard AmRhein

Architecture: Reference Sites on the Internet   147
  Jeanne M. Brown

Internet Reference Resources in Language and Literature   153
  Pam Day

World History Internet Resources   161
  Sarah Landeryou

Reference Sources on the Internet in United States History   167
  Stanley D. Nash

LEISURE STUDIES

Entertainment Resources on the Internet 179
Allison Cowgill

Reference on the Internet: Sports 187
Bruce Weaver

SCIENCES

Internet Reference Resources for the Life Sciences 191
Kathleen A. Clark

Ready Reference Web Sites in Earth and Physical Sciences 203
Edward Lener
Flora G. Shrode

Health and Medicine 215
Eric H. Schnell

Reference on the Internet: Environment 223
Bruce Weaver

Index 227

ABOUT THE EDITOR

Karen R. Diaz is both Reference Librarian and Web Librarian at the Ohio State University Libraries. Her reference work is in the Main Library, which primarily serves the social sciences and humanities. Her position as Web Librarian includes responsibilities for coordinating the content and organizational issues of maintaining the Libraries' web presence.

Introduction:
Doing Reference "Off the Shelf"

Surfing may be fun, but it's no way to do reference. Imagine approaching your printed reference collection the way many users approach the Internet. What kind of reference librarian spends one to two hours browsing the whole collection to come up with one answer! Those who remember Ranganathan's Five Laws of Library Science will remember that one of our goals as librarians is to "save the time of the reader." But in this day and age when even Vanna White and Pennzoil have their own homepages, and a search engine keyword search finds over 200,000 hits on "Small Business," the librarian faces a challenge to find the exact piece of information needed without having to wade through irrelevant, unreliable and out of date material.

This volume is an attempt to provide reference librarians with a core list of resources in a variety of subject areas available on the Internet. The contributors have provided introductions that in many cases outline the strengths of the "Internet collection" and why and when a librarian should make use of this collection for reference purposes. A review of these introductions makes it clear that the Internet has not yet replaced paper resources, but also cannot be ignored by those wishing to provide timely information and access to resources beyond what any library could hope to collect in-house.

There seem to be four core issues that reference librarians face to

---

Karen R. Diaz is both Reference Librarian and Web Librarian at the Ohio State University Libraries. Her reference work is in the Main Library which primarily serves the social sciences and humanities. Her position as Web Librarian includes responsibilities for coordinating the content and organizational issues of maintaining the Libraries' web presence.

[Haworth co-indexing entry note]: "Introduction: Doing Reference 'Off the Shelf.' " Diaz, Karen R. Co-published simultaneously in *The Reference Librarian* (The Haworth Press, Inc.) No. 57, 1997, pp. 1-3; and: *Reference Sources on the Internet: Off the Shelf and Onto the Web* (ed: Karen R. Diaz) The Haworth Press, Inc., 1997, pp. 1-3. Single or multiple copies of this article are available for a fee from The Haworth Document Delivery Service [1-800-342-9678, 9:00 a.m. - 5:00 p.m. (EST). E-mail address: getinfo@haworth.com].

master the Internet for reference purposes. These issues are nothing new, but are just practiced on a new playing field. They include understanding the search tools available, learning what sources or providers of information are most reliable, framing the reference need in light of the arrangement of the collection, and just plain knowing the core resources that exist.

Stacey Kimmel has provided an excellent article that gives an outline of the various types of search engines that exist as well as a visual cue to which engines search what types of data. While many may argue that there is not an adequate search engine yet to be found, understanding the idiosyncracies of what is there is still an important step in using the engines effectively. For instance, some search engines will pick up discussions on newsgroups as well as homepages while others will find data available for FTP. Knowing these differences can save a lot of time when you know you need one kind of data source and not another. It is also worth mentioning that one search engine of choice among librarians is definitely Yahoo! A Yahoo! sub-category was cited by most contributors to this volume as a great collection site for a variety of resources. Yahoo!'s combination of subject organization and keyword searching within the category is recognizable as organization long employed by libraries.

Librarians have always recognized the importance of buying information from reliable sources. When paying for information, there can be an expectation that the provider has placed some sort of quality control in the production of the product. Where such accountability does not exist however, new methods must be applied to gain a sense of reliability of the data. Five major types of information providers exist on the Internet: official organizations and professional associations, government, educational institutions, commercial organizations and individuals.

Gary McMillan provides some interesting insight into the issue of reliable data providers in his introduction to resources for social problems. He suggests that homepages of official organizations and professional associations are much more reliable than those of individuals with a personal chip-on-their-shoulder or agenda to advance. As another major provider, government sites provide a level of authority one would expect to be reliable. University pages provide an interesting mix of college or department sites containing official university information, research projects and pages that are very authoritative, and unofficial pages of individuals who simply attend or work for the institution but have a pet topic or agenda to present. While commercial sites can be relied upon as being the authoritative source for their own products, one can also expect a bit of propaganda. Commercial sites that exist for the sole purpose of doling out information of a certain type, that is serving as a distributor or publisher, will become increasingly subject to the same level of accountability that exists in print resources, where a good reputation is everything. Finally, sites provided by individuals will be as reliable and as authoritative as the individual him/herself. One site listed here is an encyclopedia maintained by an MD. However, many sites maintained by individuals simply gather and point to other sites. One site maintained by an individual had already disappeared from the time the article was mailed to the time it arrived for review. The page creator had left behind a written statement saying he was no longer going to be able to maintain the page because it was a full time job!

Thirdly, reference librarians will continue to have to use their skills to frame the reference question within the context of how information is organized and how it is distributed. Librarians will have to continue consideration of likely sources of information production and distribution, terminology most appropriate for the intellectual level of the user's need, or appropriateness of seeking out the likely provider of data rather than posing a keyword search to snare whatever might be out there.

But, beyond these larger issues that loom, the old-fashioned technique of simply learning the core resources remains. Here you will find some specific resources culled by the contributors to this publication. The standard disclaimer exists as does anytime someone attempts to put in writing a list of these sometimes elusive materials . . . they may have moved or disappeared by the time you see this! However, selections were partly based on the fact that they will likely still exist. I hope you will be delighted by the discovery of many of them, and will find them useful in your eternal quest to "save the time of the reader."

Karen R. Diaz

GENERAL

WWW Search Tools in Reference Services

Stacey Kimmel

SUMMARY. An introduction to World Wide Web Search tools for reference services, including robot-generated services, review/rating services, metasearch engines, and subject directories. *[Article copies available for a fee from The Haworth Document Delivery Service: 1-800-342-9678. E-mail address: getinfo@haworth.com]*

INTRODUCTION

The World Wide Web (WWW) has become an important component of library reference services. Many libraries have introduced WWW stations in public areas, and reference librarians have added Web searching to their repertoire of professional skills. The dynamic nature of the Web and its explosive growth make it a challenging environment for online searching.

Stacey Kimmel is currently the Collection Manager for Education, Psychology, and Management at North Carolina State University in Raleigh, NC. She has seven years of reference experience.

[Haworth co-indexing entry note]: "WWW Search Tools in Reference Services." Kimmel, Stacey. Co-published simultaneously in *The Reference Librarian* (The Haworth Press, Inc.) No. 57, 1997, pp. 5-20; and: *Reference Sources on the Internet: Off the Shelf and Onto the Web* (ed: Karen R. Diaz) The Haworth Press, Inc., 1997, pp. 5-20. Single or multiple copies of this article are available for a fee from The Haworth Document Delivery Service [1-800-342-9678, 9:00 a.m. - 5:00 p.m. (EST). E-mail address: getinfo@haworth.com].

5

Internet search tools such as Yahoo!, AltaVista, and Excite organize Web-space by categorizing or indexing its resources. The popularity of these tools has surpassed expectations, and some host millions of searches per day (Grimes, 1996). Comparisons of search tools have appeared in the literature, and most have reported wide variation in functionality, coverage, and ease of use (Venditto, 1996; Zorn, 1996; Stanley, 1996). This article will discuss characteristics of search tools, the types of tools available, and the use of selected products for reference services.

CHARACTERISTICS OF WWW SEARCH SERVICES

Although most WWW search services are business ventures, they differ from other commercial end-user services. Unlike SilverPlatter and First-search, most Web search services are freely available to anyone connected to the Internet. Advertisers, rather than libraries or searchers, are paying customers in this model, and different commercial forces drive these services. To use search tools wisely, librarians and patrons must understand some basic characteristics of WWW services and their users.

- *Most Web search tools sell advertising.* Online advertising is one of the largest revenue generators for the World Wide Web. Web advertising revenue for 1996 is expected to reach over $300 million, and revenues by the year 2000 could reach $5 billion (Hickman, 1996). Following the *Thomas Register of American Manufacturers* and the *Yellow Pages* model, most WWW search tools combine advertisements with information services. Some of the most popular Web search tools are sponsored by companies that sell advertising space. While ads subsidize the cost of maintaining search services, there are drawbacks to this model. At minimum, advertising banners on Web sites can distract users and obscure relevant search cues. Advertising can also affect the search experience more directly. In June 1996, for example, OpenText Corporation announced a "preferred listing" service that allowed Web sites to pay for a higher ranking in the OpenText index search results (*Internet News Pointers*, 1996). This feature bypassed the algorithm that ranks retrieval by relevance of content. The announcement drew a negative reaction on listservs and news sources (MacKinnon, 1996; Wingfield, 1996), and it was never implemented. Since advertiser interests impact the development of search services, librarians should follow trends in marketing and advertising that might affect the user.
- *Search tools serve a general consumer market.* The Internet is a rich source of entertainment and consumer resources, and a large per-

centage of search engine use is for popular topics. Andrews (1996 April 29) analyzed search logs from the major search engines and found that a frequently occurring search topic in all tools was *Baywatch*. Searches on sex, business, and consumer topics dominated the list of topics.

Because busy search services can command higher advertising rates, most services aim for broad consumer appeal. Internet directories often have extensive listings under entertainment, travel, and shopping; some services sponsor sweepstakes or other attractions. Lebedev (1996) conducted searches in eleven search engines on specialized chemistry and physics topics and found that scientific publications account for only 10 to 20% of total retrieval.

- *Services are constantly changing.* Many Web searching tools are diversifying and expanding their services. Veteran sites such as Lycos and Yahoo! are adding new products such as news, stock prices, and WWW site reviews (Andrews, 1996 May 20). Newly established services have begun to tap specialized markets (Andrews, 1996 September 23). The *StreetEye search engine (http://www.streeteye.com)* maintains a database of stock quotes, financial and market data, and other financial resources. The University of Evansville's peer-reviewed *Argos search engine (http://argos.evansville.edu)* caters to the needs of classical and medieval scholars *(Chronicle of Higher Education, 1996)*.

The technology used by these services is also developing rapidly. New user interfaces are more personalized, better able to anticipate user needs, and easier to use (Frook, 1996). *Firefly Online (http://www.firefly.com)* creates a profile of user music preferences and presents reviews that match the user's musical tastes. Other software agents, such as WebCompass, are loaded on the user's desktop computer. WebCompass conducts periodic Web searches in the background, without intervention, and creates a local database of items that match user interests (Baldazo, 1996).

TYPES OF SEARCH TOOLS

Web search services have evolved from single-tool utilities to multifaceted "destination sites" that offer a suite of integrated services. While it can be difficult to categorize these increasingly complex services, individual tools fit loosely into one of four types: search engines, directories, metasearch engines, and review/rating sites.

Search Engines/Robot-Generated Databases

A search engine allows Internet users to search a robot-generated database of WWW resources by subject or keyword. There are more than 100 search engines available through Yahoo!'s *Searching the Web* page, and the features of each tool vary considerably. To understand the differences among products it is helpful to know how search engines and their databases are created. Search engines have several components: *robots* retrieve documents from the Web; *indexers* extract information from the documents and build the database; and the *interface* mediates database searches.

Robots

A robot (also called spider, crawler, agent, or wanderer) is a program that retrieves documents to build the search engine database. This program resides on the host computer and uses the standard protocols (e.g., http, FTP, gopher) to retrieve documents in Webspace. The robot starts with a known WWW site, retrieves the homepage, and systematically follows hypertext links it finds therein. By following links recursively, the robot learns about new sites on the Web. Algorithms determine which hypertext links a robot will harvest among many possible links. Some robots are programmed to retrieve top-level documents from a large number of servers (a breadth-first approach), while others capture most or all of the documents on each server (a depth-first approach). Search engines may employ a workforce of robots to construct and maintain a database.

Indexers

The indexer extracts information from the retrieved documents to store in the database. Different search engines retain different parts of the documents, but most services retain at least the words in HTML titles, links, and headers. Some extract frequently occurring words, while others index the full text of documents. Recently, search engines have begun indexing images, netnews group postings, FTP sites, and other resources along with HTML documents. Search engine databases vary widely in content. This variation stems from differences in the indexing strategy and the robot's method of harvesting documents.

Interface

The user interface of the search engine accepts user input, queries the database, and displays the matches found in the database. The interface can be shareware or commercial search software. Features may include Boolean logic, truncation, proximity searching, ranking of documents, as well as more specialized capabilities such as limiting by date, image searching, and stopword searching.

COMPARISONS OF SEARCH ENGINES

Figure 1 provides a comparison chart for selected search engines. All of the search tools reviewed here offer solid search features and attempt comprehensive coverage of the Web. Standard features include relevance ranking of results, Boolean AND, OR, and NOT (or equivalent), and adjacency or proximity searching. All tools but Lycos offer case-sensitive searching and field-based searching, and all but Lycos index the full text of the document. Lycos creates abstracts from document content.

Database size, measured as the number of URLs or documents in the database, has been a source of competition among search engines (*How to count URLs,* 1996). The meaning of this measure is difficult to judge for several reasons. Some engines count only documents that have been retrieved and fully indexed, while others count links within indexed documents. Search services that devote computing resources to updating old links may grow more slowly than those that devote all resources to finding new links. Furthermore, some engines delete duplicate and dead links.

AltaVista (Digital Equipment, Inc.)
http://www.altavista.com

AltaVista offers full-text searching of Usenet and the World Wide Web. Its extensive search options rival those of commercial search services. Field-based searching, embedded truncation, and stopword searches are available in this search engine. The Simple menu provides examples to help users conduct Boolean and phrase searches. An Advanced menu is also available, but the range of AltaVista' s capabilities are not well expressed in the menu options. Users must read the Help pages to find instructions for using the "near" operator and nested searching, for example. The Help pages also explain the Ranking Criteria feature, which can be critical to successful searching. Searchers should generally include at least one keyword in the Ranking Criteria entry line for optimal ranking of results.

AltaVista has a reputation for retrieving more hits than other search engines and for locating obscure items. The AltaVista ranking feature sometimes performs unevenly, however, and low relevance documents may appear at the top of results. A search for "Stanford University" and "Wall Street Journal" failed to list these organization homepages in the first 30 hits, while Infoseek and Lycos listed the homepages in the first 10 hits. AltaVista updates its index every 4 to 6 weeks, and frequently visited links are updated first.

Recommendation: AltaVista is unrivaled for handling complex search strategies and for providing comprehensive results. It can often locate instances of obscure terms buried within a document. For very broad searches or common terms, AltaVista results may overwhelm the user.

HotBot (HotWired, Inc.)
http://www.hotbot.com

HotBot also covers Usenet and the Web in full text, and it offers above-average search capabilities. It is the only search engine that allows searchers to set defaults for a search session, and unlike AltaVista it provides an elaborate menu structure to help users perform advanced searching. Beginners can follow onscreen cues to limit searches by organization type (.com, .edu, etc.), update date, geographic location of server, and a wide variety of media types (Acrobat, VRML, file extensions such as GIF, Java, etc.). HotBot does not support stopword searching or truncation. The FAQ states that the database is designed to be updated weekly, but at the time of this writing the updating process was not implemented.

Recommendation: HotBot is an innovative product with a few significant deficiencies. The ability to set session defaults makes HotBot useful for extended search sessions, and its well-designed menus help inexperienced searchers formulate complex searches.

InfoSeek Ultra (InfoSeek, Inc.)
http://ultra.infoseek.com/

Infoseek services combine full-text searching of Usenet and Webspace with an assortment of news and review services. InfoSeek Ultra rivals AltaVista in its range of features, and like AltaVista it requires some command memorization. While Infoseek Ultra does not support truncation, it uses a software technology that automatically finds plurals, variant word endings, and similar words. For example, the keyword "harddisk" would also retrieve "hard disk." Infoseek's ranking algorithm has been praised for its ability to guess which documents are relevant (Venditto, 1996). Stopwords such as "the, us, and "be" are searchable. Updates are added in real-time (instantaneously) rather than in batches, but the length of time required to update the entire database is not provided.

FIGURE 1. Search Engines Compared

SERVICE	COVERAGE	FULL TEXT	BOOL-EAN	ADJ	NEST ()	FIELD SEARCH	MEDIA	RANK	DUPL. DETECT	TRUN-CATE	SIMI-LAR	CASE SENS	BACK-WARD
AltaVista www.altavista.com	30M URLs & Usenet	*•	•	•	•	•	•	•		•		•	
HotBot www.hotbot.com	54M URLs & Usenet	•	•	•		•	•	•	•			•	•
Ultraseek www.infoseek.com	50M URLs, Usenet, more	*•	•	•		•		•	•	•	•	•	•
Lycos www.lycos.com	66M URLs, FTP, gopher		•	•			•	•		•			
Opentext www.opentext.com	1.5M URLs & Usenet	*•	•	•		•		•	•	•	•	•	

KEY FULL TEXT = full text of documents indexed; BOOLEAN = AND/OR/NOT; ADJ = adjacency or proximity searching; NEST() = nested Boolean; FIELD SEARCH = field-based searching (title, headers, etc.); MEDIA = search by media (images, etc.); RANK = results ranked by relevance; DUPL. DETECT = URL duplicate detection; TRUNCATE = truncation or wildcards; SIMILAR = find similar sites; CASE SENS = case sensitive; BACKWARD = finding links that link, or refer to a homepage.

*• Word-by-word indexing (no stopwords)

11

Recommendation: This versatile tool is recommended for nearly any kind of search, and its ranking mechanism appears to work more reliably than AltaVista's does. Its no frills interface requires the user to learn the command language.

Lycos Search Engine (Lycos, Inc.)
http://www.lycos.com

Lycos covers Web, FTP, and gopherspace. It does not index documents in full text, but it extracts significant words and other parts of each document to create an abstract. Lycos uses natural language processing software developed at Carnegie-Mellon University. Simple and advanced menus are available, but search syntax and user commands are de-emphasized in this system. Proximity searching and Boolean logic are handled automatically–documents containing several keywords or keywords adjacent to one another are ranked high in results. Searchers sacrifice some control for this ease of use; there is no means for nested logic, phrase searching or field searching. Most terms less than three characters long are discarded, so searches such as "windows 95" fail or yield many false hits.

Lycos uses a patented ranking algorithm that lists popular sites highest in search retrieval. Popularity is determined by counting the number of WWW pages that point to a site. However, searches for two popular Internet sites ("White House" and "Microsoft Corporation") did not list either homepage in its first 20 results. Unlike other search engines, the Lycos database is built cumulatively–documents are visited only once, and records are not updated.

Recommendation: Lycos performs better with broad topics and concepts than with phrases, proper names and organizations, and obscure topics. Inexperienced users may prefer its simple interface and natural language features, but it is not recommended for phrase searches or complex search strategies.

OpenText Index (Opentext Corporation)
http://www.opentext.com

OpenText Index covers Webspace and newsgroups in full-text. This tool's search features are impressive, but its greatest strength lies in its ability to perform precise searches. OpenText searches stopwords and numbers, and it is the only index to allow the user to specify word order in a phrase. Choosing the [followed by] menu option lets the user find "race horse" but not "horse race." Searches such as "100 best companies," "to be or not to be," and "south [followed by] africa" can be performed successfully in this database. Its Simple and Power Search screens clearly articulate the search features and guide the user in building a search. The OpenText database is small in size, but in practice its search results are comparable to its competitors. It does not provide information about frequency of database updates.

Recommendation: OpenText's sophisticated features and well-designed interface will appeal to both beginning and experienced searchers. It is a good choice for searching phrases and search strings.

SUBJECT DIRECTORIES

WWW-based directories attempt to categorize resources in a hierarchical structure. Directories are smaller in size than search engines, and coverage is selective rather than comprehensive. Most directories use humans to select and index resources. Human resource selectors build the listings by accepting online submissions from users, using robots to gather new URLs, and browsing update services and announcement lists. However, selection policies are often unavailable.

Most directories offer keyword searching of the links and text in the menu structure. For this reason, directories are most appropriate for general topics, organizations and conferences, or topics that are meaty enough to warrant a homepage. General subject headings (magazines, software, etc.) are often assigned consistently so that searchers can make use of a controlled vocabulary.

As the World Wide Web grows, directory services will become increasingly unwieldy to manage and use. Experts have warned that directory services will soon confront limitations in scalability (Steinberg, 1996), and new strategies for building directories are needed. The use of human intervention to maintain directories may become infeasible in the future.

Lycos A2Z (Lycos, Inc.)
http://www.lycos.com

The Lycos A2Z directory is generated from Lycos search engine statistics. The search engine tracks the "most linked-to sites," the sites with the greatest number of links pointing to them. This popularity is taken as an indication of value to the Internet community, and sites are added to the A2Z directory. This method of collecting sites is efficient as it requires little human intervention. The A2Z directory reflects the interests of the majority of searchers rather than the quality of content, however. The directory divides 40,000 sites into 16 categories and 800 subcategories. The Lycos search interface can be used to search the directory by keyword.

Recommendation: A2Z is best suited for casual browsing or for searching topics of popular or current interest.

Galaxy (Tradewave Corporation)
http://www.tradewave.com

Tradewave's Galaxy organizes more than 100,000 gopher, telnet, and WWW sites in an 11-category directory with many subcategories. The Galaxy menu structure is simple to use but not as tightly constructed as Yahoo!'s menus. Galaxy users can search the directory as well as other resources using a full-featured WAIS index. A selection of broad subject headings (e.g., new items, articles, books, collections) group topics within each category or subcategory. Tradewave uses guest editors, but very little editorial control appears to be exercised in some sections. Links to personal diaries can be found under "Articles," for example. As one of the oldest directories on the WWW, Galaxy's menus are well-developed and resource rich. Its basic services have not changed for over a year, however, a considerable length of time on the Internet.

Recommendation: Galaxy's size and coverage are its strongest features, but development appears to have stalled–this service is quickly being outpaced by its competitors. Galaxy can be used to supplement search results from other services.

Yahoo! (Yahoo, Inc.)
http://www.yahoo.com

Yahoo! is perhaps the best known Web directory. Its classification scheme is well-constructed and the menu hierarchy is easy to navigate. Yahoo!'s directory includes more than 300,000 sites and newsgroups, and it has expanded its services to include Reuters news, an online magazine, My Yahoo! (a version of Yahoo! tailored to user interests), National Yahoo! sites (France, Germany, Japan, etc.) and other resources. Yahoo! provides useful visual cues. New or recommended sites are tagged as such, and numbers to the right of a link indicate how many sites are listed under that choice. The @ sign indicates that the heading is found elsewhere in the hierarchy, and each page displays the user's location in the menu hierarchy.

The Yahoo! search engine has solid basic features, and users can search the entire directory or limit to specified subsections. Yahoo! uses a controlled vocabulary that can greatly enhance search retrieval. Users can conduct a Boolean search for "plato" and the subject heading "software" to quickly locate the Plato Education Systems software company. All resources that appear in the directory are hand-selected, and Yahoo! reserves the right to refuse submissions. There is no written selection policy.

Yahoo! has automated much of the directory's routine maintenance, but 35 full-time staff are involved in selecting and indexing resources for the directory (Brandt, 1996). The scalability of this strategy will be put to the test in the coming years.

Recommendation: Yahoo!'s aggressive development of new services and continued investment in the original directory make this one of the most useful tools on the Web. It is a good place to find ready reference sources (directories, weather, etc.), homepages of services and organizations, businesses, and current interest topics.

METASEARCH ENGINES

Metasearch engines allow users to search several services simultaneously and view results in one list. These services perform pre-search processing to prepare the query for each search engine, and most offer post-search processing to compile retrieval results. The potential usefulness of metasearchers has been demonstrated by studies showing that there is little overlap in the retrieval of different search engines (Venditto, 1996). Because each engine tends to give unique results, metasearch engines provide a means of gathering the most highest-ranked records from different engines.

These services have limitations. Usually only a subset of each engine's hits are retrieved from each service. Searches in metasearch engines tend to take longer because additional processing is needed to gather and compile results, and because the search is only as fast as the slowest engine. The biggest drawback of metasearch engines is that capabilities of individual engines are inaccessible through the metasearcher interface. If metasearchers could tailor a search to each engine's unique capabilities, the value of results would be enhanced.

Notess (1996) states that metasearchers are best used for single-term or other simple searches. Metasearchers can also function much like the OneSearch function in DIALOG, pointing to the one best resource for a given question. Metasearch services need further development before they can be truly useful in reference services.

Metacrawler
http://metacrawler.cs.washington.edu

Metacrawler performs searches of Lycos, WebCrawler, Excite, AltaVista, Yahoo!, HotBot, and Galaxy. It supports basic Boolean queries and phrase searching. Searchers can elect to conduct a fast search, which displays whatever results are returned within five seconds, or a comprehensive search, which searches all available search engines regardless of time required. A pull-down menu offers a choice of sorting results by relevance or location (domains such as .com, .edu, country, etc.), and a configuration menu lets searchers turn on advanced display capabilities available through Java and frames.

Recommendation: Metacrawler's sophisticated sort and display features set it apart from other metasearchers, particularly for users with Java- and frames-capable browsers.

SavvySearch
http://www.cs.colostate.edu/~dreiling/smartform.html

SavvySearch covers the major search engines and directories, as well as additional categories such as reference, technical reports, news, people, software, academic, references, images, and entertainment. The additional categories tap specialized sources that might be useful on occasion, but these should not be routinely selected. SavvySearch selects three services initially and then presents users with options for expanding the search to other resources. SavvySearch supports AND, OR, and phrase searches and lets users select brief, normal or verbose displays. Results can be grouped by resource or integrated into one list, and up to 50 hits from each resource can be retrieved. SavvySearch can be slow to perform, and users may experience sporadic search failures.

Recommendation: SavvySearch offers "one-stop-shopping" that helps the user expand a query to a wide range of resources. Its slow response time and frequent timeout messages can be problematic in reference services.

Profusion Search (University of Kansas)
http://www.designlab.ukans.edu/profusion/

The Profusion metasearcher is a relatively new search service that covers AltaVista, InfoSeek, Lycos, Excite, WebCrawler, and OpenText. Searchers can select up to three search engines or let Profusion select them. Boolean operators and many other standard search features are currently unsupported. Profusion detects and removes duplicates, prefetches documents and removes dead links, and merges relevance rankings of each engine. The result is an integrated list of the most relevant materials available when the search is run. There is also an update service that allows users to receive daily, weekly, or monthly e-mail updates of their search.

Recommendation: Profusion cannot accommodate complex searches but works well for searches requiring only one or two keywords. This tool's post-search processing and other innovative features make it a service to watch for future developments.

REVIEW/RATING SERVICES

Review/rating services provide numeric ratings and/or evaluative summaries of selected Web resources. Reviewers may be volunteers or paid employees, but names and qualifications are often unavailable. Review services may add hundreds of reviews per week from user suggestions or editor selections.

Searchers looking for systematic, detailed evaluations of WWW sites will be disappointed with the content of most Web review sites. Rettig (1996) notes that the quality of WWW review services is weak by librarians' standards. At the time of this writing, only one review site provided a detailed editorial or selection policy. Despite these shortcomings, review sites perform a filtering function and some users prefer them.

Argus Clearinghouse (Argus Associates, Inc.)
http://www.clearinghouse.net

Formerly the University of Michigan's Clearinghouse for Subject-Oriented Internet Resource Guides, Argus is now managed by librarians affiliated with Argus Associates, Inc. This site selects and evaluates user-contributed subject guides to Internet Resources. It currently hosts or points to more than 400 guides which can be searched by keyword or browsed in 12 broad subject categories. A detailed collection development policy, ratings information, and submission guidelines for authors are available. Sites are rated on a scale of 1 to 5 on level of resource description (objective data), level of resource evaluation (subjective evaluation), guide design, guide organizational schemes, and guide meta-information (information about the guide, its authors, etc.). The guides include diverse topics such as AIDS, popular music, the sixties, herpetology, artificial intelligence, women and technology, ecotravel, and homeschooling.

Recommendation: Users preparing to conduct an exhaustive search should check to see if Argus covers the topic. This site's well-articulated mission and selection policies provide a level of quality control absent in other review sites.

Excite Review Service (Excite, Inc.)
http://www.excite.com

Excite has the basic features needed for searching its database of 60,000 reviews, but it does not support proximity operators or truncation. The Excite Concept Search feature automatically searches for synonyms of keywords. For example, the keyword "aging" will also retrieve the word "elderly." Reviews are written in a popular journalistic style and usually less than 50 words long. Sites are assigned a rating from 1 to 4, and subject headings are assigned to each review. Users can browse the site reviews in the Excite subject directory, which mirrors the content of the database. Categories in the directory are strongly oriented to consumer interests (e.g., shopping, hobbies, and entertainment). Excite uses paid journalists as reviewers, and biographies of reviewers are available. No criteria for ratings or inclusion are provided.

Recommendation: Excite provides light reading for the casual user, but the descriptions and ratings have little to offer in the way of critical evaluation.

Top 5% (Lycos, Inc)
http://point.lycos.com/

The Top 5% review site is hosted by Lycos and uses the Lycos search engine. Sites are arranged in a 15-category directory. Each is assigned a numeric rating for content, presentation, and experience. Directory listings can be sorted by any of the rating criteria, by date, or alphabetically. Top 5% offers the fairly thorough descriptions of a site's content, usually between 50 and 100 words long. Beyond the numeric ratings, evaluation of sites is not provided. Lycos provides no information on the reviewers or editorial policies, but entertainment appears to be a factor in selection. Sites such as "The Page at Pooh Corner" appear in the Education category, and the heading "Conspiracies and Hoaxes" appears on the top level page.

Recommendation: Top 5% can be used to locate content or descriptive summaries for WWW sites.

CONCLUSION

When the Internet is deemed appropriate for a search, librarians need to identify the best tool for the task at hand. knowing the strengths and weaknesses of each service will help staff quickly locate answers to ready reference questions. For in-depth or comprehensive searching it is advisable to try several services as there is little overlap among the databases' content.

Web directories are ideally suited for finding reference sources and services, as well as for finding homepages on a topic, organization, or event. Yahoo!'s elegant structure and investment in human indexing provide fertile ground for research. Search engines are appropriate for comprehensive topic searches or for locating a specific or obscure piece of information. Infoseek and AltaVista offer robust search capabilities through a command interface, while the HotBot and OpenText services each offer a strong assortment of features in an easier menu format. Lycos handles simple and broad topics well.

Other search services are in need of refinement. Metasearchers must undergo further development to meet the demands of a reference environment, but can be used to sample results from different search engines and resources. Most review/rating sites are "novelty" browsing services rather than bona fide research tools. Argus is the exception to this rule; while limited in coverage, it provides selection policies and evaluation criteria that are worthy of emulation.

REFERENCES

Andrews, W. (1996 September 23). A new breed of search service. *Webweek, 2*(14): 21.

Andrews, W. (1996 May 20). Feeling the heat: Engines rev up in search of new content. *Webweek, 2*(6): 7.

Andrews, W. (1996 April 29). It ain't just bits and bytes. *Webweek, 2*(5): 10.

Baldazo, R. (1996). Quarterdeck harnesses leading-edge metasearch technology. *Byte, (21)*3: 97.

Brandt, R. (1996). Tim Koogle defends Yahoo's outrageous valuation. *Upside, 8*(7): 30-34.

Frook, J. (1996 September 16). Net sites to get more personal. *Communications-Week, 6*(28): 63.

Grimes, R. (1996, April). Searched and found on the Internet. *Digital Age, 15*(4): 4.

Hickman, A. (1996 November 5). Dollars from cyberspace. *PC Magazine, 15*(19): 34.

How to count URLs [WWW document]. URL: http://www.excite.com/ice/counting.html

Lebedev, A. (1996 September 29). *Best search engines for finding scientific information on the Web* [WWW document]. URL: http://www.chem.msu.su/eng/comparison.html

Lycos attempts a transformation (1996 September 23). *Webweek, 2*(14): 4.

MacKinnon, P. (1996 June 19). *Relevancy and ranking . . . By wealth* [WWW document]. URL: http://sunsite.berkeley.edu/Web4Lib/

Most scholars agree that Internet search engines are terrible tools for academic research (1996 October 18). *Chronicle of Higher Education, 43*(8): A23.

Notess, G. (1996). Internet Onesearch with the mega search engines. *Online, 20*(6): 36-39.

OpenText search engine offers advertisers preferred ranking (1996 June 24). *Internet News Pointers.* URL: http://enigma.phys.utk.edu/webnews/6-24.html

Rettig, J. (1996). Beyond cool: Analog models for reviewing digital resources. *Online, 20*(5): 52.

Stanley, T. (1996 March 22). AltaVista vs. Lycos. *Ariadne, 2.* URL: http://ukoln.bath.ac.uk/ariadne/issue2/engines/

Steinberg, S. (1996). Seek and ye shall find (maybe). *Wired, 4*(5): 108-114, 172-182.

Venditto, G. (1996). Search engine showdown. *Internet World, 7*(5): 78.

Wingfield, N. (1996 June 21) *Engine sells results, draws fire* [WWW document]. URL: http://www.news.com/News/Item/0,4,1635,00.html

Zorn, P., Emanoil, M., & Marshall, L. (1996). Advanced Web searching: Tricks of the trade. *Online, 20*(3): 15-28.

Career and Employment Resources on the Internet

Rachel F. Fenske

SUMMARY. This article presents an annotated list of career and employment web sites to assist librarians and job seekers with locating information on all aspects of career and job searching. General indexes to career and employment resources are provided, along with sites specializing in career fairs, résumé services, relocation and newsgroups. The aim of this paper is to present stable, comprehensive, and well maintained sites that provide resources and services without charge. However, some sites that charge for services, such as résumé evaluation and writing, have been included because they also offer links to other sites and information that could be useful to a job searcher. *[Article copies available for a fee from The Haworth Document Delivery Service: 1-800-342-9678. E-mail address: getinfo@haworth.com]*

Many job seekers dread the thought of looking for a new job or making a career change. However, in recent years, the Internet has simplified the job process by empowering users with searching tools and the ability to "link" on the World Wide Web. Users can now instantly acquire information on job opportunities and locale, satisfying all their crucial job search-

Rachel F. Fenske is Instructional Services Librarian at Eastern Washington University, Cheney, WA. She holds a MLS from the University of Alabama and a BA in Communication from the University of South Alabama.

Address correspondence to: Rachel F. Fenske, JFK Library, Eastern Washington University, MS-84, 816 F. Street, Cheney, WA 99004. E-mail: rfenske@ewu.edu

[Haworth co-indexing entry note]: "Career and Employment Resources on the Internet." Fenske, Rachel F. Co-published simultaneously in *The Reference Librarian* (The Haworth Press, Inc.) No. 57, 1997, pp. 21-30; and: *Reference Sources on the Internet: Off the Shelf and Onto the Web* (ed: Karen R. Diaz) The Haworth Press, Inc., 1997, pp. 21-30. Single or multiple copies of this article are available for a fee from The Haworth Document Delivery Service [1-800-342-9678, 9:00 a.m. - 5:00 p.m. (EST). E-mail address: getinfo@haworth.com].

ing and relocation information needs. Not only can job seekers locate a vast array of career opportunities in virtually any field, information can also be found about specific job markets. Market profiles, economic indicators, and demographics help job seekers determine the potential job outlook for a specific region. Many web sites provide "agents" that work to match a job seeker's personal profile with newly posted job announcements on the Internet. The searcher is kept updated about potential leads through e-mail notification. Users will find sites offering guides and other services to help them create effective résumés, as well as tips on the interview process, relocation services, career fair events, and much more.

The following annotated list is intended to provide information specialists and job seekers with organized and comprehensive career web sites. They are considered stable and well maintained, and should provide users with a good starting point in their career search.

INDEXES

Academic Position Network
http://www.umn.edu/apn/

The job postings on this site list faculty, administrative, and staff positions available at higher education, research, and vocational institutions. The search features allow a user to customize a search by keyword, state, institution type, and position type. The full text of the job announcement along with the position description is also searchable. Graduate fellowships, assistantships, and post-doctoral positions are also listed. The job database includes postings from institutions in the United States, Canada, Japan, and several other countries. Although, this site does not allow a user to submit or post a résumé electronically, it is a nice web site that serves the needs of job seekers in the field of academia.

America's Job Bank
http://www.ajb.dni.us/

America's Job Bank links job seekers to state employment service offices that provide information on private as well as government jobs. The easy search capabilities enable a user to search by keyword, DOT, Occupational or Military code as well as menu searching. Users can search the nationwide database or individual state job banks if a state web server is available. Links to over 200 employment agencies nationwide are provided, enabling a user to search agency job postings as well as state employment offices.

Best Jobs U.S.A.
http://www.bestjobsusa.com/

Produced by Recourse Communications, Inc., Best Jobs USA provides job seekers with a database of job listings ranging from administrative/secretarial to manufacturing and engineering. Listings are provided from Fortune 500 companies to start up businesses. Best Jobs USA has an excellent link to career fairs enabling users to locate events in cities other than the major metropolitan areas. Job seekers can submit their résumé to a confidential database by e-mail, fax, or mail. Articles about employment and the job search are also provided. (See full description of Best Jobs career fair link under the category Career Fairs in this article.)

CareerPath
http://www.careerpath.com/

An excellent site listing jobs primarily from over 20 of the nation's leading newspapers, including *The Atlanta Journal-Constitution, The New York Times, San Jose Mercury News, Sacramento Bee,* and *The Boston Globe.* Users can select one or more newspapers to search by job category or keyword. Users can link to specific newspapers to locate information such as industry statistics, profiles of an area's top employers and can also read about local employment news from the newpaper's business pages. Pay scale comparisons for major cities along with median household incomes, geographical population statistics, and information on the area's climate are also provided. Tips on writing effective cover letters, preparing résumés, and helpful hints on the interview process are also included. A highly recommended web site providing comprehensive job market information as well as job postings.

Career Magazine
http://www.careermag.com/

Career Magazine, produced by NCS, Inc., is a well organized and comprehensive career web site. Job seekers can search for job opportunities by location, skill, and title. Jobs posted include technical as well as non-technical positions such as retail, marketing, medical, management, sales and much more. The employer database provides information on the goals and mission of a company and the ability to search for job opportunities available within the company. In addition, job seekers can network with one another by engaging in discussion groups and forums seeking advice on the job search process. For a minimal fee, the Résumé Bank allows users to post résumés on the Internet for up to 6 months. A calendar of upcoming career fairs is also available.

Career Mosaic
http://www.careermosaic.com/cm

Career Mosaic, created by Bernard Hodes Advertising, Inc., a recruitment and advertising communications agency, provides a worldwide database of job listings. Job seekers can search an employer database, post résumés, locate job fairs, and have access to international employment opportunities. Top employers in the high tech, banking and finance, insurance, health care, retailing, and communications industry are just a few of the fields this site covers. By providing links to company home pages, users can gain valuable insight into a company's mission statement and history, products and services, press releases, and employment opportunities.

Catapult
http://www.jobweb.org/catapult/catapult.htm

Aimed at recent graduates and career counselors, this comprehensive site provides job listings, industry information, relocation services, professional associations, and other valuable resources for an individual embarking on a career search. Career decisions are made easy with links to resources describing specific career choices and links to internship programs. Catapult provides information on occupations that best suit a particular major or discipline. Résumé guides, articles on the job market, and career fairs are also provided. Students interested in pursuing graduate or professional school can link to home pages of institutions of higher education to locate information on specific programs.

Cool Works
http://www.coolworks.com/showme/

Cool Works is a great web site for those seeking adventure and the great outdoors in their new job. Whether a user is looking for a job on a cruise ship, in a national park, resort location, or a volunteer position, Cool Works provide listings of available opportunities. Listings of positions in the Peace Corps, VISTA (Volunteers in Service to America) and AMERICORPS are provided along with major resorts around the country.

FedWorld Federal Jobs
http://www.fedworld.gov/jobs/jobsearch.html

FedWorld job database, maintained by the Office of Personnel Management, lists job announcements for over 1,500 government positions. Listings are searchable by keyword, state, series, and grade. Updates occur everyday except Sunday and Monday. Information provided is brief, however, contact names and numbers are given for those seeking more information about an available position. For those familiar with the government employment system, this site will be most valuable.

A Guide to Job Resources by US Region
http://www.wm.edu/csrv/career/stualum/jregion.html

This web site, developed by the Career Services at the College of William and Mary, enables a job seeker to locate jobs according to a specific career field or location. Users can locate jobs in their field by following links to numerous career categories including art, business, media, health care, science and technology and sports. To locate a job by location, users are linked to employment sites such as local newspaper want ads, federal job links, and job hotlines. Short-term employment such as seasonal, summer, volunteer, or fellowship programs, as well as research positions, can also be located. The Career Resource Index provides links to a wealth of information on all aspects of career planning and the job search. This site is very well organized and comprehensive.

JobTrak
http://www.jobtrak.com/

Primarily targeted to undergraduate students and recent graduates, Job-Trak provides full and part-time job positions from over 400 college career centers. To access job postings from the career center, a user must be a student or alumni from a participating institution and obtain a password to search the available listings. For users unable to search a participating institution's career center job postings, the site offers other searching options. Job seekers can link to top employer's home pages locating employment opportunities, information relating to the products and services of the company, press releases, and cover stories. Events such as trade shows, exhibits and conferences are also provided. Domestic, international, government, and non-profit business web sites are also accessible. Individuals seeking advice on professional and graduate school programs, financial aid, and graduate school applications will be pleased with the many links that provide assistance and help guides. Internships available to undergraduate and graduate students are also featured on this web site.

Monster Board
http://www.monster.com/

The Monster Board is a comprehensive employment site. With over 50,000 postings from top companies in the retail, banking, manufacturing and high technology industry, a user can locate jobs by location, discipline, or keyword. The search features also allow users to conduct job searches for entry level positions as well as internships. Monster Board includes job opportunities in the United States, as well as abroad. The employer profile database allows users to locate information about a corporation's work environment, culture, products and services, history, benefits, and career opportunities. Job search agents are available, and will review incoming job listings according to a user's personal profile, posting them to a user's e-mail account. This service enables a user to retrieve desired job opportunities when not online. Users may also network with others by engaging in discussion groups and surveys. Links to major career fair companies are also provided, giving the job seeker an extensive calendar of career fair events. The Monster Board Career Center enables users to seek help with résumé preparation, career planning decisions, in addition to providing a wealth of additional career web sites.

Online Career Center
http://www.occ.com/

The Online Career Center (OCC) provides access to job listings searchable by keyword and location. Job seekers can locate information on career fairs and events, select "agents" to review job opportunities matching their specific profiles, and electronically post and submit résumés. OCC On Campus provides links to over 800 colleges and universities worldwide, enabling job seekers to access college placement centers, alumni associations, résumé help guides, and other educational resources. OCC Career Forum allows users to network and share information regarding career and employment interests. This multi-faceted web site provides a wealth of information for those engaged in career and employment searching.

The Riley Guide
http://www.jobtrak.com/jobguide

The Riley Guide, produced by Margaret Riley, librarian and author of "The Guide to Internet Job Searching," is one of the most comprehensive web sites on career planning and employment. The beginning job seeker can locate valuable information on career planning, résumé preparation, interviewing, as well as tips for their Internet career search. Hundreds of job listings covering all fields and disciplines, in the private and public sector, are given. International as well as domestic job listings are provided. Networking sites and additional links to other job related resources make this an excellent site for those looking for a career change or seeking employment.

CAREER FAIRS

The following sites are links to companies specializing in career fairs. While many web sites link you to career fair events, the sites listed below may provide the user with more information on the career fair event than other links.

Best Jobs USA
http://www.bestjobsusa.com/

Use this main web site address to link to the career fair events. Career fair listings will include those in secondary employment markets such as San Antonio, Memphis, and Madison, WI and will not include events in major markets such as Boston, Chicago, or New York. Advertisement of a job fair in a particular region will be provided three weeks in advance with a list of participating companies in attendance as they are confirmed. Specific information such as arrival and registration times, as well as the exact location of the fair, is provided. Users can link to city postings to retrieve maps of the area and fair site. If users are seeking relocation and do not find a career fair listed in a desired market, RCI representatives encourage job seekers to call the toll free number for the latest updates (1-800-707-3190). The confidential résumé database enables users to submit résumés electronically, by fax, or by mail, and are kept on file for 1-3 years. Employers participating in the career fair have access to a job seeker's résumé upon authorization from the user. The résumés are not shared with any other firms such as headhunting or recruiting offices.

Candidates may be considered for local, pre-arranged, private interviews. This is a nice web site that expands career fair listings to secondary markets.

The Lendman Group
http://www.lendman.com/

Conducting job fairs for over 30 years, the Lendman Group provides candidates with career fairs targeting the sales and management, and technical needs of various companies. Schedules of past and upcoming fairs throughout major cities are provided. Users can pre-register for fairs, enabling the Lendman Group to forward résumés and credentials to prospective employers. A list of participating employers is provided. Guidelines on electronic submission of résumés is supplied and encouraged. Articles from the Lendman's Career Magazine are provided to help the job seeker gain insight and tips on the interview process, résumé planning, and other employment related issues. Links to other career related sources are also provided.

National Career Centers USA, Inc.
http://www.foto.com/nccjobfair/

National Career Centers list career fairs primarily in the sales and business industry and high tech fields including computer programming, MIS, Research & Development, and engineering. The calendar of events provides the user with the date, city, hotel, and type of career fair. The events are listed quarterly giving users a good lead date for fair locations in a specific market. Fairs are scheduled for smaller markets as well as major cities. Companies participating in each type of fair are listed once clients are confirmed. Résumés can be submitted by fax and are only provided to company representatives attending the fair.

Westech Career Expo
http://www.careerexpo.com/pub/westech/

Westech Career Expo is a comprehensive career fair site providing a calendar of events up to one year in advance. Exhibitors are listed two weeks in advance with updates daily. The listings provide detailed information about the event and provides the user with the exact location of the fair and a map of the area. If users cannot attend the fair, they can post their résumé to a database. This résumé database is only available to the participating representatives of Westech Career Expo.

RÉSUMÉ SERVICES

Résumé Doctor
http://www1.mhv.net/~acorn/Acorn.html

Résumé Doctor, created by Fred Nagel, President of Acorn Career Counseling and Résumé Writing, is a résumé writing service that helps users create résumés that market their skills and experience. A valuable feature of this site is that it provides links to other resources that post résumés, with no charge to the user, on general employment networks, as well as specific career web sites. If a user decides to have their résumé reviewed by a career counselor and revisions are recommended, a fee for this service will be quoted. This web site provides valuable links and a potentially useful service to assist users in creating effective résumés and achieving suitable interviews.

RELOCATION SERVICES

Salary Relocation Calculator
http://www.homefair.com/homefair/cmr/salcalc.html

Supported by the Center for Mobility Resources, this site provides users with cost of living comparisons and other relocation information. Information in this site is collected from local, national, and government sources using local real estate boards and chambers of commerce. This site includes a "relocation wizard," which enables users to create a customized timeline to plan and organize their upcoming move. Links to real estate companies and apartment listings make this a great site to visit once a job has been found.

MEGALISTS

The following MegaLists pull together some of the more useful Internet accessible sites on career development and the job search. Two of the MegaLists provide descriptions along with ratings of each resource. The sites provided are chosen for their stability and usefulness.

Emory Colossal List of Career Links
http://www.emory.edu/CAREER/Links.html

Supported by Emory University, this site provides a description and rating of each web resource.

JobHunt: On-Line Job Mega-List
http://www.job-hunt.org/

This site, produced and maintained by Dane Spearing, has won numerous Internet awards and is quite impressive.

Job Search and Employment Opportunities: Best Bets from the Net
http://www.lib.umich.edu/chdocs/employment/

A great MegaList of career related resources providing a description and evaluation of some of the best resources around.

NEWSGROUPS

DejaNews
http://www.dejanews.com/forms/dnq.html

DejaNews, a Usenet newsgroup search utility, enables job seekers to post questions and talk to others on all topics relating to employment, career development, and the job search. The extensive searching capabilities allow users to target their search retrieving relevant articles from archived files of the Usenet newsgroup file.

A Virtual Government Documents Reference Collection

Deborah R. Hollis

SUMMARY. World Wide Web technology has reached the highest levels of U.S. government. Many changes are taking place at the federal level of government. Every cabinet level agency has a homepage and subordinate agencies are making gains in this new technology on a daily basis. This article highlights the web sites of the executive, legislative, and judicial branches of government. Well known government publications which are found in any traditional government documents reference collection are noted and recommended for both bookmarking and local web site development. The downside of electronic access is discussed as well. *[Article copies available for a fee from The Haworth Document Delivery Service: 1-800-342-9678. E-mail address: getinfo@haworth.com]*

INTRODUCTION

Is a virtual reference collection of government publications possible in the electronic environment? What kind of government information is currently available on the Internet and what can the student, scholar, business

Deborah R. Hollis is Government Publications Librarian for State & Foreign Documents, University Libraries, Campus Box 184, University of Colorado at Boulder, Boulder, CO 80309-0184.

The author wishes to thank Terry W. Fahy of the Center for Human Resource Research at The Ohio State University and Patricia McClure of the Government Publications Library at the University of Colorado at Boulder for their editorial assistance.

[Haworth co-indexing entry note]: "A Virtual Government Documents Reference Collection." Hollis, Deborah R. Co-published simultaneously in *The Reference Librarian* (The Haworth Press, Inc.) No. 57, 1997, pp. 31-43; and: *Reference Sources on the Internet: Off the Shelf and Onto the Web* (ed: Karen R. Diaz) The Haworth Press, Inc., 1997, pp. 31-43. Single or multiple copies of this article are available for a fee from The Haworth Document Delivery Service [1-800-342-9678, 9:00 a.m. - 5:00 p.m. (EST). E-mail address: getinfo@haworth.com].

person or public patron find that is of value on the World Wide Web? There is a lot to be excited about with regard to government-produced information, yet there are issues that should concern various constituencies. Under the Government Printing Office (GPO) Electronic Information Access Enhancement Act passed by Congress in 1993, the public is getting a rapidly expanding list of publications delivered free of charge over the Internet.[1] Fewer publications will be issued in standard formats from now on. Users are downloading electronic documents at the rate of more than two million per month.[2]

That the federal government is embracing new technology is evident in the Fall 1996 edition of the well known *Federal Yellow Book: Who's Who In Federal Departments and Agencies.* Internet homepage URLs are provided at the cabinet level of government as well as e-mail addresses for employees who have them. Independent agencies ranging from the Commodity Futures Trading Commission to the United States Information Agency have URLs as well.[3]

This kind of access allows the average citizen to bypass the media and yes, even libraries, for their information needs, but access is limited to those with the financial and technical support. Libraries still need to serve those who cannot access government information in their homes, schools, or offices. While the ability to access publications in a timely manner is indeed appealing, a major issue of access arises when the *only* way to obtain a document is electronically. The Commerce Department provides an excellent example of access issues and electronic government-produced information. The Census Bureau has plans to replace paper distribution with Internet-only distribution.[4] In conjunction with Internet-only availability three levels of access will be designed with a fee set by the Census Bureau at certain levels. The problems with this new approach are apparent, but hopefully designated federal depository libraries will absorb the cost of fee-based access to provide free access to state citizens. This is already the case with *Stat-USA,* a fee-based business and economic web site maintained by the Department of Commerce: many federal depositories purchased subscriptions to this service to provide free access to public patrons. While there are many benefits inherent in the use of electronic information, including more timely and broader public access, there is no conclusive data at this time to support the assertion that it will result in significant savings to either depository libraries or the Government.[5]

Other issues of electronic information distribution involve libraries, staff, and budgets. More electronic information means the additional responsibility of training staff to assist patrons in the use of Internet resources, and budgets are strained when libraries bear the burden of hardware and software purchases. Many electronic government publications are in the portable data file (PDF) format and require a system with enough random access memory (RAM) to handle the simultaneous use of various software packages. Electronic access is not easy if the required technical tools are not available. These are a combination of management and access issues. Library administrators will continue to be challenged to provide quality public service and access to these important information sources.

Federal information on the Web has developed beyond a public relations and directory format to actual data and full text publications. The format of federal web sites is becoming standardized. These web sites vary in design yet most explain and/or contain some variation of the following:

- the mission of the agency or office
- regional office or lab information; directory information; organizational structure
- links to the subordinate bureaus, agencies, divisions, etc.
- hot topics, news releases and/or current events newsletters in full text
- catalogs of publications that can be ordered if not the full text publications
- descriptions of agency programs, services and initiatives
- a "what's new" at the agency or on the web site feature
- statistical, sometimes interactive, data that can be downloaded
- descriptions of research funded and grant information
- regulations and standards; sections of the U.S. Code that pertain to that particular agency
- contacts for the appropriate Freedom of Information Act (FOIA) and Privacy Act (PA) Officers and Coordinators

The following web sites were identified for their usefulness to bibliographers for government publications. These sites provide legislative analysis, statistical resources, and the full text of publications which can be found in most traditional government publications reference collections.

EXECUTIVE BRANCH

The President
http://www.whitehouse.gov

Find out what was really said at the White House press briefing. Full-text press briefings, press releases, the President's radio addresses, Executive Orders, and more. Take a virtual tour of the White House and find out about the history of the building and its former tenants. Has historic documents such as the *Declaration of Independence, the U.S. Constitution, NAFTA,* and *GATT* in full text. Provides links to the President's Cabinet and federal agencies and commissions such as NASA, FDIC, EPA. Bookmark this to reach all sites discussed in this article including the legislative and judicial branches of government.

Department of Agriculture
http://www.usda.gov

Full-text publications about a multitude of agricultural issues. The 1994 and 1995-1996 editions of *Agricultural Statistics* are available in .PDF format under the National Agricultural Statistics Service homepage. The *Adobe Acrobat* reader is a linked site for those needing to download the software to view the full text.

Department of Commerce
http://www.doc.gov

Access to *Stat-USA* (business, economic, social, and environmental information), *Fedworld,* patent and trademark database, the Census Bureau (see below), weather information from NOAA, and the National Institute for Standards and Technology (NIST). This is a MUST bookmark site as well as the following subagency:

U.S. Census Bureau
http://www.census.gov

Should just be titled "statistics-R-us." Hundreds of reports about population, housing, and living conditions in the United States. Reports date from 1992 to the present. The 1995 and 1996 *Statistical Abstract of the U.S.* are available in full text but the web surfer must have *Adobe Acrobat* reader software which can be retrieved from (http://www.shareware.com). The *Statistical Abstract* will be password restricted in the near future.

Department of Defense
http://www.dtic.dla.mil/defenselink

Annual report to the President and Congress, defense directives, important speeches concerning defense issues, and a defense fact file that contains information prepared for the media about aircraft, weapons, etc. Links to homepages for the Air Force, Army, Navy, Marine Corps, Coast Guard, National Guard, and the Joint Chiefs of Staff. Great for high school students, military buffs, and anyone interested in military affairs and history.

Department of Education
http://www.ed.gov

Many full text publications about a wide range of educational issues ranging from student financial aid to statistical information. Publications date from 1993 to the present. Best of all this site has *The Condition of Education, 1996* and *Digest of Education Statistics* and *The Projections of Education Statistics to 2006* available in full text.

Department of Energy
http://www.doe.gov

Energy related reports. Has *DOE Reports Bibliographic* database which contains citations for DOE sponsored scientific and technical reports covering the period of January 1, 1994 to present. Also has the *Human Subjects Research Projects* database which began in 1994. Can search by subject or DOE or non-DOE site that conducts research involving human subjects.

Department of Health and Human Services
http://www.os.dhhs.gov

Coordinates consumer health related web sites that cover a wide range of topics. Examples include links to homepages for Alzheimer's Disease, cancer, and adoption information. Links to the Consumer Information Center in Pueblo, Colorado where full text federal consumer publications are available to download. Links to the full text version of the *Catalog of Federal Domestic Assistance*. Has the *1994 Green Book: Data and information on selected social welfare programs*. Links to the Centers for Disease Control and *Grateful Med* on the Internet, and much more.

Department of Housing and Urban Development
http://www.hud.gov

Explains various housing programs designed to assist the first time home buyer, the elderly, low-income families, and migrant farm workers.

Good consumer information site about home ownership. Provides access to current *Commerce Business Daily (CBD)* issue as well as archive of *CBD* from 1995 to the present. Has funding and contracting information for community planners and business people. Lists HUD home sales by state and city.

Department of the Interior
http://www.doi.gov

Links to DOI and its subagencies; the National Park Service, U.S. Fish and Wildlife, Land Management, Reclamation, Minerals Management Service, Office of Surface Mining and U.S. Geological Survey. A fun and informative surfing experience. Links to the Bureau of Indian Affairs which has the 1996 *American Indian Tribal Directory,* the official list of U.S. federally recognized tribes.

Department of Justice
http://www.usdoj.gov

A must for anyone conducting criminal justice and law enforcement research. Of major importance are the Bureau of Justice Statistics and National Criminal Justice Reference homepages. Can access many full text reports such as the 1995 preliminary findings of the *National Crime Victimization Survey, Drugs and Crime Facts, 1994,* and the well known *Sourcebook of Criminal Justice Statistics.* Another site of interest includes: *Federal Bureau of Investigation (FBI) (http://www.fbi.gov)* Lists the Ten Most Wanted Fugitives, current cases, e.g., TWA Flight 800 and the Unabomber, preliminary results of 1995 Hate Crime Statistics.

Department of Labor
http://www.dol.gov

The link to the Bureau of Labor Statistics (BLS) has the most interesting information. A project of possible interest to academic reference librarians is the National Longitudinal Survey of Youth (NLSY) Bibliography, a searchable database (http://www.chrr.ohio-state.edu/nls-bib/). This annotated bibliography identifies every research project, publication, dissertation, etc., that used the federally funded NLSY data, begun in 1968, to analyze every imaginable labor market experience in the United States. This site is an excellent example of government research that becomes more accessible via the Internet. The *Occupational Outlook Handbook* is available in full text.

Department of State
http://www.state.gov

Current full text issues of *Dispatch Magazine* available in ASCII files or PDF. Full text access to *1995 Country Reports on Economic Policy* and *Trade Practices* and *Human Rights Reports.* Press releases about current U.S. foreign policy. Has information about the Foreign Service examination and career opportunities.

Department of Transportation
http://www.dot.gov

Access to full text DOT regulations, orders, policies and legislation. Of interest to some, a *Fatigue Resource Directory* with links to research and a directory of sleep disorder clinics in the country. Links to DOT bulletin boards like the *Hazardous Materials Information Exchange BBS, Fedworld,* and *OST Human Resources BBS.*

Department of the Treasury
http://www.ustreas.gov

Good consumer information about savings bonds and T-bills. Links to the IRS and downloadable 1992-1996 tax forms, instructions and publications. Secret Service, U.S. Customs, and small business information links.

Department of Veterans Affairs
http://www.va.gov

Good site of consumer related information regarding veterans rights, benefits, and services with limited statistics about the veteran population. Has a *National Cemetery System* page that might interest genealogists. This site lists all of the 114 military cemeteries in the U.S. (and Puerto Rico) and under "Burial Location Assistance" explains how a genealogist can request (free of charge) to find out whether a relative is buried in one these VA cemeteries.

Other Agencies of Note

Central Intelligence Agency
http://www.odci.gov/cia

Has the *World Factbook, Chiefs of State and Cabinet Members of Foreign Governments,* and *Handbook of International Economic Statistics, 1995.*

Environmental Protection Agency
http://www.epa.gov

Full-text fact sheets about radon, asbestos, etc., and consumer guides about myriad environmental issues. Superfund site information by state and Toxic Release Inventory (TRI) for local community information. Has much to offer.

Social Security Administration
http://www.ssa.gov/

Good consumer information site for guides in applying for social security benefits. Has full-text pamphlets that can be downloaded.

LEGISLATIVE BRANCH

http://www.access.gpo.gov (Select GPO Access)
http://thomas.loc.gov
telnet://locis.loc.gov

The three major free Internet sites for legislative analysis are *GPO Access, Thomas,* and the Library of Congress Information System (*LOCIS*). These sites help the student/researcher track proposed legislation through Congress. The full text of bills, information about bill sponsors, status of bills, transcripts of what is said on the floor of Congress (the *Congressional Record*), and much more is now available electronically. *GPO Access* and *Thomas* are available via the world wide web but *LOCIS* is only available through Telnet.[6] *LOCIS* is a valuable resource since it provides summary bill information and legislative histories beginning with the 93rd Congress (1973). The following chart compares the three sites and highlights the strengths and weaknesses of each:

CHART 1. Comparison of Legislative Tools on the Internet[7]

	GPO Access www.access.gpo.gov	Thomas thomas.loc.gov	Library of Congress Information System (LOCIS) telnet://locis.loc.gov
Dates of Coverage	Varies. Begins with legislative sources from 103rd Congress (1993) but most coverage from 1994 to present.	Varies. Most legislative sources from 104th Congress (1995) to the present.	Begins with the 93rd Congress (1973) to the present.
Scope	Comprehensive. Legislation PL103-40 mandates complete publication of many sources and the speed of publication. Full text of bills available.	Selected. Fewer publications included in the databases. More editorial work is involved in building the links–so coverage is generally not as complete or speedy. Includes selected historical publications. Full text of bills available from 1993 to present.	Detailed legislative histories and digests of bills. Full text of bills not available.
Ease of use	Structure of the database makes it more complex to use. Advanced searches in some databases, e.g., *Federal Register*, simplify searching with check boxes. Help screens are available.	Structure of the database makes it easy to use. Best for high school audience or above. Help screens available.	Cryptic until used a couple of times. Help screens are available.
Boolean logic available	yes–Similar to Boolean logic used in many databases.	yes–but complex. See the "About Thomas" section for assistance.	yes–Type "help c" for samples of the "combine" syntax.
Proximity searching	no	yes. Uses the INQUERY information retrieval system. Has good instructions for use.	Begins with 99th Congress. Instructions found under the "help" menu. Select "searching file" and then "subject."
Controlled vocabulary searching (assigned subject headings)	no	yes–but buried	yes. Use "s" and term/s to search the controlled vocabulary index.
Keyword searching	yes	yes	yes. Use "r" which stands for "retrieve" for keyword searching

CHART 1 (continued)

	GPO Access www.access.gpo.gov	Thomas thomas.loc.gov	Library of Congress Information System (LOCIS) telnet://locis.loc.gov
Simultaneous searching of multiple databases	yes	no	yes
Legislative histories	yes–In the *History of Bills* database.	yes–Under the *Bill Summary and Status* section.	yes–From 1973 to present.
Bill status	yes–Select the *History of Bills* database. Coverage from 1994 to present.	yes–*Bill Summary and Status*. Other versions of the bill, debate in the *Congressional Record*, Committee prints are all linked. From 1995 to present.	yes
Hot bills marked	no	yes	yes
Links to key documents	no	yes–Use the *Bill Summary and Status*. Linked to other versions of bill, *Congressional Record*, and Committee prints.	no
Vetoed bills identified	yes–Located in *History of Bills* database.	yes–located under the *Bill Summary and Status* section.	yes

Only *GPO Access* is considered official since it is the result of PL103-40 passed by Congress in 1993. *Thomas* is the result of the Republican revolution and like *LOCIS* is maintained by the Library of Congress. These sites differ from the fee-based services of *Legi-slate* and *LEXIS/ NEXIS* in their historical coverage of information and the availability of full-text hearings before Congress. *GPO Access* and *Thomas* are strong for current legislative analysis while *LOCIS* provides coverage from 1973 to the present but lacks full-text bills. The major weakness of all three free legislative World Wide Web sites is the lack of congressional hearing transcripts.

JUDICIAL BRANCH

FedWorld/FLITE Supreme Court Decisions
http://www.fedworld.gov/supcourt/

Contains the full text of 7,407 U.S. Supreme Court Decisions from 1937 to 1975. Decisions available as ASCII text files that can be read on browser's screen or saved to hard drive and accessed by using most word processor programs.[8]

GPO Access
http://www.access.gpo.gov

Provides same coverage as *Fedworld*; Supreme Court Decisions from 1937 to 1975.

Decisions of the United States Supreme Court:
A Service of the Legal Information Institute, Cornell
http://www.law.cornell.edu/supct/

Maintained by Cornell Law School. Provides the Court calendar for 1996-1997, decisions of the U.S. Court of Appeals, and biographical information about each justice as well as their recent opinions. Has recent Court decisions (since 1990) and selected historic decisions.

United States Federal Judiciary
http://www.uscourts.gov/

Functions as a clearinghouse for information from and about the Judicial Branch of the U.S. Government.

WEB SITES FOR GOVERNMENT PUBLICATIONS LIBRARIANS

National Security Archive
http://www.seas.gwu.edu/nsarchive/

All of the previous resources are unclassified in nature. The National Security Archive (NSA) constructed an excellent web site that identifies their major declassified microfiche collections. NSA is an independent non-governmental research institute and library located at The George Washington University in Washington, D.C.[9] The Archive collects and publishes declassified documents acquired through the Freedom of Information Act (FOIA).[10]

U.S. Government Printing Office
http://www.access.gpo.gov

Bookmark this site to keep abreast of developments of federal electronic information. A one-stop shopping place for a wealth of government information products. Links to the Superintendent of Documents web page. *GPO Access* provides many full-text publications for legislative analysis.

University of Idaho
http://drseuss.lib.uidaho.edu:80/govdoc/otherdep.html

Organized links to web pages of Federal Depository Library Program (FDLP) members. Has great link to the University of Memphis called *Migrating Government Publications* which tracks all of the paper editions of government publications that are currently available in full text on the Internet by title or SuDoc classification.

University of Michigan
http://www.lib.umich.edu/libhome/Documents.center/doclibs.html

One-stop shopping site for organized links to ALA, ALA/GODORT and its task forces, ARL, various state GODORT organizations, federal depositories; identifies United Nations depositories, links to index of GPO's *Administrative Notes* since 1980 and full text since 1995. Links to basic depository library documents, ceased SuDocs numbers, and information about the Depository Library Council.

University of Colorado at Boulder
http://www.colorado.edu/libraries/govpubs

Just one fine example of how government documents librarians can respond to the transition of government information to a new medium. This site is developed and maintained to meet the research needs of the campus, local community, and state and congressional constituencies.

CONCLUSION

It is apparent that the federal level of government is embracing new technology with a vengeance and is preparing to cross that bridge into the

21st century. The much valued printed reference sources that librarians have relied on are making the transition as well. Librarians have an opportunity to assist the public in identifying and organizing these important web sites. While there are positive and negative issues that result from these changes, the public can still benefit from greater access to these important research tools. Libraries will continue to be the key in providing access to government information for all citizens regardless of economic status or computer ownership.

REFERENCES

1. Wayne P. Kelley, "Testimony Before the Committee on Rules and Administration, United States Senate, Tuesday, June 18, 1996," *Administrative Notes: Newsletter of the Federal Depository Library Program*, vol. 17, no. 9, July 15, 1996, p. 9.

2. Ibid., p. 9-10.

3. *Federal Yellow Book: Who's Who In Federal Departments and Agencies*, Washington, D.C. : Washington Monitor, 1996, p. xii-xiii.

4. Timothy Byrne, Deborah Hollis, and Margaret Jobe, "Cybercitizenry: Government Information in Transition," *Colorado Libraries*, Fall 1995, p. 29.

5. Wayne P. Kelley, "Panel Discussion before the Federal Librarians Round Table (FLRT), 1996 Annual ALA Conference, New York, NY, July 6, 1996," *Administrative Notes: Newsletter of the Federal Depository Library Program*, vol. 17, no. 10, July 25, 1996, p. 2.

6. Netscape does NOT include a telnet "client" application. A client application may be downloaded from (http://www.shareware.com) for any platform (Mac, Windows, Windows 95, etc.). After this is installed configure *Netscape* to open the telnet client by opening the "Options" pull down menu. Choose "General Preferences," and then choose "Apps." After Netscape is configured to "open" the telnet client it will automatically open whenever a telnet address is entered in the Web URL (Uniform Resource Locator) format. Written by Margaret Jobe in her guide *U.S. Legislative Information on the Internet,* Government Publications Library, University of Colorado at Boulder, Sept. 25, 1996, p. 6.

7. Margaret Jobe, *U.S. Legislative Information on the Internet,* Government Publications Library, University of Colorado at Boulder, September 25, 1996, abridged version of chart on p. 1-4.

8. "U.S. Supreme Court," *Fedworld,* http://www.fedworld.gov/supcourt/ (December 13, 1996).

9. *National Security Archive* web page. http://www.seas.gwu.edu/nsarchive/ (December 30, 1996).

10. Ibid.

Patent Resources on the Internet:
A Reference Librarian's Guide

Lisa Pillow

SUMMARY. This article profiles web sites that are intended for browsing and reference in patent searching. The web provides limited information and cannot be considered a resource for comprehensive patent research. *[Article copies available for a fee from The Haworth Document Delivery Service: 1-800-342-9678. E-mail address: getinfo@ haworth.com]*

INTRODUCTION

When it comes to it patents, librarians and patrons alike should understand that not all patent sources on the Internet are free and like most Internet sources, little substance and standardized quality control exists.[1] Given the nature of the use of intellectual property protection as a highly technical area, authority is everything. This becomes crucial when considering what sources can be used for reference. Because freely accessible resources allow searching without the constraints of costs for connect times, the Internet resources profiled in this article are intended for browsing and reference for *some* valuable patent information and not for extensive patent searching.

So what is available for retrieving free and relevant patent information on the Internet? When limiting the sources to those that offer free access, the majority of the information available on the Internet is general in

---

Lisa Pillow is Reference Librarian, Main Library, Ohio State University.

[Haworth co-indexing entry note]: "Patent Resources on the Internet: A Reference Librarian's Guide." Pillow, Lisa. Co-published simultaneously in *The Reference Librarian* (The Haworth Press, Inc.) No. 57, 1997, pp. 45-49; and: *Reference Sources on the Internet: Off the Shelf and Onto the Web* (ed: Karen R. Diaz) The Haworth Press, Inc., 1997, pp. 45-49. Single or multiple copies of this article are available for a fee from The Haworth Document Delivery Service [1-800-342-9678, 9:00 a.m. - 5:00 p.m. (EST). E-mail address: getinfo@haworth.com].

scope. Many sites offer basic facts about patents, downloadable U.S. patent applications, application procedures, answers to frequently asked questions, definitions of intellectual property, and links to the major free sites such as the United States Patent and Trademark Office (USPTO) homepage, the U.S. Bibliographic Patent Database, the AIDS Patent Database, and foreign patent office sites.

RESOURCES

United States Patent and Trademark Office (USPTO) Home Page
URL: http://www.uspto.gov

This homepage offers useful information about the USPTO including press releases, current fees for patent applications, PTO information contacts, a roster of patent attorneys and agents authorized to practice before the USPTO, and a complete list of addresses and telephone numbers of each Patent and Trademark Depository Libraries in the United States and Puerto Rico. Full-text brochures, *Basic Facts About Patents and Basic Facts About Registering a Trademark* are available, as well as a downloadable patent application, U.S. and international legal materials including the Patent Cooperation Treaty, the Disclosure Document Program, along with links to other intellectual property websites including the European Patent Office, the United Kingdom Patent Office, the World Intellectual Property Organization, and the United States Copyright Office.

USPTO provides access to two patent databases: the *U.S. Patent Bibliographic Database* which includes bibliographic data from 1976 to the present, and the *AIDS Patent Database* which includes the full text and images of AIDS related patents issued by the U.S., European and Japanese Patent offices in English from 1995 to 1996.

U.S. Patent Database

As of November 9, 1995, the U.S. Patent Office made searchable bibliographic data of U.S. patents issued from 1976 to the present available on the Internet for free retrieval. As Nancy Lambert wrote in 1995, "The PTO patent database is mostly for the patent-information-deprived,"[2] and not an alternative to the patent information disseminated by the USPTO through the Patent and Trademark Depository Library Program (PTDLP). The PTDLs, approximately eighty, are located in the 50 states and Puerto Rico and provide free access to USPTO electronic products such as CASSIS (Classification and Search Support Information System) which contains searchable patents back to 1790. The PTDLs also have print resources such as the *Official Gazette* and *The Manual of Classification* which are essential when conducting extensive patent searches. The patent abstracts on the Internet database are searchable by keyword using Boolean or advanced searching. The Boolean option enables searching using operators and/or selected fields like title, inventor or abstract. Options are also available for searching the entire database or specific years and ranking the results chronologically or by relevancy. The advanced search protocol uses command strings for complex Boolean searching, field search, and right truncation. Tables for U.S. Patent Field Codes are available on the advanced search page. As with the Boolean search, results can be ranked chronologically or by relevance. Detailed help screens and query examples are available to assist users with formulating searches.

Once the results are listed, users can access the patent abstract(s) which include the date of filing and/or the date the patent was granted, the name(s) and address(es) of the inventor(s), related application data, application number, the class and subclasses related to each claim, and references cited, essentially all the information found on the front page of a full-text patent. Some of this information is linked to additional information. These links are mainly related to the references cited and provide access to abstracts of cited patents or to class and subclass information, which subsequently links the user to the U.S. Patent Classification definitions for each class and subclass.

The *U.S. Patent Database* is useful for finding quick bibliographic information, such as names of an inventor of a particular patent or finding the title of a patent when all the information a patron has is the patent number. It is also important to keep in mind that this database is not retrospective and that it only includes patents filed and/or granted since 1976.

Patent AIDS Database

The AIDS Patent Database provides access to over 1,500 images and text of U.S., European and Japanese patents related to AIDS. The database has been established through a joint venture between the U.S. Commerce Department, the National Science Foundation (NSF) and the Clearinghouse for Networked Information Discovery and Retrieval (CNDIR). The database is comprised of three indexes, (1) U.S. patents, (2) European patents, and (3) Japanese patents which must be searched individually. The database allows searching and browsing. If the browsing option is chosen, AIDS related patents are listed by patent number, with the most recent listed first. The search option allows search strings including field searching. A table containing searchable fields and tags are on the search screen, and indicates if the individual fields are searchable in all of the indexes or only certain indexes. Once relevant hits are listed, the full-text and images of the patents can be accessed. The site offers a link which cross-references the index to find like patents. Like the *U.S. Patent Database,* this site offers excellent help screens including how to formulate queries. Text and images are in English and cover the time period from January 1995 to December 1996.

IBM Patent Server Home Page
URL: http://patent.womplex.ibm.com/

The IBM Patent Server accesses over 26 years of U.S. patent descriptions from January 5, 1971 to the present. It differs from the USPTO Internet database in that it also include images of patents granted in the last ten years. The database can be searched in its entirety or from 1995 to the present. Like the USPTO Internet database, it allows searching by keyword, patent number, Boolean text search or advanced text search. The advanced text search allows specific field searching, but not with search string commands because the fields are searchable directly from the screen.

Patent Searching Tutorial, University of Texas, Austin
URL: http://www.lib.utexas.edu:80/Libs/ENG/PTUT/og.html

Nancy Green, a librarian at the Richard W. McKinney Engineering Library at the University of Texas in Austin, has created a patent tutorial for users of the library's Patent and Trademark Depository Library materials. While some of the information is specific to the McKinney Engineering Library, most of the tutorial can be used by anyone who wants an introduction on doing a basic patent search with the services provided by a PTDL or plans to in the future. As a patent librarian, Ms. Green has created a tutorial which takes the user step by step through a basic patent search for an invention using all of the tools necessary to conduct an initial search. Often novice patrons are confused about the patent classification system and definitions. By clicking on specific icons, the user can get an introduction to the patent classification system and the *Index to Patent Classification* with illustrations and easy to follow explanations. The tutorial is an excellent introduction to the sometimes mysterious world of patent searching for first time searchers and illustrates the use of both the paper and electronic patent depository materials needed to conduct a basic patent search. PTDLs may find this particularly useful to show patrons when the reference desk is busy, the phone is ringing, and time is not immediately at hand. Ms. Green also has created a trademark search tutorial which can be found at: *http://www.lib.utexas.edu/Libs/Eng/PTUT/ptut.html*

SOURCES

1. Nancy Lambert, "The Idiot's Guide to Patent Resources on the Internet," *Searcher* 3(1995 May): 34-39.
2. Nancy Lambert, "More Patents–Lots More–on the Internet," *Searcher* 3(1995 Nov/Dec): 24-27.

BUSINESS AND SOCIAL SCIENCES

Reference Sources on the Internet: Geography and International Studies

Susan E. Clark

SUMMARY. Many web sites on the Internet are useful in helping answer reference questions in geography and international studies. This paper describes web sites which provide maps, gazetteers and country information. Also included are web guides which collect and organize numerous links to geographical and international sites. *[Article copies available for a fee from The Haworth Document Delivery Service: 1-800-342-9678. E-mail address: getinfo@haworth.com]*

Geography on the Internet is great fun. There are so many sites to explore; in fact, there's a whole world to explore. The challenge lies in finding what you need quickly, since it's very easy to be distracted by the profusion of interesting sources.

Susan E. Clark is Reference Librarian/Bibliographic Instruction Coordinator, William Knox Holt Memorial Library, University of the Pacific, 3501 Pacific Ave., Stockton, CA 95211. E-mail: sclark@uop.edu

[Haworth co-indexing entry note]: "Reference Sources on the Internet: Geography and International Studies." Clark, Susan E. Co-published simultaneously in *The Reference Librarian* (The Haworth Press, Inc.) No. 57, 1997, pp. 51-54; and: *Reference Sources on the Internet: Off the Shelf and Onto the Web* (ed: Karen R. Diaz) The Haworth Press, Inc., 1997, pp. 51-54. Single or multiple copies of this article are available for a fee from The Haworth Document Delivery Service [1-800-342-9678, 9:00 a.m. - 5:00 p.m. (EST). E-mail address: getinfo@haworth.com].

MAPS AND GAZETTEERS

Many sites on the Web offer maps, from simple reference maps to very detailed maps. Although a computer monitor cannot approach the quality of a finely-printed map, the following sites are useful for quick look-ups at the reference desk as well as extended browsing.

The *Perry-Castaneda Library Map Collection* (University of Texas) *(http://www.lib.utexas.edu/Libs/PCL/Map_collection/Map_collection.html)* is an interesting site which provides electronic maps from the collections of the University of Texas. The library staff have scanned about 1,900 public domain maps from their collection. Included are maps of world cities from the U.S. Department of State, country maps from the CIA, maps of national parks, historical maps and more. The site also provides many links to other map resources on the Web.

Most libraries own at least one of the National Geographic Society's superb atlases. If you're at a computer without an atlas close at hand, try the *National Geographic Map Machine* at *http://www.nationalgeographic. com/ngs/maps/cartographic.html*. This site includes political and physical maps of countries and regions of the world. Although lacking the fine resolution and detail of printed maps, these online maps can be handy for ready reference. The site also includes facts, flags, and profiles of countries of the world.

A number of commercial sites provide online maps that can be useful for ready reference. One example is *Magellan Maps (http://pathfinder. com/travel/maps/index.html)*. Point to this site for quick and colorful on-line maps of Paris, Singapore, and many other cities. For links to more map sites on the Web, go to *Yahoo Maps (http://www.yahoo.com/Science/ Geography/Maps/)* and select from a variety of sites, both educational and commercial.

Gazetteers or geographical dictionaries have always been standard reference tools. For an online gazetteer, go to the U.S. Census Bureau's *U.S. Gazetteer (http://www.census.gov/cgi-bin/gazetteer)*, which links to the Census Bureau's TIGER Mapping Service to provide detailed maps of U.S. locations. Just type in the name of any town or city (this site does not search for physical features) and receive a map on the screen that can be customized with the user's choice of features such as highways, railroads, congressional districts, county boundaries, parks, latitude and longitude.

To search for physical features such as mountains or lakes, as well as cities and other place names, try the *USGS Geographic Names Information System* at *http://www-nmd.usgs.gov/www/gnis/*. According to the USGS, "The GNIS is our nation's official repository of domestic geographic names information." Containing information on about two million place names and features in the United States, this site uses the TIGER Mapping Service (U.S. Census Bureau) to provide online maps to the user. For international place names, point to the *GEOnet Names Server* at *http://164.214.2.59/gns/html/index.html.* This international gazetteer is maintained by the National Imagery and Mapping Agency in cooperation with the U.S. Board on Geographic Names. Searchable by geographic name (physical or cultural), the site provides latitude and longitude but does not link to a mapping program.

COUNTRY INFORMATION

A familiar source for most reference librarians, the CIA *World Factbook (http://www.odci.gov/cia/publications/95fact/index.html)* is useful for statistics and brief information on the countries of the world. It also includes a basic reference map for each country and maps of world regions. Another source of country information, U.S. State Department *Background Notes* are kept in pamphlet form in many libraries. The full text of these reports on about 200 countries is available at *http://www. state.gov/www/background_notes/.* Each report includes statistics and basic information on a country's geography, people, economy, government, history and politics.

For more in-depth country information, go to the Library of Congress *Country Studies (http://lcweb2.loc.gov/frd/cs/cshome.html).* Many libraries purchase these studies in book form for their detailed information on the politics, economy, history, geography, culture and people of each country in the series. Although the online versions currently lack the books' illustrations and bibliographies, they contain full text for about 70 countries at this time. Some of the studies have not been updated for several years, yet the information on social structure, ethnic groups, status of women, human rights and many other topics is invaluable and can be difficult to find in other sources.

Another way to access country information is through the *Electronic Embassy (http://www.embassy.org/),* which provides links to foreign embassies in Washington, DC. Many embassy home pages provide detailed information on their countries: economics, politics, culture and travel information. Of course the user will want to keep in mind the potential for bias in government-sponsored sites.

INTERNATIONAL ORGANIZATIONS

International organizations are important sources for international relations information, treaties and other policy documents. A frequently-visited site at many reference desks is the *United Nations* home page at *http://www.un.org/*. This site provides detailed information about the U.N.'s history, structure and functions, U.N. news and events, and links to numerous full-text documents such as resolutions, committee reports and conference publications. Other international organizations have useful home pages, such as the *Association of Southeast Asian Nations (http://www.asean.or.id/)* and the *Organization of American States (http://www.oas.org/)*. Many other international organizations can be found through the web guides listed below.

WEB GUIDES FOR GEOGRAPHY AND INTERNATIONAL STUDIES

There are several useful web guides which have collected and organized links to sites related to geography and international studies. *Geographical, Cultural, and People-Related Links (http://www.cs.uidaho.edu/~connie/interests-geography.html)* is very helpful for finding links to sites about the people of the world and their cultures, languages and religions, as well as links to countries by region. Another excellent web guide is *International and Area Studies (http://www.clark.net/pub/lschank/web/country.html)*. This site provides links to country web sites as well as international organizations (government and non-governmental), international news sources, treaties and other documents, universities and much more. Another well-organized guide to international information and organizations is *IANWeb* (International Affairs Network) at *http://www.pitt.edu/~ian/resource/statist.htm*.

Web guides by region can be very helpful to the librarian and researcher. A few well-organized regional guides are: *African Studies WWW* (U. Penn) *(http://www.sas.upenn.edu/African_Studies/AS.html); Asian Studies WWW Virtual Library (http://coombs.anu.edu.au/WWWVL-AsianStudies.html); European Home Page (http://s700.uminho.pt/europa.html); Latin American Studies (http://lanic.utexas.edu/las.html); Middle Eastern Studies (http://menic.utexas.edu/mes.html); and REESWeb: Russian and Eastern European Studies (http://www.pitt.edu/~cjp/rees.html)*.

There are a myriad of sources on the Internet for geography and international studies. The above sites are only a sample of what's available. Researchers interested in these subjects are often explorers by nature. They have much to discover on the World Wide Web!

Education Resources

Margaret M. Jobe

SUMMARY. Governmental, non-profit, and commercial organizations are putting a variety of materials online which provide access to information previously published in print, or on stand-alone fee-based databases. Although it is still difficult to locate information efficiently on the Internet, access to relevant materials has been improved by subject-organized online indexes of resources. These indexes take some of the chaos out of locating relevant materials. Rapid growth in online in electronic publishing combined with access to resources via organized indexes to online information make the Internet useful to reference librarians and educators. This article lists some of the resources and access points for information relevant to educators and librarians. *[Article copies available for a fee from The Haworth Document Delivery Service: 1-800-342-9678. E-mail address: getinfo@haworth.com]*

INTRODUCTION

Promoted aggressively by individuals such as Vice President Al Gore, the Internet is covered extensively in the media. Gore, credited with coining the phrase "information superhighway" seventeen years ago,[1] is an advocate for the National Information Infrastructure (NII) which proposes to bring Internet and telecommunications connectivity to every school in

Margaret M. Jobe is International Documents Librarian and Webmaster, Government Publications Library, University of Colorado at Boulder, Campus Box 184, Boulder, CO 80309-0184.

[Haworth co-indexing entry note]: "Education Resources." Jobe, Margaret M. Co-published simultaneously in *The Reference Librarian* (The Haworth Press, Inc.) No. 57, 1997, pp. 55-62; and: *Reference Sources on the Internet: Off the Shelf and Onto the Web* (ed: Karen R. Diaz) The Haworth Press, Inc., 1997, pp. 55-62. Single or multiple copies of this article are available for a fee from The Haworth Document Delivery Service [1-800-342-9678, 9:00 a.m. - 5:00 p.m. (EST). E-mail address: getinfo@haworth.com].

the United States. Even before the dream of the NII becomes a reality, educators and those who serve them are exploring use of the Internet in an educational setting. Educators are using telecommunications for information collection, two-way communication, distance learning, and transfer of instructional software and simulations.[2] Future uses of the NII are envisioned to include universal access for students, simulations, easy-to use interfaces for persons with disabilities, and multimedia interactive learning programs.[3] Although the schools report insufficient numbers of computers, modems, telephone lines, and other equipment,[4] educators and librarians are beginning to use the Internet for classroom and reference activities as federal agencies, commercial publishers, educational organizations, and individuals publish relevant materials electronically.

With the maturing of the World Wide Web (WWW) technology, state, local, and federal agencies are exploiting the Web to deliver information which was previously available only in print or on stand-alone databases. For example, the Department of Education has mounted Web editions of popular reference tools like the *Digest of Education Statistics, Youth Indicators,* and *Student Guide to Financial Aid.* It has also created online access to the last five years of the ERIC database, which combines the two print indexes *Research in Education* (RIE) and *Current Index to Journals in Education* (CIJE). ERIC, previously available in print, online from fee-based services and on leased or purchased CD-ROMs, is now freely available to anyone with Internet access. The department has been able to take advantage of Web technology to capture a larger audience for its publications and information.

Commercial and non-profit organizations are using the Internet to mount online versions of popular reference tools. Both Peterson's, publisher of popular college guide products, and the College Entrance Examination Board, which administers many of the required college examinations, have introduced Web sites with advanced search and retrieval capabilities. Library patrons and students can use the Peterson's and College Board sites to locate colleges and universities which meet their specific needs. Armed with information gleaned from these two sites, the user can then access the home page of individual schools by using a locational tool like Christina DeMello's College and University Home Pages, which indexes higher education Web sites worldwide. While individual Web sites vary widely in their content and organization, they often include such information as admissions policies, course catalogs, graduation requirements, and faculty directories. The process of choosing a school could potentially be transformed by the electronic campus "visit."

Although the Internet lacks a centralized catalog of resources, individuals and organizations are creating subject-classified indexes, often called "hotlists," which link Internet-accessible resources in an organized format. The organization and content of hotlists vary widely, reflecting the personalities of the creators. Teachers and librarians can use hotlists to find information on creating an acceptable use policy for the Internet in a classroom or library setting, to locate projects on which their students can collaborate with other schools, and to find Internet resources which complement and enrich the curriculum. Hotlists can link to vendors of educational material, to experts willing to respond to e-mail queries, and to educational organizations.

The following resources, stable-over-time, well-organized, and consistently updated, provide good access to educational information on the Internet.

FEDERAL OR FEDERALLY-FUNDED WEB SITES

Ask ERIC (http://ericir.syr.edu/). This site for education professionals includes information on educational practice and research. Major components of the site are the "Question and Answer Service" and "Virtual Library." Educational practitioners use the Q and A service to submit a question to an information specialist. Within 48 hours, Ask ERIC will respond with *ERIC* database searches, *ERIC Digests*, and Internet resources. The "Virtual Library" includes lesson plans, guides to educational television series, access to the *ERIC* database, searchable full-text *ERIC Digests* (summaries of current educational research), Ask ERIC Info-Guides (topical guides to Internet and *ERIC* resources), *Goals 2000* initiatives, educational conference calendars, and archives of education-related listservs, including LM_NET, K12ADMIN, and KIDSPHERE. The site also has links to the individual *ERIC* Clearinghouses which contribute to the *ERIC* database and print products. The Ask ERIC site includes links to the earlier gopher-based version of the site which can be found at *gopher://ericir.syr.edu/.* Both the Web and gopher sites are individually searchable from the search screen, but the Web and gopher versions are not fully integrated. For example, a search for "acceptable use" in the gopher search interface retrieves a significant number of policies on acceptable use of the Internet contributed by individual school districts. A search for the same terms in the Web search interface yields very different results: documents retrieved are lesson plans, and Ask ERIC Infoguides which contain both terms but do not relate to acceptable use of the Internet

in schools. Both components should be searched for comprehensive results.
   Department of Education (http://www.ed.gov/). Teachers can use the Department of Education as a starting point when searching for federal programs, statistics, and initiatives. The site features press releases, notices from the department which appeared in the *Federal Register,* a searchable *ERIC* database 1991-1996, the department's budget, directories of offices and individuals, and a wide variety of publications about its research efforts and programs of the department. Sample titles include: *Preparing Your Child for College,* [titles in] the *Helping Your Child* series, resource directories, professional publications for teachers and a wide variety of statistical publications. The statistical publications include standard reference tools like Digest of Education Statistics, *Condition of Education,* and *Youth Indicators* in hypertext markup language (HTML) format for on-screen viewing and printing or Adobe Acrobat® .pdf format for downloading and printing of a typeset-quality document. Some older publications are available in a compressed .zip format. The decompressed files include a mixture of ASCII text files, GIF images, and spreadsheet files. Pages include instructions and downloadable viewing and decompression software. *Edsearch: Education Statistics on Disk,* a searchable database of 2,000 tables, charts, and text files from major publications, is also available for download. It requires an IBM-compatible personal computer with 640k of memory, hard disk drive, and DOS 3.1 or higher.
   This fully searchable site also includes links to educational resources and to other sites which are fully or partially funded by the department including the *ERIC* Clearinghouses and regional educational laboratories. Search results can be limited to type of document (*ERIC Digests,* legislative documents) and include separate search interfaces for individual datasets, such the *Thesaurus of ERIC Descriptors,* to further refine searches.

COMPANIES AND ORGANIZATIONS

   College Board Online (http://www.collegeboard.org/). The College Entrance Examination Board (College Board) features an impressive array of information. The ExPan College Search feature allows the user to select from level of education, major, location and other features to get a scrollable list of institutions offering the appropriate area of study and degree. Information included for each institution is gathered from annual surveys sent to them by the College Board, and include addresses, costs, admission requirements and deadlines, housing, accreditation, majors, and foreign student information. The ExPAN Scholarship Search feature allows the user to fill in an online questionnaire to retrieve a list of potential scholarship opportunities. Use of the ExPAN databases requires careful reading of the onscreen instructions since some of the choices are not intuitive. College Board recommends using Netscape Navigator® to access some of its databases because of browser conflicts. The College Board site also includes sample test questions, online test registration forms, financial aid worksheets and calculators, statistics about test scores, and other information. A demonstration version of SAT preparation software can be downloaded from the site. The *One-on-One with SAT* software runs on an IBM-compatible PC, 386 or better, with Windows® 3.1 or higher, VGA monitor, 10 MB space on the hard drive and 4 MB RAM.

Peterson's Education and Career Center (http://www.petersons.com/). Peterson's went online in January of 1995. The site features interactive versions of Peterson guides to colleges and graduate and professional schools. Most files are retrieved with easy-to-use scroll down menus. Undergraduate programs can be located alphabetically, geographically, by length of study (two and four year colleges), by major, religious affiliation, keyword search of descriptions, and by colleges which accept a universal electronic application form. This electronic form can be downloaded in either Windows 3.X and higher or Mac OS 7.0 and higher formats. The Peterson's site is under continuous development. At the present time, the amount of information available for each school varies widely but can include information for international students, e-mail inquiry forms directed to individual universities, and information about graduate and undergraduate programs with links to more detailed information about selected programs. The in-depth descriptions of institutions are also keyword searchable and include hotlinks to either campus or admissions office Web sites. Entries for the schools also include citations to page numbers of the relevant printed Peterson's guide to consult for additional information. The undergraduate and graduate sections of the service are the most well-developed. Peterson's is adding information about private K-12 schools, distance learning programs, international study, summer programs, and financial information. All pages follow a consistent format for ease-of-use.

CLASSIFIED LISTS OF RESOURCES (HOTLISTS)

Blue Web'n Applications Library (http://www.kn.pacbell.com/wired/bluewebn/). This is searchable, browsable index of Internet-based curricular resources for the K-12 education community. Resources are grouped by topic and subdivided into the following groups: Lessons, Activities, Projects, Resources, References, and Tools. Definitions of the groupings and criteria for inclusion in the site are online. Materials are also arranged by content and subcontent areas labelled with a Dewey classification number. Each resource includes a short description and star-rating. Blue Web'n offers an e-mail registration service to receive page updates which list sites recently added with the following information for each resource: site name and address, rating, description, audience (grade level), content areas, and type of application.

Education World (http://www.education-world.com/). Sponsored by American Fidelity, this site features original material ("Experts Say"), online forums, and an index of links on all aspects of education. It is oriented to the practicing teacher, K-12 and college-bound student, and parents. Its 20,000 links include information on college preparation and financial aid, lesson plans, educational organizations, vendors of educational materials, educational institutions by state, and educational resources by curriculum area. Education World features online reviews of selected sites on the basis of content, aesthetics, and organization. Some links at the site include brief annotations. The "Education News" section features stories which have appeared in online editions of newspapers and press releases of educational organizations. The site is both browsable and searchable. It offers online forms (to get on) mailing lists which provide site updates and site reviews.

Kathy Schrock's Guide for Educators (http://www.capecod.net/ schrockguide/). A library media specialist, Kathy Schrock, has created an easy-to-use classified list of Internet resources to support curriculum and professional development. It groups Internet resources into twenty broad topics subdivided into smaller ones. For example, "Arts and Literature" leads to pages for "Art and Architecture," "Literature and Language Arts," and "Performing Arts." Schrock includes a short descriptive statement for each resource and has created a set of website evaluation tools for use by elementary, middle, and secondary school students. The site includes links to search tools and guides to using them effectively. Other features include an alphabetic index to all sites, a listing of new sites for the current month, and an e-mail registration service for information on updated pages.

University of Arkansas at Little Rock College of Education ONLINE (http://www.ualr.edu/~coedept/index.html). Thomas Teeter, Associate College of Education Dean, compiled this comprehensive educational resource index. Resources are grouped into broad areas including those specifically for all educators, and financial, news, weather, and other information of interest to many audiences. Some of the material is information specific to the University of Arkansas at Little Rock. The "ERIC on the Internet" page links to all of the searchable *ERIC* databases and to *ERIC* Clearinghouses. This page features "Quick Search" boxes beneath the hotlink and description to allow direct querying of databases. The "Education Web Index" page includes links to subject lists and search tools available at Education World, Excite, Galaxy, Infoseek, Lycos, Magellan, Web Crawler, WWW Virtual Library, and Yahoo!. Teeter employs a unique approach which, in effect, puts the "table of contents" for each tool online–beneath the icon for each service is a link to the top level education index with the subheadings displayed and directly linked. This approach makes it easy to select the appropriate category or subcategory from these popular Internet indexes before initiating the connection. Teeter also includes concise descriptive annotations of site contents with each link.

World Lecture Hall (http://www.utexas.edu/world/lecture/index.html). This is a classified list of links to examples of how the Internet can be used in instruction. Materials linked from the site include course syllabi, assignments, lecture notes, exams, class calendars, and multimedia textbooks. The site includes a form which can be used to submit additions to the site, a "What's New" feature, and links to pages for U.S. universities, community colleges, and K-12 school pages worldwide.

HOTLIST DIRECTORIES OF K-12 SCHOOLS, COLLEGES AND UNIVERSITIES

College and University Home Pages–Alphabetical Listing (http://www.mit.edu:8001/people/cdemello/univ.html). This site includes links to over 3,000 colleges and universities worldwide. College and University Home Pages is mirrored (copies available on additional servers) at several sites internationally and is available for download in UNIX tar format. Access is by two separate indexes, the alphabetical arrangement cited above and by a geographic listing at *http://www.mit.edu:8001/people/cdemello/geog.html.*

HotList of K-12 Internet School Sites–USA (http://rrnet.com/~gleason/k12.html). The HotList is an index of elementary, middle, and high school home pages on the Web organized by state. Pages for each state also include a state flag graphic, small profile map, and links to school districts, state departments of education, and state home pages.

REFERENCES

1. White House. "Al Gore–National Information Infrastructure." n.d. [Online] Available: http://www.whitehouse.gov/WH/EOP/OVP/html/nii1.html (13 Dec. 1996).

2. United States National Information Infrastructure Virtual Library. "A Few Illustrations of NII Applications in Education." n.d. [Online] Available: http://nii.nist.gov/applic/educ/esexmp.html (13 Dec. 1996).

3. Ibid.

4. U. S. General Accounting Office. *School Facilities: America's Schools Not Designed or Equipped for the 21st Century.* 1995. [Online]. Available: http://www.access.gpo.gov/su_docs/aces/aces160.shtml (13 Dec. 1996).

Reference Sources on the Internet: Psychology

Lorrie A. Knight

SUMMARY. Reference librarians will find numerous opportunities for effective patron referrals on the Internet. This paper describes selected sites from organizations, academic departments and the private sector which offer useful information. The sites included are chosen for their uniqueness, credibility, and usefulness. *[Article copies available for a fee from The Haworth Document Delivery Service: 1-800-342-9678. E-mail address: getinfo@haworth.com]*

The field of psychology generates numerous requests for information from patrons for a variety of reasons–personal, professional and educational. Reference librarians must often probe for the reason for the inquiry before recommending an appropriate resource. This is especially important when using the Internet as a source of psychology information. Although a large quantity of information is available, much of it is targeted toward specific audiences. Certain sites will appeal to those seeking help with particular problems, others to patrons researching papers. This article reviews sites selected for their value to reference librarians, for the diversity of their content, and for their effectiveness as gateways to additional resources or for their uniqueness.

Lorrie A. Knight is Electronic Services Reference Librarian, William Knox Holt Memorial Library, University of the Pacific, 3501 Pacific Ave., Stockton, CA 95211. E-mail: lknight@uop.edu

[Haworth co-indexing entry note]: "Reference Sources on the Internet: Psychology." Knight, Lorrie A. Co-published simultaneously in *The Reference Librarian* (The Haworth Press, Inc.) No. 57, 1997, pp. 63-67; and: *Reference Sources on the Internet: Off the Shelf and Onto the Web* (ed: Karen R. Diaz) The Haworth Press, Inc., 1997, pp. 63-67. Single or multiple copies of this article are available for a fee from The Haworth Document Delivery Service [1-800-342-9678, 9:00 a.m. - 5:00 p.m. (EST). E-mail address: getinfo@haworth.com].

ORGANIZATIONS

Professional organizations play a key role in the dissemination of information and serve as bridges between the practitioner and the academic communities. Today, professional societies use their websites to augment their important communications responsibilities. *PsychNet (http://www. apa.org/)* is the Internet service of the American Psychological Association. Designed to enhance the study, practice and understanding of mental health issues, components include articles from the APA Monitor, discussion of public policies and descriptions of APA publications and products. The site also offers extensive resource lists, divided by the interest of the user. Reference librarians will particularly appreciate the *Information for Students (http://www.apa.org/science/stu.html)* which offers guides to library research and suggestions for locating published and unpublished psychological tests. Employment postings and funding opportunities are also described.

Another excellent website is that of the *American Psychological Society (http://psych.hanover.edu/aps/)*. This organization's site is directed toward the support of teaching and research. Faculty and students will find sample course materials, links to Internet-based experiments, pointers to funding and employment agencies, and directories of discussion lists and electronic journals. This website is of special value to academic librarians and university students, as it provides information about career selection, graduate schools and APA style guidelines. APS is also sponsoring an ongoing project to "rate" Internet resources via user feedback.

DIRECTORIES

A frequently used reference tool is the directory, and web-based directories are equally valuable. Wesleyan University provides a *Listing of U.S. Psychology PhD Programs (http://www.wesleyan.edu/psyc/psyc260/ranking. htm)*. The site provides a list of 185 programs, quality ranked according to a 1995 National Research Council study. In addition to this quick tabulation of rankings, users can link directly to either the institution or academic department. A similar site, *Psychology Departments Around the World (http://psy.ucsd.edu/otherpsy.html)*, is hosted by UCSD. This site offers a straightforward alphabetical list of academic departments of psychology, both in the U.S. and abroad. Users may connect directly to the departments named. No rankings or geographical listings are available.

Two timely directories document the growth of online discussion groups and journals. *Mailing Lists Related to Psychology (http://www.nova. edu/Inter-Links/health/psy/psychlist.html)* is generated weekly through a keyword search of a database of listservs maintained at Dartmouth. A referral to this site will provide patrons with information about a wide array of self-help groups and online learning opportunities. *Links to Psychological Journals (http://www.wiso.uni-augsburg.de/sozio/hartmann/psycho/ journals.html)* provides links to and descriptions of more than 700 online psychology and social science journals. Users may choose between an annotated list, with information about contents or a basic alphabetical arrangement.

REFERENCE TOOLS

Internet sites that offer content are the "reference books" of the Internet and the number and quality of these sites is as varied as the special interests which they represent. One of the most interesting websites is *Internet Mental Health (http://199.45.66.207/)* an encyclopedia of mental health information. It is provided as a public service by Phillip L. Long, MD. There are three useful components of the site. Using frames technology, the user can select a disorder, such as anorexia, and locate its American or European description, information about treatment and abstracts of relevant articles or booklets. Similarly, one can select a medication then click to locate a summary of its chemistry, indicators, contra-indicators, dosage and citations to current research. The third section of the site provides links to WWW resources for specific psychological conditions.

Mind and Body–Rene Descartes to William James (http://serendip. brynmawr.edu/Mind/Table.html) is a WWW version of an exhibit held in honor of the Centennial Celebration of the American Psychological Association, August 7 to December 15, 1992. It offers a look at the growth of experimental psychology as a discipline. Although limited by the lack of an internal search engine, it is an interesting example of the potential value of content-rich sites.

The librarian's dilemma, requests for illustrations, is partially ameliorated through *PsychArt (http://loki.sonoma.edu:80/psychology/psychart. html)* a public domain portrait gallery of famous psychologists. Portraits of Adler, Freud, Jung, Rogers, Binet, Rogers, and Skinner are currently available. The images are available for non-profit use and may be saved in a variety of formats. This is a very useful resource for students or Web publishers in the field of psychology.

A significant help to researchers is the *ERIC/AE Test Locator (http:// ericae2.educ.cua.edu/testcol.htm),* a joint project of the ERIC Clearinghouse, Educational Testing Service and the *Buros Institute of Mental Measurements (http://www.unl.edu/buros/home.html)*. At these sites, reference librarians and library patrons can use enhanced keyword searching to locate psychological tests. In addition to the title of the test and ordering information, patrons can also search for citations to test reviews in Buros publications.

MEGA-LISTS

The most significant type of Internet source for psychology is the mega-list, the single website which attempts to gather and organize all of a certain type of resource. Mega-lists are often a mixed blessing. Some are so lengthy as to be without selective value; others are poorly organized and become unwieldy. Many subscribe to the "I'll point at your site if you point at mine" school of thought. The mega-lists identified here are noteworthy for good organization, selectivity of resources listed, and of value to the librarian guiding patrons to information.

A number one site for the reference desk is *PsychWeb (http://www.gasou.edu/psychweb/)*, an Internet service provided by Russ Dewey at Georgia Southern University. Comprehensive and well organized, this site concentrates on the academic researcher and provides links to books and articles, resource gateways and career information. Of special value is the section called "Tips for Psychology students" which offers suggestions about graduate programs, research opportunities, and even a crib sheet for the APA style manual. There is also a good collection of mental health and self-help links, useful to students and the general public alike.

The *WebPsych Partnership (http://www.cmhc.com/webpsych/)* is a unique presence in the arena of Internet based psychology resources. WebPsych is a confederation of web developers who agree, via an electronic discussion list, to conform to certain guidelines in their publishing efforts. The guidelines are designed to ensure high quality in the pages of WebPsych partners. In addition to this unique cooperative effort, Web-Psych is also an excellent gateway to useful resources. There is no single orientation among the pages listed; in fact, the websites listed run the gamut from the psychology of dreams to online tests for depression. Patrons seeking online psychology information might well begin by investigating the annotated directory found at the WebPsych page.

PsycSite (http://www.unipissing.ca/psyc/psycsite.htm) is another academically directed website. Despite a graphic that is much too large and time consuming to load, this site provides excellent links to scholarly and scientific resources. There are also good pointers to university pages, listservs and professional organizations. Sites dealing with selfhelp or parapsychology are not included, nor are there content annotations. The strength of this site lies in its excellent presentation and organization.

MegaPsych (http://members.gnn.com/user/megapsych.htm) by John W. Nichols is designed for psychology faculty and students. Well organized and annotated, MegaPsych offers pointers to more than 200 discussion lists, 50 useful websites, and a variety of additional links. Two unique features of this site are pointers to quotations and a link to a searchable file of antiquarian books.

Cognitive and Psychological Science on the Internet (http://www-psych.stanford.edu/cogsci/) is one of the pioneers of psychology mega-sites. In addition to a collection of more than 750 pointers, the author of the site also provides a paper describing the methodology of its construction. Major components of the site include academic programs, organizations and conferences, electronic journals and publishers, and software for psychologists. The scope of coverage is very broad. It should be noted that the current web editor is seeking a replacement and the location of the site may change.

CONCLUSION

Psychology resources on the Internet are a true reflection of the many dimensions of the field. They demonstrate the zest for collaboration and communication inherent in the discipline and practice of psychology. However, the sites are often very tightly focussed and of interest only to a select audience. At another extreme, many sites are so sprawling as to confuse most patrons. The sites described in this article were selected to suggest the type of web-based resource of use for reference work. At present, librarians hoping to incorporate web-based resources into their reference programs would do well to adopt a referral rather than content seeking strategy. Patrons seeking very specialized information will find many avenues for cautious exploration. Students will find practical and useful educational tools. Academic researchers will find burgeoning opportunities for online collaboration and publication.

Social Problems
and Human Services/Social Sciences
Solutions on the Internet

Gary McMillan

SUMMARY. This article describes several omnibus social work/human services web sites with "social problems" links. Strategies are also suggested–and examples provided–for identifying additional Internet resources by framing the search in the context of lifespan development and in terms of institutional stakeholders. *[Article copies available for a fee from The Haworth Document Delivery Service: 1-800-342-9678. E-mail address: getinfo@haworth.com]*

INTRODUCTION

Reference work related to social issues and problems often requires considerable ingenuity and diplomacy. The electronic availability of information does not allay concerns of equity and social justice in how "problems" are identified, characterized, and addressed. Information on the Internet is no less "value-laden" than print sources (and perhaps far less scrutinized) and access issues loom large for marginalized, oppressed, and resource poor constituencies. Renewed vigilance is needed to ensure cultural sensitivity and ideological balance in reference service.

Gary McMillan is Head of the Social Work Library and Anthropology/Sociology Bibliographer, Howard University, 601 Howard Place, NW, Washington, DC 20059.

[Haworth co-indexing entry note]: "Social Problems and Human Services/Social Sciences Solutions on the Internet." McMillan, Gary. Co-published simultaneously in *The Reference Librarian* (The Haworth Press, Inc.) No. 57, 1997, pp. 69-75; and: *Reference Sources on the Internet: Off the Shelf and Onto the Web* (ed: Karen R. Diaz) The Haworth Press, Inc., 1997, pp. 69-75. Single or multiple copies of this article are available for a fee from The Haworth Document Delivery Service [1-800-342-9678, 9:00 a.m. - 5:00 p.m. (EST). E-mail address: getinfo@haworth.com].

Nevertheless, the Internet is burgeoning as a seemingly limitless resource on every imaginable social problem. It is equally an excellent vehicle for promoting public education, disseminating data and research finds, fostering technology transfer in the development and delivery of services, and advocating for and supporting indigenous self-help groups and clients' rights movements. The challenge is to distinguish that which is practical and useful from that which is speculation, propaganda, and/or personal catharsis. Seeking leads from recognized academic, voluntary, research, and professional organizations often provides surer results than key word searching via one of the many Internet search engines.

The specificity of a reference question and the context which frames the request will indicate whether the patron is at the stage of browsing or focused information gathering. Following are sites which each serve as a useful beginning point. Naturally, they often represent alternative paths to the same URLs as well as provide cross-references (via hot links) to one another.

GATEWAY WEB SITES

U.S. Department of Health and Human Services (HHS)
http://odphp2.osophs.dhhs.gov/consumer.htm

Many social problems fall under the purview of the Department's divisions, institutes, centers and offices. This consumer-oriented, content-focused web site provides links for roughly 50 topics (and growing) from aging, AIDS, alcohol abuse, and Alzheimer's disease to sexually transmitted diseases, smoking, Social Security, substance abuse, and women's health. Especially useful is the hot link to "statistics." For searchers who have a special interest in a specific HHS unit, organizational access is provided through the *HHS Agencies page (http://www.os.dhhs.gov/).*

Social Work and Social Services Web Sites/George Warren Brown
School of Social Work at Washington University in St. Louis
http://www.gwbssw.wustl.edu/%7Egwbhome/websites.html

This is among the most comprehensive privately-developed, problem-focused web sites for human services with over one hundred topics represented, including clinical populations (e.g., ADHD, borderline personality, dissociation, and schizophrenia), social groups (e.g., children and youth, families, gender, men, and women), and social work practice resources (e.g., ethics, genograms, measurement and assessment scales, social work licensing, and writing scholarly papers).

The following sites are organized less systematically but have some distinctive strengths.

Pat McClendon's Social Work Resources
http://users.aol.com/McClendon/socialwk.html

This site is particularly strong for social work resources related to clinical practice and mental health, also providing links to social work schools, professional organizations, social workers on the web, and historical information about social work and social workers.

Social Work Links/University of Chicago
http://http.bsd.uchicago.edu/~r-tell/swlinks.html

This site seems particularly strong regarding computers and technology in human services, and provides unique links to information about *The Settlement House* and to *Chugman's Empowerment for the Oppressed* web page.

Web Resources for Social Workers/Colorado State University
http://www.colostate.edu/Depts/SocWork/webstuff.html

This site provides a fast track to information by, about, and for organizations, including nonprofit, philanthropic, national and international organizations; social work/social services websites, news groups, and discussion lists; and links for activists and organizers (e.g., *Poor People's Convention, People's Internet Directory,* the *Left Side of the Web,* and the *Democratic Socialists of America*).

YAHOO! Social Work
http://www.yahoo.com/Social_Science/Social_Work/

This site highlights conferences, institutes, journals, and organizations, with a hot link to the *Social Work Cafe* (links for social workers, social work students, and other professionals with an e-mail list of social workers and students internationally).

LIFESPAN RESOURCES ON THE NET

The Welfare State is often characterized as a "cradle to grave" social safety net. Because problems are often more associated with some stages of life than others, tapping into web sites from a lifespan perspective can be very useful.

National Center for Education in Maternal and Child Health
http://www.ncemch.georgetown.edu/

The Center is a partnership of the federal Maternal and Child Health Bureau and Georgetown University's Graduate Public Policy Program. This site provides access to NCEMCH databases, bibliographies and other reference resources, and information about Maternal & Child Health Bureau-funded projects. See also *The Parent's Page (http://www.efn.org/~djz/birth/babylist.html)* on resources for parents-to-be as well as for parents of infants and small children.

Child & Adolescent Development: Mental Health Net
http://cmhcsys.com/guide/pro03.htm

This site aims to provide a comprehensive gateway to child and adolescent development online information resources, both professional and self-help.

Family Law Advisor
http://www.divorcenet.com/

This site provides leads to interactive bulletin boards related to many adult and family concerns: adoption, divorce, custody and visitation, stepfamilies, and grandparents rights as well as links to a reading room and library, e-zines, book reviews, quotations, an annotated divorce law dictionary, and state and local resources.

Administration on Aging and the Aging Network
http://www.aoa.dhhs.gov/aoa/pages/aoa.html

This is the federal web site for information and resources (e.g., fact sheets and directories) related to the Older Americans Act, the White House Conference on Aging, and the aging services network nationwide. Two of the best nongovernmental aging information sites are the *American Association of Retired Persons Webplace (http://www.aarp.org/index.html)* and the *Ethel Percy Andrus Center Gerontology Library's World Wide Web Resources on Aging (http://www-lib.usc.edu/Info/Gero/gerourl.htm)*.

Grief and Bereavement/Growth House Inc.
http://www.growthhouse.org/death.html

Coping with widowhood is merely one of the many topics touched upon at this death and dying-related web site.

SPECIAL INTEREST ORGANIZATIONS

The traditional behavioral and social sciences disciplines (and their subdisciplines) offer distinctive theoretical perspectives on social issues and problems. In addition, many professions, especially social work, public health, and related health and human services fields, contribute to these perspectives a substantial body of research and practice wisdom regarding social interventions. The Gale Research Companies' print (the *Encyclopedia of Associations* and the *Research Centers Directory,* in particular) and commercial online directories are invaluable for identifying academic and professional associations to be hunted for on the Internet. Also, the *Library of Congress' National Referral Center Master File (telnet://locis. loc.gov;* then choose: *"Organizations"*) indexes and describes over thirteen thousand organizations. Following are examples of private and public organizations with excellent web sites related to some perennial "hot topics":

Alcoholism:
National Clearinghouse for Alcohol & Drug Information
http://www.health.org/

This federal web site includes PREVLINE, an electronic gateway to searchable databases and substance abuse prevention materials related to alcohol, tobacco, and drugs.

Community Organizing/Activism:
Economic Democracy Information Network (EDIN)
gopher://garnet.berkeley.edu:1250/1/

EDIN bills itself as "the voice of community organizations on the Information Superhighway." Major topical headings at this gopher site are: the economy; defense conversion and peace resources; labor issues; race and racism; gender and sexuality; human rights and civil liberties;

education and youth issues; housing, health and poverty; progressive magazines and on-line news services; political and non-profit organizations and movements, fast facts from EDIN, and other community-based resources.

Crime and Victimization:
The Corrections Connection
http://www.corrections.com/index.html

The Connection is sponsored by the American Correctional Association, the American Jail Association, the American Probation & Parole Association, and the National Commission on Correctional Health Care. It provides a criminal justice links directory and highlights issues related to crime and victimization, children and juveniles, domestic violence and family support, substance abuse, and research and education.

Homelessness:
National Coalition for the Homeless (NCH)
http://nch.ari.net/

The NCH Online Library provides a searchable bibliographic database with references to research on homelessness, housing, and poverty as well as directories of local, state, and national homeless/housing organizations including lists of contact people, e-mail addresses, and over 100 web pages. See also: *American Homeless Society (http://www.gtii.com/members/lannin/ ruben.htm), The Homeless Page (http://www.teleport.com/~ronl/homeless. html),* and the *Homeless Home Page at Communications for a Sustainable Future (http://csf.Colorado.EDU/homeless/).*

Poverty:
Institute for Research on Poverty (IRP) at the University
of Wisconsin-Madison
http://www.ssc.wisc.edu/irp/

IRP is one of the best known academic poverty research institutes. Its web site provides access to the full-text of newsletter features, discussion papers, and relevant links. See also: *YAHOO's! Poverty (http://www.yahoo. com/Society_and_Culture/Poverty/)* and *YAHOO's! Welfare Reform (http:// www.yahoo.com/Government/Politics/Political_Issues/Welfare_Reform/).* On a particular note, the text of the often asked for *Welfare Reform Act,* formally the Personal Responsibility and Work Opportunity Reconciliation Act of 1996, may be found at *http://thomas.loc.gov/cgi-bin/bdquery/z?d104: HR03734:.*

Sexuality:
Planned Parenthood Information Resources
http://www.ppfa.org/ppfa/resource.html

This site references resources on abortion, AIDS/HIV, contraception, family planning, men's and women's health, reproductive rights, sexually transmitted diseases, teenage pregnancy, world population, and related issues. For the nexus of sexuality and victimization, see Chris Bartley's *Sexual Assault Information Page (http://www.cs.utk.edu/~bartley/saInfoPage. html),* an information and referral service focusing on acquaintance rape, child sexual abuse/assault, incest, rape, ritual abuse, sexual assault, and sexual harassment.

Internet Resources for Reference: Finance and Investment

Brent Alan Mai

SUMMARY. Thanks to the Internet, the average investor today has access to more information about potential investments and their performance than has been available at any time in the past. When called upon to aid in filtering through this information, the business reference librarian is also faced with the challenge of knowing what is "out there" and how to find it. This article identifies sites that provide information about stocks and their exchanges, mutual funds, bonds, company annual reports, and taxes. *[Article copies available for a fee from The Haworth Document Delivery Service: 1-800-342-9678. E-mail address: getinfo@haworth.com]*

INTRODUCTION

The Internet has made the average investor's life both easier and more complicated. While it is possible to get more information than ever before about a potential investment opportunity, it is also possible to be led astray more quickly by misinformation and even disinformation. As in the print world, it is quite legal to offer advice–right or wrong. To tweak an old cliché, some electronic advice isn't worth the wire or airwave over which it came.

An attempt has been made here to identify a few Web sites (hereafter

Brent Alan Mai is Assistant Professor of Library Science at Purdue University, 1340 Krannert Building, West Lafayette, IN 47907-1340.

[Haworth co-indexing entry note]: "Internet Resources for Reference: Finance and Investment." Mai, Brent Alan. Co-published simultaneously in *The Reference Librarian* (The Haworth Press, Inc.) No. 57, 1997, pp. 77-83; and: *Reference Sources on the Internet: Off the Shelf and Onto the Web* (ed: Karen R. Diaz) The Haworth Press, Inc., 1997, pp. 77-83. Single or multiple copies of this article are available for a fee from The Haworth Document Delivery Service [1-800-342-9678, 9:00 a.m. - 5:00 p.m. (EST). E-mail address: getinfo@haworth.com].

77

referred to as sites) that provide basic information about finance and investing which may be helpful to the Business Reference Librarian. Most of them include links to a range of other products and services, some of which are free and some of which are fee-based.

META SITES

http://www.wsrn.com

Wall Street Research Net claims over 140,000 links chosen because they may "help professional and private investors perform fundamental research on actively traded companies and mutual funds and locate important economic data that moves markets." The company research section provides well-organized access to various kinds of information about a company, from EDGAR filings to 15-minute delayed stock quotes.

http://www.webfinance.net

The *Web Finance* site includes several finance and investment links including a list of banks, investment banks, and brokerage firms. This list is not completely comprehensive because it includes only those banks and firms with homepages of their own (to which links are provided). There is a mutual funds link which lists mutual fund providers and links to their homepages as well. Under the "miscellaneous" link are further links to the Fannie Mae and Sallie Mae homepages among others. Following the "Who's Hot, Who's Not" link from the Web Finance homepage, one finds a weekly ranking of brokerage stocks by performance compared to the S&P 500 Index for the same period.

DEFINITIONS

http://www.webinvestors.com

The *Web Investor's Dictionary* is an excellent resource for identifying the real meaning behind the terms and phrases that the big investors and stock traders throw around every day (e.g., naked position). Another source of definitions is the individual exchanges listed below which also offer glossaries of trading terms.

http://www.tiaa-cref.org/dict.html

Here TIAA-CREF provides a *Dictionary of Financial Terms*. It is fairly comprehensive and also offers a section of definitions specific to how TIAA-CREF does things.

STOCK AND MUTUAL FUND QUOTES

http://www.stockmaster.com

Stockmaster is a free site which provides for searching by company or fund name and ticker symbol. The stock quotes are provided by S&P Comstock and are on a 20-minute delay. In addition, a graph indicates the stock's performance over the last year. The mutual fund quotes are for the close of trading on the previous day with a graph indicating performance over the last 3-4 years. This is also an excellent site for identifying a company's ticker symbol and the exchange on which it is trading.

http://www.usa.ft.com

This *Financial Times* site requires free registration to get to most of the information it offers, including the daily closing price and other key market data on 3,000 equities traded on the London Stock Exchange.

ANNUAL REPORTS

http://www.sec.gov

EDGAR (the Electronic Data Gathering, Analysis, and Retrieval system) performs automated collection, validation, indexing, acceptance, and forwarding of submissions by companies and others who are required by law to file forms with the U.S. Securities and Exchange Commission (SEC). As of 6 May 1996, all public domestic companies are required to make their filings on *EDGAR* with very limited exemptions. There are many other Internet sites which provide fee-based access to *EDGAR* filings and there are definitely some advantages to their value added searching capabilities. Nevertheless, the SEC site does provide free links to all filings since 1994. *EDGAR* filings are posted to the SEC site 24 hours after the date of filing. There are several other interesting features on the SEC site such as proposed and final SEC rulings, ticker symbol look-up, and mutual fund activity reports.

http://www.prars.com

For those who insist on having the "real thing" in their hands, *PRARS* is an online ordering service for company financials, including annual reports, prospectuses, and 10Ks. Over 3,200 public companies are listed alphabetically and by industry. Simply complete the requested information and an annual report for the company or industry you specified will be put in the traditional mail within 24-hours. This is not an exhaustive site, but it does include a large number of companies. This service is free to U.S. addresses. Contact *PRARS* for pricing information for non-U.S. addresses.

EXCHANGES

New York
http://www.nyse.com

The Internet site of the *New York Stock Exchange* offers a listing of its member companies and the Exchange's Annual Report. There is also an extensive glossary of terms often heard in the stock trading culture. A running list of new NYSE listing companies by the date of their first listing is included. The current list goes back about 10 months.

American
http://www.amex.com

The *American Stock Exchange* site, too, lists its member companies. There is also a link to the revised edition of the *Dictionary of Financial Risk Management* [direct link: *http://utah.e1.com/ames/findic*] by Gary Gastineau and Mark Kritzman. It has a searchable interface.

NASDAQ
http://www.nasdaq.com

On the *NASDAQ* site, choose "Company Look-Up" to search for a particular issue. This site also provides a glossary of stock trading terms, but it is not as extensive as that provided on the NYSE site.

Chicago Board of Trade
http://www.cbot.com

Follow the MarketPlex, then Market Information links to obtain free 10-minute delayed futures quotes, 30-minute delayed options quotes, and settlement prices from the *Chicago Board of Trade*. There is also a listing of futures and options commodity symbols and contract specifications. This contract specifications link serves as a glossary for many of the terms used by commodity traders.

Tokyo
http://www.tse.or.jp

The *Tokyo Stock Exchange* site is available in Japanese or English. It provides complete listings of the companies that trade in the 1st, 2nd, and Foreign Sections. The companies are grouped by industry sector. Links to company homepages are provided, when available.

STOCK INDEXES

http://www.stockinfo.standardpoor.com/idxinfo.htm

This *Standard & Poors* site lists the S&P 100, S&P 500, MidCap 400, SmallCap 600, and Supercomposite 1500 closing averages as of the close of trading on the previous trading day. Listings of the companies that make up each index are given along with each company's ticker symbol. Separate lists group these respective companies by industry.

http://www.exchange.de/fwb/indices.html

Although located in Germany, the *DAX* site does provide English-language information about a host of the Deutsche Börse composite indexes including the DAX, MDAX, DAX 100, and CDAX. Links to the individual company homepages are provided, when available. Other links on this site provide information about German bonds.

http://www.bloomberg.com/markets

Follow the Bloomberg *"World Equities"* link to locate a comprehensive geographic list of all the major international stock indexes. The current or most recent trading day's index figures are listed.

TAXES

http://www.irs.ustreas.gov

The *IRS* site includes all sorts of documents relating to the taxing of America. This site tends to be slow to load. Whenever possible, select the "text only version" to speed it up. It is possible to download tax forms and instructions in PDF format from this site. There are links to about 40 of the state tax sites, some of which also provide for downloading of forms. The *Revenue Canada* site *[http://www.revcan.ca]* provides similar federal tax information for Canadians including tax forms in PDF format.

http://www.yahoo.com/business

The taxes link from *Yahoo's!* business homepage provides further links to a variety of tax-related resources, including Ernst & Young's Top 25 Most Common Tax Preparation Errors and 50 Easily Overlooked Tax Deductions for Individuals.

MUTUAL FUNDS

http://www.cs.cmu.edu/~jdg/funds.html

The Mutual Fund Company Directory provides extensive lists of mutual fund companies around the world. It is organized by country and each entry includes the fund name, toll-free number, and a link to the fund's homepage, if available.

BONDS

http://www.bonds-online.com

Bonds Online includes data and links to resources covering treasury, municipal, and corporate bonds and bond funds. Most of the treasury information is coming from the *U.S. Treasury Department* site [direct link: *http://www.ustreas.gov*]. There is also a handy link to the Federal Reserve Bank of New York's *Treasury Bond Calculator* [direct link: *http://www.ny. frb.org/pihome/svg_bnds/sb_val.html*] which will calculate the current value of a savings bond based on its series and issue date. Through the *Bonds Online* site, it is also possible to obtain valuations of prices of municipal bonds. This free service is provided by R.W. Smith & Associates who will respond by email within 48 hours (2 business days) of any inquiry. Links are provided to the major corporate bond rating companies (Moody's, S&P, Fitch, and Duff & Phelps), but there is little actual ratings information available for free through them. The corporate bonds link does offer a nice chart which compares the ratings schemes of the four above-mentioned companies. Following the "Bond Professor" link will lead to a nice glossary of terms used in the bond trading industry.

Internet Resources for Reference: General Business and Company Information

Brent Alan Mai

SUMMARY. It did not take long for the business world to notice the potential marketing opportunities provided by the Internet. The number of businesses providing information via the Internet and those actually "doing business" over the Internet continues to grow at an outstanding rate. The business reference librarian is then faced with the challenge of providing knowledgeable access to these businesses and their information. This article outlines a few of the thousands of sites which are helpful in obtaining general business information and company-specific information. Also included are a couple sites helpful for answering questions about agribusiness and the programs of the Small Business Administration. *[Article copies available for a fee from The Haworth Document Delivery Service: 1-800-342-9678. E-mail address: getinfo@haworth.com]*

INTRODUCTION

The business world impacts everything and everyone. As a result, many business Web sites (hereafter referred to as sites) fall into other "Reference" categories. For example, the government provides access to in-

Brent Alan Mai is Assistant Professor of Library Science at Purdue University, 1340 Krannert Building, West Lafayette, IN 47907-1340.

[Haworth co-indexing entry note]: "Internet Resources for Reference: General Business and Company Information." Mai, Brent Alan. Co-published simultaneously in *The Reference Librarian* (The Haworth Press, Inc.) No. 57, 1997, pp. 85-92; and: *Reference Sources on the Internet: Off the Shelf and Onto the Web* (ed: Karen R. Diaz) The Haworth Press, Inc., 1997, pp. 85-92. Single or multiple copies of this article are available for a fee from The Haworth Document Delivery Service [1-800-342-9678, 9:00 a.m. - 5:00 p.m. (EST). E-mail address: getinfo@haworth.com].

85

formation such as Census statistics that can be quite useful to businesses doing a demographic analysis for marketing.

With all the business-related sites available today, it is not possible to list them all. The following are but a few which one may find useful for assistance with general business-related reference questions. There are separate articles for Finance and Investment and International Trade which list sites of interest to those specific business sub-groups. Currency exchange rates, a frequently asked business reference question, are found in the International Trade paper.

META SITES

http://web.idirect.com/~tiger/supersit.htm

Entitled *Worldclass Supersite,* this site provides access and commentary on 600 top business sites in 70 countries. According to the site's homepage, the links have been chosen based upon their usefulness to world commerce, timeliness, ease of use, and presentation. The Supersite has six sections: reference, news, learning, money, trade, and networking. A seventh section examines how over 160 globally-active companies of various sizes, sectors, and countries of origin are using the Internet to promote themselves internationally. This would be a good site to recommend to the "powers that be" within your organization if they are just beginning to investigate Web site development.

http://biz.yahoo.com

This Yahoo! business site is very well organized and easy to use. In typical Yahoo! fashion, it draws upon resources from far and wide. The homepage accesses business, financial, company, and industry information as well as up-to-date news and stock quotes. The company information section puts everything at your fingertips, listing companies in alphabetical order with links to three categories: news, profiles, and quotes. The company profiles are provided by Hoover's, but Yahoo! adds additional links from the profile to the company's homepage (if available), company news, stock prices, and EDGAR filings.

http://www.bnet.att.com

This is the *AT&T Business Network* site. Although duplicative of many of the other meta sites, it does have an excellent annotated listing of company information providers including those that are fee-based (follow Business Bookmarks to Companies to Company Profiles).

http://www.brint.com

This site, called *"A Business Researcher's Interests,"* is perhaps not one for use in quick reference, but is an excellent resource for more in-depth reference questions and for self-education about the hottest topics in business. Having received a host of excellent reviews in the mainline business press, it is definitely a site worth investigating. It provides access to hundreds of full-text papers, magazines and journals; case studies; and thousands of other resources of business interest.

http://www.stat-usa.gov

STAT-USA is a primary point for access to government statistics of all kinds. Government depository institutions have each been given one password and there are some locations which have received site-licensed access. For the general user, the subscription cost is $150/year. This site contains a wealth of business-related information which could be useful in reference work. For example, the section entitled "Frequently Requested Statistical Releases" includes all types of economic data from GDP figures and interest rates to housing starts and retail sales. A searchable version of *Commerce Business Daily* is available here as well as the *Survey of Current Business* since 1994. Most of the applications on this site require Adobe Acrobat software which can be downloaded.

DEFINITIONS

http://www.onelook.com/browse.html

There are many sites for business dictionaries. The *Onelook* site is a convenient place to start because it offers links to a variety of dictionaries arranged by subject. Under the "Business" heading is found links to the *Washington Post*'s Business Glossary, the TIAA-CREF Dictionary of Financial Terms, and a Home Buyer's Vocabulary Guide. There are also a couple of law dictionaries under the "Business" heading which are useful for someone who is writing or evaluating a contract.

COMPANY DIRECTORIES AND HOMEPAGES

http://www.companiesonline.com

This is a free Dun & Bradstreet site claiming to include over 60,000 companies. Each entry lists the company's address, telephone number, and

Duns Number (of course). For publicly traded companies, the ticker symbol and exchange are indicated. Company homepages are also linked where available. By completing a registration form, it is possible to gain access to just a bit more information like categorized sales and employment figures. There are many opportunities to select D&B services which are available for a fee.

http://www.hoovers.com

The Hoover's electronic company information is as varied as are its print publications. One of the free sites that is particularly valuable for the Business Reference Librarian follows the "Search for Company Information" icon. There it is possible to search for companies by name, ticker symbol, industry, location, and annual sales. This search retrieves what Hoover's calls a "Company Capsule" that includes basic company identification information. Another free link is a searchable index for a company's homepage address. For a subscription fee of $9.95 per month, the Hoover's company profiles database is also available. Covering more than 2,600 public and private companies in the U.S. and around the world, the company profiles database provides company identification information, corporate history, current events effecting the company, several years of EDGAR filings, a list of officers, a list of competitors, and a link to the company's homepage, if available.

http://www.bizweb.com

This site indexes over 9,300 companies with a presence on the Internet in over 120 "industry" categories. It is keyword searchable with Boolean operators capability. Although there is a category for the Fortune 500, this site's focus is on the consumer. There are consequently many links to companies that provide only an online catalog.

http://networth.galt.com/www/home/equity/irr

This free site provides quick access to over 2,100 public companies which have a presence on the Internet. Its focus is much more geared toward the investor who wants to analyze a company. Its search engine also allows for pulling up only those companies who are part of the Dow 30 Industrials, S&P 500, S&P SmallCap 600, S&P MidCap 400, Fortune 500, and NASDAQ 100.

TELEPHONE DIRECTORIES

http://www.switchboard.com

Switchboard claims to have 11 million business listings at its site. Its data is licensed from Database America. *Switchboard* provides company name, address (including ZIP Code), and telephone number. It is possible to search by company name (city and state may be added for a narrower search) or by a pull-down menu of 264 business categories which resemble Yellow Pages headings. The categories may also be searched freetext. *Switchboard* also claims to have 93 million personal listings at this site. This site is relatively speedy compared to some of the others.

http://s18.bigyellow.com

As one of the larger sites, *Big Yellow* draws its data from NYNEX's own database plus Database America. It claims to list the addresses and telephone numbers of over 16 million businesses (ZIP Codes included). Yellow Pages categories are available for searching. GTE offers a similar site called *SuperPages* [direct link: *http://yp.gte.net*] which claims to list 11 million businesses (ZIP Codes included) from 5,000 Yellow Pages directories. The *SuperPages* are also capable of reverse searching, which is a function not offered by many other such sites.

http://www.yellownet.com

Recently revamped, the *YellowNet* site now claims to have 17 million business listings licensed from Database America. It too provides for category searching and narrowing by location. It also has a feature that allows for searching a Metro area even if the exact city is not known. For example, specifying Dallas in a metro search will also bring up businesses in Plano and Richardson. The biggest drawback of this site is that ZIP Codes are not provided. Only the business name, street address, city, state, and telephone number are available.

http://www.abii.com

American Business Information, Inc. has two separate telephone directories. The first one, called Lookup USA, has a White Pages format where businesses can be looked up by name. The second one, as its name (American Yellow Pages) intimates, provides for searching for businesses by

Yellow Pages-style categories. *ABII* does its own data gathering and claims to call each of the 15 million businesses at least once a year to verify the data. They also use "a sophisticated multivariate-regression model to determine probable credit worthiness" which takes the form of a "credit score" for each business. ZIP Codes are included here.

CHAMBERS OF COMMERCE

http://www.uschamber.org/mall

The site of the U.S. Chambers of Commerce is searchable through what it calls the *Chamber Mall*. Use this search function to locate a link to a local Chamber of Commerce with a presence on the Internet. Chambers located abroad are also included. It is also possible to search the Chamber Mall by location, industry, product, or company. Searching by company will access links to the sites of some of the 215,000 businesses which are members of the Chamber.

http://chamber-of-commerce.com:80

This is the *International Chamber of Commerce* site. Use this site to locate the contact information of a particular Chamber by name or geographic location.

MARKETING AND ADVERTISING

http://www.utexas.edu/coc/adv/world

This site, provided by the Advertising Department of the University of Texas at Austin, is packed with links to almost any combination of marketing and advertising sites. The demographic information section links to a variety of sites including those of the U.S. Census Bureau and Statistics Canada.

AGRIBUSINESS

http://www.ttu.edu/~aecovl/

This is the *Agricultural Economics Virtual Library* maintained at Texas Tech University. It serves mainly as a gateway to hundreds of other worldwide sites relating to business in agriculture including those from the USDA and FAO.

http://usda.mannlib.cornell.edu/usda/usda.html

The Mann Library at Cornell University serves as the official site for the *USDA Economics and Statistics System*. Currently there are nearly 300 reports and datasets from USDA's three economics agencies: the Economic Research Service (ERS), the National Agricultural Statistics Service (NASS), and the World Agricultural Outlook Board (WAOB). Many files are updated daily. The datasets are often in tabular format and will be displayed as Excel or Lotus 123 spreadsheets if your search software is set to recognize those file types.

http://www.milcom.com/fintrac/home.html

The *Global Agribusiness Information Network* (GAIN) provides quick access to daily wholesale prices of vegetables, fruit, miscellaneous tropical fruit, oriental vegetables, onions/potatoes, herbs, and flowers at most of the major metropolitan markets in the U.S., Canada, Mexico, and Europe. There is also a searchable index of the market information provided at this site. Under the "Postharvest Information" icon are reports detailing the handling, packaging, and storage requirements for a variety of fresh produce items from anthora to yams.

GOVERNMENT

http://www.business.gov

The *U.S. Business Advisor* site was developed by the Small Business Administration (SBA) and National Performance Review (NPR). Under the "How to" icon is a table of links to helpful business resources from disaster assistance to how to file W-2 Wage and Tax Statements.

http://www.sbaonline.sba.gov

The *Small Business Administration* (SBA) site provides links to information about starting, financing, and expanding a business. Through a clickable map, it is also possible to link to all of the SBA local office sites around the country. A relatively new link at this site is *ACE-Net*, the Internet-based network sponsored by the SBA's Office of Advocacy that gives new options to both small companies looking for investors and investors looking for promising opportunities.

COST OF LIVING

http://www.homefair.com/homefair/cmr/salcalc.html

There are many places on the Internet where one can find salary calculators, but this one with data provided by the Center for Mobility Resources is quite easy to use. How accurate it is may be debatable, but it is an excellent resource for a quick salary equivalency check across the U.S. and Canada.

BUSINESS SCHOOLS

http://www.yahoo.com/Business_and_Economy/Business_Schools/

A recently added feature of this *Yahoo!* business site is a linkable list of over 450 business schools from around the world. Business institutes are listed as well as the business programs of major academic universities. Some of these links (the bold-face ones) go to yet another *Yahoo!* index while others go directly to the institution's business school homepage. This site is still growing, so if the institution being sought today was not listed there now, check again tomorrow.

NONPROFIT BUSINESS

http://www.clark.net/pub/pwalker/home.html

Phillip Walker of United Way has compiled an index of sites with nonprofit-related information. Listed here are the names of foreign and domestic foundations and other grant sources along with connections to their respective homepages.

Internet Resources for Reference: International Trade

Brent Alan Mai

SUMMARY. The proliferation of international trade agreements serves as ample evidence of the importance of international trade in today's business environment. Countries and their companies have become more interrelated, and the opportunities for use of the Internet with its "no-boundaries" mindset have provided an excellent platform through which business information can be shared regardless of its original location. This article identifies a few of the thousands of Internet sites that can be helpful to the business reference librarian confronted with questions regarding international trade. The sites for the major trade agreements are listed along with a currency exchange calculator which can handle date-specific historical conversions. *[Article copies available for a fee from The Haworth Document Delivery Service: 1-800-342-9678. E-mail address: getinfo@haworth.com]*

INTRODUCTION

In theory and increasingly in practice, the Internet knows no geographic boundaries. This makes it an excellent medium through which to exchange international business information. As access to the Internet continues to expand globally, additional resources in the realm of international trade

Brent Alan Mai is Assistant Professor of Library Science at Purdue University, 1340 Krannert Building, West Lafayette, IN 47907-1340.

[Haworth co-indexing entry note]: "Internet Resources for Reference: International Trade." Mai, Brent Alan. Co-published simultaneously in *The Reference Librarian* (The Haworth Press, Inc.) No. 57, 1997, pp. 93-96; and: *Reference Sources on the Internet: Off the Shelf and Onto the Web* (ed: Karen R. Diaz) The Haworth Press, Inc., 1997, pp. 93-96. Single or multiple copies of this article are available for a fee from The Haworth Document Delivery Service [1-800-342-9678, 9:00 a.m. - 5:00 p.m. (EST). E-mail address: getinfo@haworth.com].

become available on an almost daily basis. Likewise, Web sites (hereafter referred to as sites) are altered almost daily and some disappear completely. Listed here are a few of the resources available in this field that appear to be reliably available and appropriate for reference related librarianship.

META SITES

http://ciber.bus.msu.edu/busres.htm

This site is sponsored by *CIBER* (Center for International Business Education and Research) at Michigan State University. The homepage begins with a topical index of the links that it provides. The links run the gamut from periodicals dealing with international business topics through company directories and government resources. Of particular interest are 31 links to international trade information.

http://www.uncc.edu/lis/library/reference/intbus/vibehome.htm

This site is the home of *VIBES* (Virtual International Business and Economic Sources). It is maintained by University of North Carolina at Charlotte's Jeanie Welch, Dun & Bradstreet's Online Champion of the Year for 1996. This well-indexed site provides links to a host of resources including exchange rates, international stock markets, and trade law.

http://www.stat-usa.gov

STAT-USA is a primary point for access to government statistics of all kinds including the National Trade Data Bank (NTDB). Government depository institutions have each been given one free password and there are some locations which have received site-licensed access. For the general user, the subscription cost is $150/year. Through the section on "Export and Trade Databases," one will find trade leads, market research reports, company indices, and export/import statistics.

http://www.dis.strath.ac.uk/business

For a look at business resources on the Internet from the European perspective, try this site maintained by Sheila Webber of the University of Strathclyde in Scotland. It provides links to business resources around the world that are not often found on U.S.-based sites.

DIRECTORIES

http://www.cris.com/~Serranyc

The *Import/Export Directory* provided by Serra International, Inc. is an excellent general resource for import/export questions. Included is a directory of international import/export sites arranged by country.

http://www.nafta.net/global

The *NAFTA Register* is a directory of companies trading internationally. It is designed to help users locate export service providers and trading companies who are doing business under NAFTA and to assist them in buying products and services. It is searchable by company name, type of product or service, or SIC Code.

http://www.mexconnect.com

The *Mexico Connect* site includes all types of resources related to doing business in and with Mexico. This site has been undergoing reorganization lately, but the Directory of Mexican Exporters has always been available. In it, hundreds of companies are listed by industry category.

EMBASSIES AND CONSULATES

http://www.state.gov/www/about_state/business/business_tools.html

This State Department site can assist in identifying the Economic Officers at U.S. Missions Overseas, Country Desk Officer contacts at the State Department, and Foreign Consular Offices in the United States. There are also links to the full text of the State Department's *Country Background Notes* and *Country Commercial Guides.*

NAFTA/GATT/MAASTRICHT TREATIES

http://itl.irv.uit.no/trade_law/nav/freetrade.html

This international trade law site provides the full text of several trade law agreements including NAFTA (the North American Free Trade

Agreement), GATT (the General Agreement on Tariffs and Trade), and the Maastricht Treaty on European Union. There are also links to "official" and "other" commentaries on the various trade laws and their implementation.

http://iepnt1.itaiep.doc.gov/nafta/nafta2.htm

This is the official U.S. Department of Commerce, International Trade Administration NAFTA site. In addition to providing access to the full text of the NAFTA, the "NAFTA Facts" link connects to information about business practices in Mexico and Canada as well as demographic statistics.

CURRENCY EXCHANGE

http://www.olsen.ch/cgi-bin/exmenu

This currency converter site is provided by Olsen & Associates. It is simple, yet comprehensive. Specify which of the over 160 currencies needs to be converted and to which one it should be converted. It is also possible to specify a particular date (default is yesterday–and notice that the date is entered in day/month/year format) and amount to be converted (default is 1).

Selected Ethnic and Gender Studies Internet Sources for Reference Use

Lisa Pillow

SUMMARY. The purpose of this article is to give a general overview of selected reference resources dealing with ethnic and gender studies available on the Web, and to present an annotated list of said sources. *[Article copies available for a fee from The Haworth Document Delivery Service: 1-800-342-9678. E-mail address: getinfo@haworth.com]*

INTRODUCTION

As interdisciplinary and multi-disciplinary fields, ethnic and gender studies cross into a wide number of overlapping subject areas including each other. Although these distinctions may not always be easy to make, when looking at how the two disciplines are covered on the World Wide Web (WWW), the overlapping subject areas are a plus given the linking technology of Web based browsers. The purpose of this article is to give a general overview of selected reference resources dealing with ethnic and gender studies available on the Web, and to present an annotated list of said sources. For the purpose of this writing, ethnic and gender studies have been broken up into seven disciplines:

- Ethnic Studies

  - African and African American Studies
  - Asian and Asian American Studies

Lisa Pillow is Reference Librarian in the Main Library at Ohio State University.

[Haworth co-indexing entry note]: "Selected Ethnic and Gender Studies Internet Sources for Reference Use." Pillow, Lisa. Co-published simultaneously in *The Reference Librarian* (The Haworth Press, Inc.) No. 57, 1997, pp. 97-109; and: *Reference Sources on the Internet: Off the Shelf and Onto the Web* (ed: Karen R. Diaz) The Haworth Press, Inc., 1997, pp. 97-109. Single or multiple copies of this article are available for a fee from The Haworth Document Delivery Service [1-800-342-9678, 9:00 a.m. - 5:00 p.m. (EST). E-mail address: getinfo@haworth.com].

- Latino/Chicano Studies
- Native American Studies

- Gender Studies

    - Gay, Lesbian and Bisexual Studies
    - Men's Issues
    - Women's Studies

All of these disciplines are well-represented on the Web. As with most subjects on the Internet, a plethora of information exists, but not all of it is suitable for reference work. A myriad of personal and institutional web sites exist relating to studies of race, gender, and sexual orientation. The range of information can be regional, national or local. Accessible sources can range from electronic journals and articles, statistical data, and bibliographies to images and sound. Now that the vastness of the Internet and the diversity of the disciplines in general has been illustrated, what constitutes a relevant reference resource web site?

Each of the areas was searched using various search engines, including *Infoseek, Yahoo!, Lycos,* and *Magellan,* with the parameters being free accessibility and relevance for reference work. Due to the interdisciplinary nature and size of ethnic and gender studies, sites with multiple links were chosen and evaluated for content in terms of usefulness for reference. For example, while looking at many of the Women's Studies pages, links to other sites dealing with women of color were found. The same can be true when it came to searching the gay, lesbian, and bisexual sites where access to Women's Studies sources were found. Overall, coverage for all the disciplines in general is very large in scope. Most of the major web sites, meaning those with many relevant links, have tables of contents which are searchable and serve as indexes and access points to other sites. Almost all of the authors or site editors stated that the purpose of their respective sites is to serve as a comprehensive access point to similar and related sites; but none claimed to have links to all *possible* relevant access points in existence. In fact, many of the sites contained disclaimers on the use of information contained or linked.

Looking at each of the disciplines and their respective selected web sites, all of those placed in the general category of "Ethnic Studies" have developed what could be called traditional reference sources, meaning sites containing historical, biographical, and statistical resources. The same can be said for Women's Studies, but when looking at the newest disciplines dealing with sexual orientation, it seems as though the resources on the Web are not quite as developed. This makes sense considering that racial, ethnic, and gender studies, as disciplines, established programs during the 1960s and 1970s[1] whereas sexual orientation disciplines such as Gay and Lesbian Studies programs and courses are now being offered by some universities like the City College of San Francisco and University of California, Berkeley. As sexual orientation disciplines evolve into established fields of study, so should the related web sites.

ETHNIC STUDIES

African American and African Studies

African Studies WWW (University of Pennsylvania)
URL: http://www.sas.upenn.edu/African_Studies/AS.html

African Studies WWW is supported by the African Studies Center at the University of Pennsylvania. It is a great site for reference because it provides links to the additional African Studies sites applicable to reference work. The contents of this site include:

- Country Specific Information including:

  - A list of African Embassies and Diplomats in the U.S., including addresses, telephone numbers, diplomat names and titles
  - a general map of Africa
  - a list of national holidays
  - *U.S. State Department Travel Warnings and Consular Information Sheets* by country

- A searchable site for statistics with query options which accesses relevant sites and electronic articles containing statistical information. For example, a search on "women and circumcision" yielded seven relevant articles which contained some statistical information on the practice of female circumcision.
- Information pages for each country including: a map of the country, travel advisories, the related *World Fact Book* entry, news stories, and the official language/languages.

Additional links accessible from the main contents page are the African Studies Association home page, K-12 guides on Africa, and a multimedia archive. Two links, Africa Web Links: Annotated List and Black/African Internet Resources are covered in two separate entries in this article due to the valuable information covered by each.

Black/African Related Resources (Art McGee's List)
URL: http://www.sas.upenn.edu/African_Studies/Home_Page/mcgee.html

This site is a selected list of relevant links to information relating to or concerning Black and African people, culture, diaspora, and issues. At this writing, this homepage was last updated July 29, 1994, however almost all of the links were still available. The main menu includes links to information on Pan-African politics and organizations, and Black/African cultural issues. This main menu is also linked to two additional home pages maintained by Mr. McGee, Social/Progressive Activism and International/Sustainable Development and Global Networking, both of which are related subjects to Black/African Studies. The remainder of the homepage is rich with significant subject links including various other African Studies sites, subject specific archives for the Caribbean, Ethiopia, links to all aspects of Black culture including music, specifically reggae, rap, hip-hop, and blues, cinema, African American history, as well as domestic and international politics. Resources for African and African American art and art related issues are also linked to this page. An interpretive exhibit of the National civil rights Museum offers vignettes exploring the history of major civil rights events, profiles of key players, as well as subsequent triumphs and defeats of the struggle. Mr. McGee has also included sources related to subjects of the Black diaspora including resources on xenophobia, diversity, Latin Studies, Islamic resources, and various full-text documents like the Civil Rights Act of 1964. In terms of issues of development and global networking for the African continent, links are provided to such sites as the HungerWeb, the Institute for Research and Politics, UNICEF, and USAID which has a link to a regional focus on Africa. Be cautious when using some of the links in McGee's annotated list because they do require passwords. In all cases where a password is needed, McGee has included it in the annotation.

African Web Links: An Annotated Resource List
URL: http://www.sas.upenn.edu/African_Studies/Home_Page/
WWW_Links.html

This site is an on-going project which lists on-line resources related to African Studies. Subjects covered are anthropology, arts and architecture, general references, history, languages, human rights, maps, population studies, religious studies, women's issues and travel. One of the many highlights of this site is the coverage of population studies in Africa. Sometimes it is difficult to find demographic and population statistics in the traditional reference tools. The population studies link includes demographic information on some, but not all African countries, demographic indicators for 1995 and projections for the year 2000, and a link to the World Fertility Survey for Africa which contains information on fertility from various African countries. Important resource information on women's issues in Africa is also accessible through a link to the Women in Development NETwork (WIDNET) which accesses information regarding African women including health, business, law, and training. In addition, WIDNET also includes statistics on African women like population, household health, education, and labor. For example, going into the link for statistics on population, housing, and households accesses recent statistics on the ratio of women to men in selected countries, average household sizes (1970 and 1990), percentage of women living in polygamy (1990-1995) and abortions by country (1994) are available along with general vital statistics including fertility and marriage.

The Universal Black Pages (UBP)
URL: http://www.ubp.com

The stated purpose of the Universal Black Pages (UBP), is to "have a complete and comprehensive listing of African diaspora related Web pages at a central site . . . to encourage development in categories and topics which are not currently available via existing islands."[2] UBP, which was created and is developed through efforts of the Black Graduate Students Association at Georgia Institute of Technology, does not claim to be the impossible–an exhaustive source of *all* black related web sites, but the group has managed to link relevant sources without a lot of duplication. The contents page is searchable and includes the following broad subjects:

- an events calendar
- professional organizations
- educational opportunities and activities
- history
- art
- music
- entertainment
- fraternities, sororities, and living groups

Anyone who has tried to help students who are pledging to Black Greek Societies research the histories of individual chapters will appreciate the sources for fraternity and sorority information. By clicking on the fraternities, sororities, and living groups link, the user connects to the home pages of each Greek letter society and subsequent chapters of each. These home pages include the fraternity/sorority's history on the national and chapter levels. The link for educational opportunities has a guide to medical schools with a section on minorities, and a link for scholarship and internship information for graduate and undergraduate students.

The history link provides access to biographical profiles of key 19th century African Americans including Mary Church Terrell, Nat Turner, Alexander Crummell, Sojourner Truth, Harriet Tubman and Frederick Douglass. With the present interest in the history of the Negro Baseball League, access to the Negro League Homepage provides a history of blacks in baseball from pre-1900 to the present, brief biographical sketches of some players from the Jim Crow Era, a bibliography of books on the subject, and the segregation of baseball in general.

Another component of the UBP provides access to information on the Black diaspora which contains a wealth of information covering cultural and historical information on Blacks here in the U.S. and abroad. Particularly interesting are the "hot topic" links to information on the genocide and refugee crisis in Rwanda, voodoo, and the Black diaspora in Cuba, Brazil, the Caribbean, and Canada. All in all, this web site is one of the best access points for African American resources.

Asian and Asian American Studies

The Asian Community Online Network (ACON)
URL: http://www.igc.apc.org/acon/

ACON provides timely news items such as Nike's role in labor exploitation, the aftermath of Proposition 209 in California, and reviews of new electronic databases for Asian Studies. ACON also provides links to upcoming events and conference announcements, ongoing issues in the Asian community, and a link to additional WWW resources including The Anti-Asian Violence Network and the Internet Guide for Asian American Cybernauts.

Asian American Resources
URL: http://www.mit.edu/afs/athena.mit.edu/user/i/r/irie/www/aar.html

This site contains useful links to Asian American information on the Internet. Subjects include World Wide Web Servers, events, magazines, Internet resources, electronic journals, and Asian Americans in the 1990 U.S. Census. Asian American Resources serves mainly as pointer to other sites regarding Asian American information.

Asian Studies WWW Virtual Library
URL: http://coombs.anu.edu.au/WWWVL-AsianStudies.html

The Asian Studies WWW Virtual Library is a useful access tool to scholarly resources and information regarding Asian Studies. The page is divided into three broad categories: (1) Asian Studies–Regional Information; (2) Asian Studies–Countries/Territories Data; and (3) Asia-Pacific Global Data. The first division, Asian Studies–Regional Information, gathers networked materials dealing regions including the whole Asia-Pacific, South Asia, Middle East, South East Asian, Pacific Ocean, East Asia, Caucasus, and Central Asia. For example, clicking on "South Asia" accesses materials pertaining to the entire region and each of the countries therein. For instance, once in the "South Asia Resources" a link for "Bangladesh" accesses information dealing with culture, languages and linguistics, population and demographics, teaching and resources, religion and philosophy, health, embassies, flags, maps, geography, as well as government and politics in that country. The second category, Asian Studies–Countries/Territories Data, accesses the same information by country or territory from a table of contents. The last division, Asia-Pacific Global Data, accesses electronic journals, the home page's newsletter, and subject oriented bibliographies. Overall, Asian Studies WWW Virtual Library is an excellent source for getting general country information and tools for research.

Latino/Chicano Studies

Chicano!
URL: http://www.pbs.org/chicano/

Chicano! Is part of the PBS Online home page and features biographical and historical information about the Mexican American Civil Rights Movement. Almost 100 brief biographical sketches and photographs of key players in the Mexican American and the Black Civil Rights Movement are available including Ralph Abernathy, Luis Carillo, and Cesar Chàvez. Chicano! also has a time line which covers events in American history from 1840-1975 relating to civil rights and Latinos. This site can be read in either English or Spanish.

CLNet Home Page
http://clnet.ucr.edu

CLNet, which stands for the Chicana/o Latina/o Communities Through Network, is "an emerging digital library on Latinas/os in the United States."[3] It is part of a collaborative effort between the Chicano/Latino

Electronic Network (CLEN), the University of California, Riverside, UCLA, and the University of California at Santa Barbara. CLNet provides links to statistical sources including CLNet Statistical Abstract which contains data generated by the Bureau of the Census and the Bureau of Labor Statistics which including the following information on Latinos/Chicanos:

- general population
- family
- health insurance
- income
- occupation
- residential segregation
- fertility
- household characteristics
- labor force status
- origin of birth
- voting
- education
- government assistance
- housing
- marital status
- resident population
- census information

Felipe's Things Latino
URL: http://edb518ea.edb.utexas.edu/html/latinos.html

This site accesses a variety of useful reference sources, in English and/or Spanish, related to Latino customs and culture, education history, music, politics, and religion. The "Reference/Referencias" link accesses an English to Spanish dictionary, an automatic Spanish verb conjugator, and a Spanish to English dictionary. Access to the Stanford University Libraries' research guide to Chicano/Latino Studies leads to the proper Library of Congress subject headings for Hispanic Americans, a bibliography of encyclopedias and handbooks, and periodical indexes that can help identify articles in scholarly journals. Felipe's Things Latino also serves as an access point to a variety of relevant sites on the Web.

Latin American Network Information Center (LANIC)
URL: http://info.lanic.utexas.edu

LANIC has both a country directory and a subject directory. The country directory provides access to profiles of South American countries and the Caribbean. The subject directory is divided into broad areas including, agriculture, government, indigenous peoples, maps, statistics, reference, art, literature, human rights, languages, and women. LANIC also serves as a link to other Internet tools and home pages.

Native American Studies

Index of Native American Resources on the Internet
URL: http://hanksville.phast.umass.edu/misc/NAresources.html

This index provides access to web sites in broad subject areas including culture, language, art, nations, history, health bibliographies, education, indigenous knowledge, and media. It also has a link to the Aboriginal Studies WWW Virtual Library. Also included is a link to rated and reviewed access points that access this site which according to Karen M. Strom, the author of this page, are an estimated 700 web sites.[4] Historical material on this page includes a historic map showing the western Indian territories, a directory of Native American library collections located in California, Cherokee sources including genealogy, Algonquian place names as location markers, and Native American issues in general. The link titled "Indigenous Knowledge" includes information about Native American astrology, life sciences, and traditional foods and health.

Native Web
URL: http://www.maxwell.syr.edu/nativeweb

NativeWeb is accessible by subject categories, geographic regions, nations and includes information links for languages, education, law and legal literature, organizations, bibliographies, dictionaries, and historical material. Of particular interest are the Native Web's access points for Native American dictionaries which include: *Cherokee-English Dictionary* (downloadable), *Klamath Meta Data Dictionary, Mayan Epigraphic Database* (hieroglyphics transliterated), *Short Navajo Talking Wordlist,* and *Ojibwe-English-Ojibwe Dictionary.* Additional information sites are also given including student organization home pages and gopher sites, a directory of Native American Tribes, Native fellowships, grants, scholarships and jobs, a list of federally recognized tribes of the United States, and additional WWW, Gopher and FTP sites regarding Native Americans.

GENDER STUDIES

Gay/Lesbian/Bisexual Resources

FeMiNa–Lesbians and BiSexuals
http://www.femina.com/femina/lesbians

This particular site offers an excellent access point to other Internet sources pertaining to lesbians and bisexuals. Links to same-sex marriage information, organization directories, and political action committees, gay and lesbian rights, and university student run organizations prove useful for reference use.

Lesbian Links
URL: http://www.lesbian.org/

As part of a collaborative effort between Lesbian.org and WWWomen, Lesbian Links provides a comprehensive and timely searchable database of lesbian sites on the Internet. The broad subject areas covered include advocacy and activism, arts and entertainment, health and sexuality, and links to other web pages by and about lesbians.

Infoqueer
URL: http://www.infoqueer.org/queer/qis

Infoqeer is another good access point to other links on the Internet regarding gays, lesbians, and bisexuals. The contents page is divided into two major categories, (1) information servers by subject and (2) information servers by geographic areas. The former includes arts and culture, colleges and universities, organizations, publications, transgender and transsexual, and women's sites. Servers by geographic area include Africa and the Middle East, Asia/Pacific Region, Central and South American and the Caribbean, Europe and the former USSR, and North America.

Rainbow Query
URL: http://www.glweb.com/RainbowQuery/Categories/Reference.html

The reference component of the Rainbow Query provides access to business guides, city guides, databases, regional guides and travel guides. It also provides an access point to an annotated list of links to other gay, lesbian, and bisexual resources.

Queer Resources Directory (QRD)
URL: http://www.qrd.org/QRD/

The QRD contains 18,223 files about "everything queer."[5] Topics covered include religion, family, health, culture, history, worldwide gay/lesbian links, political activism and organization directories. QRD serves as a good access point to other electronic resources on the Internet.

Men's Issues

The World Wide Web Virtual Library: The Men's Issues Page
URL: http://info-sys.home.vix.com/men

Yes Virginia, there *is* a Men's Issues Page. And it is an exhaustive access point for the Men's Movement and issues affecting men. The author, David Throop, states that the mission of this page is "To cover the several men's movements encyclopedically."[6] The page is intended to maintain a comprehensive list of men's movement web links, periodicals, and organizations. It is also the stated goal of this site "to serve as an online reference source for statistics, studies and bibliographies of interest to the men's movements."[7] The page is setup as a hierarchial topical index with major and lesser collections. Among the links listed as "Major Collections" are:

- recommended books for Men's Movements,
- domestic violence; battered men
- fatherhood and fatherlessness
- health
- rape, violence and abuse

Lists listed as "Lesser Collections" include:

- academia
- attitude, including men bashing
- patriarchy
- romance, marriage and relationships
- veterans' issues

The Men's Issues Page also has a detailed subject index which includes 1,041 links ranging from AIDS to welfare. This page should not be dismissed as a collection of white male backlashing. It does contain useful information such as health care spending on men's health, cardiac deaths by gender, a directory of over 100 Men's Movement organizations including e-mail addresses, postal addresses, telephone and fax numbers, a list of defunct men's organizations and international listings for father's groups. Access to other home pages of interest include such subjects as men's fraternal organizations, phone hot lines, fathering, and family issues.

Women's Studies

FeMiNa
URL: http://www.femina.com/femina/culture

FeMiNa is a good source for information on women of color. The site is searchable by keyword and Boolean operators. The search can be limited to search a particular component of the site or the entire contents which includes women of color, sexuality, and political activism.

Feminist Internet Gateway
URL: http://www.feminist.org/gateway/master2.html

The Feminist Internet Gateway is a pointer to Women's Studies web sites. The gateway is divided into a broad subject index including:

- general women's issues
- global feminism
- violence against women
- women and work
- women and girls in sports
- women in politics
- women's heath, abortion rights
- Women's Studies Centers

These broad subject areas are further divided. For example, clicking on "violence against women" accesses sites dealing with domestic violence, rape on campus, sexual harassment on the job, and the Men Against Rape Homepage. Looking under women and work, there are access points to sites dealing with the "glass ceiling," the Feminist Majority's National Feminist Census, and the executive woman. This gateway is timely and relevant to current women's issues.

Selected Internet Resources in Women's Studies
URL: http://www.npl.org/research/chss/grd/resguides/women3.htm

This is a comprehensive site developed by the New York Public Library. It provides access to some of the major home pages regarding women, including the National Organization for Women, the Fourth World Conference on Women, current events, a women artists archive which includes biographies on over 100 women artists from the middle ages to the present, reproductive freedom and the U.S. Department of Labor's Women's Bureau. Like many of the Women's Studies Internet indexes, the New York Public Library gateway provides good access points using both broad and specific links.

Women's Studies Resources
URL: http://www.aaln.org/vcl/electronics/etc/acad/womstud.html

Women's Studies Resources is a major access point for women's studies and related interdisciplinary subjects including women of ethnic and racial groups. This site has a broad index which provides access to collective sites, including the Clearinghouse for Subject Oriented Resource Guides, and connects to accessible web guides including bisexual resources, feminism women's health issues, and feminist activism. Women's Studies Resources also includes links to sites dealing with anti-violence, art and music, bibliographies, cinema, conferences, history, health and medicine, and reproduction.

SOURCES

1. Gretchen M. Bataille, Miguel A. Carranza and Laurie Lisa, introduction to *Ethnic Studies in the United States: A Research Guide* (New York: Garland Publishing Inc., 1996).
2. Georgia Tech Black Graduate Students Association, "The Universal Black Pages," [http://www.gatech.edu/bgsa/blackpages.html], July 1994.
3. Regents, University of California, "CLNet," [http://clnet.ucr.edu/].
4. Karen M. Strom, "Index of Native American Resources on the Net," [http://hanksville.phast.umass.edu/misc/tome.html].
5. QRD, "Queer Resources Directory," [http://www.qrd.org/QRD/], December 1996.
6. David Throop, "Men's Issues Page," [http://info-sys.home.vix.com/men], December 1996.
7. Ibid.

Politics by Other Media:
A Guide to National Political
Information Resources on the Internet

Robert Richards

SUMMARY. Librarians have long relied on printed directories and ephemera stored in vertical files to provide access to national political information. The Internet seems an ideal medium for evanescent political information because it allows for continuous updating of information directly by political organizations, enables the creation of large collections of diverse materials, frees librarians from the labor of ordering and updating materials, and permits remote access. There follows a list of political Internet resources that have proved to be valuable for reference in academic and public libraries. *[Article copies available for a fee from The Haworth Document Delivery Service: 1-800-342-9678. E-mail address: getinfo@haworth.com]*

The Internet has become a hotbed of political activity, with politicians, political parties, action committees, and activists of every stripe stumping online . . . Through the Internet, citizens will be able to garner more detailed information about issues and candidates and participate more fully in the political process.

–Michael Neubarth, "Playing Politics"[1]

Robert Richards is Library Technician II, Government Publications Library, University of Colorado at Boulder, Campus Box 184, Boulder, CO 80309-0184.

The author wishes to thank Timothy Byrne, Deborah Renee Hollis, Margaret M. Jobe and April Peterson for their support of this research.

[Haworth co-indexing entry note]: "Politics by Other Media: A Guide to National Political Information Resources on the Internet." Richards, Robert. Co-published simultaneously in *The Reference Librarian* (The Haworth Press, Inc.) No. 57, 1997, pp. 111-125; and: *Reference Sources on the Internet: Off the Shelf and Onto the Web* (ed: Karen R. Diaz) The Haworth Press, Inc., 1997, pp. 111-125. Single or multiple copies of this article are available for a fee from The Haworth Document Delivery Service [1-800-342-9678, 9:00 a.m. - 5:00 p.m. (EST). E-mail address: getinfo@haworth.com].

Reference librarians in public and academic libraries alike recognize the value their patrons place on current information about national politics. The historical reliance of the public on libraries for political information contributed to Sidney Ditzion's choice to cast public libraries as "arsenals of a democratic culture."[2] In higher education, students and scholars need reliable political information for research in political science and communications, as well as for assignments in composition and rhetoric.

To meet the great demand for quality political information, academic and public libraries over the past century and a half drew upon a common set of resources. Newspapers, political magazines and journals provided coverage of campaigns and current events, while pamphlets and other ephemeral publications produced by political organizations offered detailed information about candidates, interest groups and their positions on issues.[3]

Librarians relied on vertical files to organize and update this rapidly changing information. For contact information on political organizations, libraries employed directories, in print and, more recently, electronic formats. These tools have served librarians well, but have several shortcomings. Vertical files cause items to be misplaced, require expensive labor to maintain and are inaccessible to remote patrons. Further, directories in print, CD-ROM and commercial online formats rapidly become outdated.[4]

If there were a perfect match between content and medium, it might be said to occur between political information and the Internet. As Paul Starobin observes, the World Wide Web allows political organizations and those interested in politics to create rich information sources available to all with access to the global network.[5] For librarians, Internet sources of political information have many advantages over other media. First, information is more current and accurate, since it can be updated continuously by the organizations themselves. Second, librarians no longer need to spend precious time ordering and filing materials. Third, World Wide Web sites can assemble in one location massive collections of diverse resources: periodical articles, press releases, candidate profiles, voting records, opinion polls, policy statements, speeches, political platforms and directory information, among others.[6] These resources can be linked in a manner that renders them easily navigable and accessible. Further, both remote and in-library patrons can directly access Internet resources.

This article joins the burgeoning body of literature that attempts to extend bibliographic control over Internet political resources.[7] The resources listed here have proven useful to me and my colleagues for answering reference questions on national politics. The list is selective, and consists largely of directories and guides to resources, rather than sites of individual organizations. As I have been unable to include resources on every issue, the reader can use the directories cited to assemble a list that will best suit her patrons' needs.

"META" SITES

Yahoo!: Politics
http://www.yahoo.com/Politics/

A well organized, selective site for Internet resources across the political spectrum, *Yahoo!* connects to thirty-seven political Internet directories, lists more than three hundred sites for national and state election results, and provides current *Reuters* news stories on U.S. politics. The "Interest Groups" and "Public Interest Groups" sections cite more than 1,000, mainly political, organizations. "Political Issues" offers connections to resources on fourteen topics, from affirmative action to welfare reform. *Yahoo!* functions as a guide or bibliography: it provides an excellent tertiary resource when more specific sources fail.

National Political Index
http://www.politicalindex.com/

NPI appears to be the most comprehensive general site for political information, and lists over 3,500 Internet sites by topic. "Hourly Political Headlines" connects to the principal online news and election coverage sites. "Federal Elected Officials" links to the webpages of the President, the House and the Senate, to allow quick identification of representatives and committee members. "Information on Federal Candidates" connects to over eighty Internet resources on national campaigns, elections and voting. The "National Political Parties" page has over one hundred links to parties and directories across the ideological spectrum, neatly grouped by category. "Political Activist Groups" provides access to over five hundred links on twenty-one political topics. The "Political Think Tanks" page, linking to forty-eight research organizations, is valuable for locating sources of recent studies.

POLITICAL PARTIES

Democratic Party Online
http://www.democrats.org

The official site of the Democratic National Committee, *DPO* includes a directory of national, state and college Democratic organizations; the official party platform, charter and bylaws; a calendar of party events in every state; the text of Presidential proclamations, statements and remarks for 1996; and historical information, complete with a "History of the Democratic Donkey." Lists of Democratic candidates and Committee press releases also appear.

Republican Main Street
http://www.rnc.org

This Republic National Committee site provides many of the same features as its Democratic counterpart: party rules, platform and history; a directory of state and related party organizations; and issue statements, press releases and some legal documents. In addition, the site features a resource which may be of particular use to librarians: the "Rising Tide Book Browser," a collection of tables of contents and sample chapters of one dozen books by noted conservative authors, and a form for ordering online.

National Political Index: National Political Parties
http://www.politicalindex.com/sect8.htm

An exhaustive directory of political party Internet sites, especially useful for its coverage of marginal parties.

CAMPAIGNS, CANDIDATES AND ELECTION RESULTS

AllPolitics: Vote 96
http://allpolitics.com/elections/

A joint venture of *Time, CNN* and *Congressional Quarterly, AllPolitics* offers extensive coverage of the 1996 campaign, including the national conventions, presidential debates, official election results and exit polls. Election results offer data at state and district level for Congressional races. The "Issues" area treats twenty-one national issues. The site also offers reports on current political news, a continuous news feed from

Associated Press, and selected political articles from *Time* dating back to 1924. *CNN* provides transcripts of the presidential debates and candidate interviews. The "Candidates" area offers schedules of primaries, biographical essays on the presidential candidates and convention delegate tallies. The site also offers political poll results from October 1995 to the present. The "States" area presents biographies of Congressional incumbents–but not challengers–and the text of *CQ* articles on Congressional events. The detailed election results and full text sources provide a wonderful resource for political researchers and voters.

CBS News: Campaign '96
http://www.cbsnews.com/campaign96/home/

This rich resource includes complete transcripts of conventions and biographical sketches of convention speakers; *CBS News* polls for 1996; extensive documentation on the primary process and campaign finance; state by state delegate counts, primary results and 1992 presidential election results; campaign finance data for all primary candidates; and thorough coverage of eighteen issues. "1996 Election Results" include national and state popular and electoral vote counts, and exit polls analyzing the vote by gender, race and other factors. The historical data, background information on the political process and wonderful primary and convention coverage distinguish this site.

Encyclopedia Britannica: American Presidential Elections, 1789-1996
http://elections.eb.com/

This useful site offers popular and electoral vote results for every presidential election in U.S. history.

PoliticsNow: Campaign '96
http://www.politicsnow.com/campaign/

This is a marvelous service of *ABC News, Los Angeles Times, National Journal, Newsweek* and *The Washington Post. PoliticsNow* offers national, state and county level election results, news stories and exit polls. "Congressional Reports" analyze election results in terms of the fates of women and minority candidates and other factors. Candidate information is the hallmark of this site: the full text of *Almanac of American Politics* provides detailed biographical essays and voting records for all members of Congress. Federal Election Commission campaign finance information on candidates is provided, but only in tabular format for downloading, not for online viewing. On the *PoliticsNow* homepage, "Poll Track" offers poll data from 1993 to the present. "The Capital Source" is a database of directory listings for "more than 7,000 government officials, interest groups, and inside-the-Beltway corporations."[8] For eleven key topics, *PoliticsNow* offers a brief overview, statistics, a timeline, profiles of recent legislation, presidential candidates' views and recent *Washington Post* articles.

Vote Smart Web
http://www.vote-smart.org/

As an antidote to the treatment of issues in the commercial media, Project Vote Smart attempts to create objective "resumes" of all presidential, Congressional and state legislative candidates.[9] For each candidate—including challengers–the service offers a biographical sketch, announcement speech, voting record and campaign finance data. *Vote Smart* surpasses other sites in issue coverage by presenting candidate "performance evaluations" by more than 70 interest groups, and candidates' responses to a questionnaire covering twenty five major issues. To help voters assess candidates' qualifications, *Vote Smart* describes the responsibilities of each office.

CAMPAIGN FINANCE

FECInfo
http://www.tray.com/fecinfo

A former Federal Election Commission employee uses FEC reports to create this mine of detailed campaign finance information. Data is included for political action committees, individual contributors of more than $200, and national candidates. For candidates, one can retrieve lists of contributions from PACs, and from individual contributors by name or zip code. One can search by candidate's name, zip code or state; by name or state of a PAC; and by name, employer or occupation of an individual contributor. Names of PACs and candidates are hotlinked, so that one can easily proceed from a search on a particular PAC to a search for all PACs that contributed to a candidate. The site also offers lists of top PACs by nine financial categories.

POLITICAL NEWS

The Christian Science Monitor Electronic Edition
http://www.csmonitor.com/

The Christian Science Monitor Archives
http://168.203.8.8/plweb-cgi/iops1.pl

In addition to offering good coverage of current national politics and a news feed from the *Associated Press, The Monitor* has placed on the Web a full text archive covering 1980 to the present. The search engine allows Boolean and field searching similar to *DIALOG*.

Los Angeles Times: Politics and Polls
http://www.latimes.com/HOME/NEWS/POLITICS/

The L.A. Times provides the full text of two weeks of political news stories, as well as detailed reports on polls, including an exit poll from the November presidential election analyzing voting by gender, region, race and other factors. *L.A. Times* political poll stories and selected data are available from March 1996 to the present.

The Washington Post
http://www.washingtonpost.com/

The Post offers the full text of political news daily in its "National Section." The "Archives" area allows the user to search by keyword for the past two weeks of the full text of *Post* articles and *Associated Press* news releases. A notice on the site states that the "Archives" will soon contain *Post* articles from 1986 to the present.

AllPolitics (http://www.allpolitics.com)

PoliticsNow (http://www.politicsnow.com)

These also provide substantial news coverage of current politics.

INCUMBENT VOTING

Congressional Quarterly Vote Watch
http://pathfinder.com/CQ/

Vote Watch provides eighteen months of voting information on significant Congressional legislation. Users may search by Member name, state, zip code, Congressional district, popular name and title keyword of bills, and subject headings. Clicking on the title of a bill in the result list evokes the text of a *CQ* article about the vote.

Vote Smart Web offers a list of incumbent voting Internet resources at:

http://www.vote-smart.org/congress/congress.html#votes

INTEREST GROUPS AND ISSUES: GENERAL DIRECTORIES

Right/Conservative:

The Right Side of the Web
http://www.clark.net/pub/jeffd/

Danky and Cherney call this "one of the best all-around web-pages containing conservative information."[10] "Conservative College Organizations and Publications" connects to more than sixty campus groups and journals. Under "Culture and Society" one finds links to directories of second amendment issue sites, Christian sites and pro-life resources. The "Economics and Foreign Policy" page connects to more than a dozen resources, including think tanks and single issue groups. In the "Reading Room," one finds a list of twenty additional conservative WWW directories. "96 Conservative Election Central" connects to the C-SPAN election site, and the home pages of dozens of Republican Congressional candidates.

Right on the Web: The Right Links
http://www.rightweb.com/links.shtml

The Right Links complements the *Right Side of the Web* by offering a clearer and more detailed arrangement of sites by nineteen categories. The coverage of Republican Party organizations and the environment also improves upon *The Right Side.*

Left/Liberal:

Turn Left: the Home of Liberalism on the Web
http://www.turnleft.com/liberal.html

This well designed site provides easy access to a range of liberal resources. Under "Politics" one finds links to more than twenty Democratic party organizations, as well as the Green Party and the New Party. The "Culture" page lists fifteen other liberal web directories. Perhaps the most valuable part of *Turn Left* is "The Issues," a catalog of more than one hundred sites on fourteen liberal issues from women's rights to "Religious Liberal Perspectives." "Fight the Right" provides links to fifteen liberal watchdog organizations and all the major conservative Internet directories.

Institute for Global Communications: Members Directory
http://www.igc.org/igc/members/index.html

Created by the premiere host of progressive resources on the Internet, the *IGC Directory* lists hundreds of individual progressive organizations. Arrangement is, regrettably, alphabetical, with no subject access.

SPECIFIC ISSUES AND GROUPS

Abortion:

The Ultimate Pro-Life Resource List
http://www.prolife.org/ultimate/

This site gathers seemingly every Internet pro-life resource into a well organized directory. The "Organizations" page is a classified list of more than seventy right-to-life organizations. "Abortion Alternatives" links to a national clearinghouse of crisis pregnancy centers, a national crisis pregnancy hotline and one dozen local crisis pregnancy center websites. The "Politics" section, however, lists only tendentious "Fact Sheets" on particular candidates and events.

The Abortion Rights Activist
http://www.cais.com/agm/main/index.html

A rich collection of pro-choice resources. "Issues and Alerts" presents information on current legislation. "Information About Abortion" has national phone numbers and hotlinks to abortion providers and documents on RU-486 and emergency contraception. "News and Events" offers weekly summaries of abortion news from May 1995 to the present. "Clinic Violence" gathers information on abortion clinic attacks, including statistics. "Tools for Activists" presents a lengthy list of abortion organizations and "Clinic Defense and Escorting Groups," and a catalog of pro-choice and pro-life Internet sites. "The Reference Library" houses texts of documents on clinic security, court decisions and laws, and links to women's medical resources.

Affirmative Action:

AffActWeb: the American Association for Affirmative Action
http://www.fga.com/aaaa/

This site, maintained by a professional organization of affirmative action administrators, offers the text of news articles from *The Washington Post* on current affirmative action issues, pages of links to materials on federal and state affirmative action policies, and a directory of pro-affirmative action organizations and Internet resources.

Yahoo!: Society and Culture: Affirmative Action
http://www.yahoo.com/text/Society_and_Culture/Affirmative_Action/

Lists more than one dozen resources, including several that express opposition to affirmative action.

Environment:

Amazing Environmental Organization Directory
http://www.webdirectory.com/

This comprehensive directory is organized as a subject tree with more than thirty major categories, ranging from "General Environmental Interest Groups" to "Recycling" and even "Arts." The service connects to other Internet directories, individual organizations and Usenet newsgroups. One can also search by keyword in title or subject.

Firearms:

National Political Index: Political Activist Groups: Firearms
http://www.politicalindex.com/sect10.htm#9

NPI links to more than twenty five second amendment-related organizations and directories.

Turn Left–The Issues: Gun Issues
http://www.turnleft.com/issues.html#gun

Turn Left lists three politically moderate sites that advocate gun control.

Gay and Lesbian Issues:

Queer Resources Directory
http://qrd.tcp.com/qrd/

QRD is a huge collection of resources on gay and lesbian culture. Especially useful are sections on "Politics, Political News and Activism," which includes articles and national opinion polls, and "Organizations, Directories & Newsletters," with the text of press releases and links to Internet sites for nearly two hundred organizations, many of them political. The full text materials make the *QRD* a valuable resource on issues and events.

Christian Resources on the Web: Christian Life: Sexuality
http://www.students.uiuc.edu/~s-schim/christian/life.html#sex

CRW links to several sites expressing opposition to homosexuality.

Immigration:

American Civil Liberties Union: Immigrants' Rights
http://www.aclu.org/issues/immigrant/hmir.html

The ACLU gathers an extensive collection of legal and policy materials on immigration, including many links to other Internet resources.

U.S. Border Control
http://www.usbc.org/

This non-profit organization lobbies on behalf of restrictions on immigration. Their website provides policy statements, the text of articles from major periodicals, and bill numbers, descriptions and in some cases the full text of pending immigration legislation.

Labor:

IGC LaborNet
http://www.igc.org/igc/labornet/index.html

A rich resource for labor related issues. "The Strike Page," updated monthly, lists labor actions throughout the U.S. and Canada. "Action

Alerts" and news stories inform users of current events. "Unions and Organizations on the Information Superhighway" is a seemingly comprehensive alphabetical directory of hundreds of labor and pro-labor groups on the Internet. The directory and strike news features are invaluable.

Religion:

People for the American Way: Religious Liberty Issues
http://www.pfaw.org/relig.htm

People for the American Way: About the Religious Right
http://www.pfaw.org/aboutrr.htm

American Civil Liberties Union: Religious Freedom
http://www.aclu.org/issues/religion/hmrf.html

These sites provide abundant information on court cases and pending legislation concerning religious liberty and the relationship between church and state. The sites offer policy statements and the texts of key bills, court decisions and news releases. The ACLU site contains two years of press releases, while PFAW hosts a sizable collection of research reports about the religious right.

Christian Resources on the Web
http://www.students.uiuc.edu/~s-schim/christian/christian.html

CRW is a user-friendly subject guide to Christian resources. The categories "Family Resources," "Pro-Life Resources," "Politics" and "Sexuality" list most of the major Christian political groups and issue sites.

Welfare:

Welfare Reform and the General Welfare
http://libertynet.org/~edcivic/welfref.html

From the Institute for Civic Values, this site comprises a wealth of materials reflecting all sides in the welfare debate. One finds here the text of welfare legislation, speeches by public officials, articles from professional journals and reports from conservative and liberal think tanks. The site provides a legislative history of the most recent federal welfare reform law, and contains links to important organizations with an interest in welfare.

Yahoo!: Government: Politics: Political Issues: Welfare Reform
http://www.yahoo.com/text/Government/Politics/Political_Issues/
Welfare_Reform/

Yahoo! links to eight additional welfare Internet sites, including several directories, and the full text of a *Washington Post* analysis of the new welfare law.

Women's Issues:

Feminist Activist Resources on the Net
http://www.igc.apc.org/women/feminist.html

This site provides access to mainstream and leftist women's rights organizations. "Women and Economic Issues" connects to materials on the Glass Ceiling Commission and the Equal Pay Act, and to a directory of more than a dozen women's political organizations. "Reproductive Rights" presents links to eighteen sites, including major advocacy organizations, directories and legal documents. "Women and Politics" connects to nine sites, including PACs, issue organizations and political participation groups. Other pages treat race and health issues. "Women's Organizations" leads to more than thirty women's organizations, both mainstream and leftist, while "Feminist Resources" gathers a weighty collection of explicitly feminist materials.

The Eagle Forum
http://www.basenet.net/~eagle/eagle.html

The Eagle Forum hosts a site that offers news on current legislation of interest to anti-feminists, links to pro-family organizations, the full text of *The Phyllis Schlafly Report* from 1994 to the present, and other Forum publications.

REFERENCES

1. Michael Neubarth, "Playing Politics," *Internet World* 6:8 (Aug. 1995): 6.
2. Sidney Ditzion, *Arsenals of a Democratic Culture: A Social History of the American Public Library Movement in New England and the Middle States from 1850 to 1900.* Foreword by Merle Curti. Chicago: American Library Association, 1947.

3. On the use of pamphlets for current affairs reference service in public libraries, see Gordon Cullingham, "The Pamphlet and Current Affairs," *Ontario Library Review* 36 (Nov. 1952): 218-219, rpt. in Michael D. G. Spencer, ed., *Readings on the Vertical File,* Englewood, Col.: Libraries Unlimited, 1993: 7. On pamphlets for political reference in academic libraries, see Tom Hodgson and Andrew Garogian, "Special Collections in College Libraries: the Vertical File," *Reference Services Review* 9:3 (July/Sep. 1981): 77-82; and Juleigh Clark, "The Vertical File in South Carolina Academic Libraries," *South Carolina Libraries* 31 (Spring 1987): 34-36, rpt. in Spencer 104-108. Robert B. Harmon notes the importance of ephemera in political science collections in *Developing the Library Collection in Political Science,* Metuchen, N.J.: Scarecrow Press, 1976.

4. Guides to reference sources in political science emphasize the importance of both ephemera and directories as information sources. See, for example, Henry E. York, *Political Science: A Guide to Reference and Information Sources,* Englewood, Col.: Libraries Unlimited, 1990; Phillip A. Smith, "Political Science," in William H. Webb et al., *Sources of Information in the Social Science: A Guide to the Literature,* 3rd. ed., Chicago: American Library Association, 1986: 503-584; and Harmon. Librarians long created their own political directories. Gale Research produced the *Encyclopedia of Associations* only irregularly from 1956 to 1975, when annual volumes began to be issued. The first commercially published directories of political action committees seem to have appeared in 1982: Edward Roeder, *PACs Americana: A Directory of Political Action Committees and Their Interests,* Washington, D. C.: Sunshine Services, 1982; and Marvin I. Weinberger and David U. Greevy, *The PAC Directory: A Complete Guide to Political Action Committees,* Cambridge, Mass.: Ballinger, 1982. For articles on attempts to use electronic databases to improve access to vertical files, see Maureen O. Carleton and Catherine G. Cheves, "The Vertical File Enters the Electronic Age," *Medical Reference Services Quarterly* 8:4 (Winter 1989): 1-10, and Eileen F. Bator, "Automating the Vertical File Index." *Special Libraries* 71:11 (Nov. 1980): 485-491.

5. Paul Starobin, "On the Square," *National Journal* 28:21 (25 May 1996): 1145.

6. "The amount of information that can be disseminated on the Internet is virtually unlimited and is not directly proportional to cost," remarks Julie Holdren. ". . . Once a site is developed, the incremental cost involved in adding anything . . . is negligible." "Cyber Soapbox," *Internet World* 6:8 (Aug. 1995): 50-51.

7. See especially ACRL Law and Political Science Section Library Instruction Committee, "Internet Resources for the 1996 Election," *College and Research Libraries News* 57:8 (Sep. 1996): 481-486; Brad Stone, "Politics '96," *Internet World* 7:11 (Nov. 1996): 44-50; John S. Makulowich, "Campaign Sites: A Potpourri of Political Punditry," *Database* 19:3 (June/July 1996): 89-91; Jim Danky and John Cherney, "Beyond Limbaugh: the Far Right's Publishing Spectrum," *Reference Services Review* 24:1 (1996): 43-56; Steven L. Hupp, "Internet Resources for Conservatism," *College and Research Libraries News* 56:7 (Jul./Aug. 1995): 464-466; Bill Mann, *Politics on the Net,* Indianapolis: Que, 1995;

Eric Lee, "Workers Unite," *Internet World* 6:8 (Aug. 1995): 64-67; Tom Sowa, "The Matrix of Hatred," *Internet World* 6:8 (Aug. 1995): 62; and G. David Garson, "Political Science and Public Administration: an Internet Guide," *Social Science Computer Review* 13:4 (1995): 453-483.

8. "The Capital Source," *PoliticsNow,* http://politicsusa.com/PoliticsUSA/CapSource/source-1.html.cgi (12 Dec. 1996).

9. Jeff Ubois, "Political Smarts: *Vote Smart* Gives Voters the Information Candidates Want to Hide," *Internet World* 7:11 (Nov. 1996): 53.

10. Danky and Cherney 56.

Economics Internet Sites
for Reference Librarians

Miles Yoshimura

SUMMARY. This article is a guide to selective Economics reference internet sites. Included are sections on statistical resources, working papers and other sites of interest to economists. *[Article copies available for a fee from The Haworth Document Delivery Service: 1-800-342-9678. E-mail address: getinfo@haworth.com]*

INTRODUCTION

There are two types of web sites that economists find especially useful for their work: statistical and working paper resources. General reference librarians will find the statistical sites of help in answering reference questions. Academic reference librarians will find the working papers sites of use, as well.

The ability to transfer data was the original intention of the Internet and has always been an important function of it. However, the web has extended the ability to present and offer access to data to the world in much more interesting and dynamic ways. The ability to make available and access data in a timely manner has made the Internet an increasingly important place for statistics. Much of the government data is made accessible over the internet before print copies of the statistical publications reach the shelves of depository libraries. Indeed the future of the print

---

Miles Yoshimura is Social Sciences Librarian, Alexander Library, Rutgers University, New Brunswick. E-mail: yoshimur@rci.rutgers.edu

[Haworth co-indexing entry note]: "Economics Internet Sites for Reference Librarians." Yoshimura, Miles. Co-published simultaneously in *The Reference Librarian* (The Haworth Press, Inc.) No. 57, 1997, pp. 127-137; and: *Reference Sources on the Internet: Off the Shelf and Onto the Web* (ed: Karen R. Diaz) The Haworth Press, Inc., 1997, pp. 127-137. Single or multiple copies of this article are available for a fee from The Haworth Document Delivery Service [1-800-342-9678, 9:00 a.m. - 5:00 p.m. (EST). E-mail address: getinfo@haworth.com].

127

copies is much in doubt. Companies, research institutions, individual academics and laymen are also putting data on the Internet. As with texts, the researcher must be aware of the reliability and source of the data that is found. If a library does not have a depository collection or machine-readable data sources, the reference librarian now has a collection of machine-readable statistical sources at their fingertips. Reference librarians will find the statistical sites invaluable for ready reference questions involving requests for the "most current" federal government data. Some, but not all, state web sites include state statistical data. International data is much more difficult to find. Many statistical offices of foreign governments have web sites, but few include statistical data. Most foreign governments do not make statistical data as readily available as the United States government does. Data from international organizations is available, but it can lag a year or two or more behind.

Bibliographic control and access to full-text working papers has been a problem for librarians and economists. But now the Internet holds the promise of being THE place for providing some level of bibliographic control as well as dissemination of them. By submitting an abstract or full text of his/her working paper, an economist provides instant access to fellow economists. Some sites provide the full text directly on the web, some allow a copy to be requested from the author by e-mail, and others allow a researcher to order a copy for a nominal fee. This self service aspect has democratized access to working papers for libraries and researchers. However, the Internet is still not a comprehensive site for all working papers, and bibliographic tools such as *EconLit* remain important for the bibliographic control of them.

Electronic journals have the potential to be the third application of promise. However, many issues regarding electronic journals have yet to be resolved (e.g., archiving, manner of access and distribution, etc.), and their use has not reached the critical mass that has been achieved by statistical and working paper sites. Unfortunately, most if not all electronic journals will be fee-based, and librarians will need to plan for this in their acquisitions budgets. Currently, only one journal is purely electronic: *Studies in Nonlinear Dynamics and Econometrics* [http://mitpress.mit.edu/SNDE/WWW/journal/index.html]; If this journal proves successful, the concern of economists for timeliness in very dynamic fields will give rise to more electronic journals.

STATISTICAL WEB SITES

When all possible statistical web sites are broken down into their component parts, the amount of statistical data available is mind-boggling.

Categorizing the individual pieces of data is equally mind-boggling. The following statistical sites were chosen for the potential they hold for the general reference librarian.

Collections of Statistical Sites

Business and Economics Numeric Data
http://www.clark.net/pub/lschank/web/ecostats.html

Larry Schankman of Mansfield University has done a very nice of job of selecting a number of business and economics statistical sites, and he provides helpful annotations.

Statistical Resources on the Web
http://www.lib.umich.edu/libhome/Documents.center/frames/statsfr.html

Grace York of the University of Michigan has created a comprehensive site of statistical resources on the Internet. It is well organized and makes effective use of "frames" (there is a "non-frame" option, as well) as a navigation and indexing device.

Economics Electronic Data Sources
http://www.libraries.rutgers.edu/rulib/socsci/econ/econ.html#menu4.1

An alternative approach to links with annotations is the "just the links, please" approach used in this list of statistical sites. This site is geared to economists who do not want to scroll through screens of annotations and who, literally, just want the links. The "Electronic Data Sources" is a section of a longer list of resources which interest economists.

United States Statistical Data

This is only a sampling of the data that is available. The annotations listed below represents only a small portion or layer of the data available at the listed sites. The user is advised to look at the entire site to get a sense of the amount of statistical data available.

Census Bureau
http://www.census.gov/

The Census Bureau provides a wealth of data. Be sure to use the "Subject A-Z" index, otherwise data can be difficult to find. There is so much data that even with the aid of the "Subject A-Z" index, the user may have a difficult time finding a known item. Reference librarians will simply have to sample this massive site to get a sense of the data available. For example, the "Subject A-Z" index lists "Census" with an innocent-looking link labeled "1990." Clicking on "1990" yields a choice of two equally innocent and uninteresting-looking links; one of those links is labeled "Lookup." By clicking on "Lookup," the user can search the contents of the 1990 Census Summary Tape File 3 (STF3). The user can search by state, county, place or tract for over 250 variables. Summary Tape File 1 (STF1) can also be searched. As a result, "Lookup" can answer many Census questions, even if the reference librarian does not have access to a depository collection.

Consumer Price Index (Bureau of Labor Statistics)
http://stats.bls.gov/cg-bin/surveymost?cu

Current Consumer Price Data–News Releases (Bureau of Labor Statistics)
http://stats.bls.gov/news.release/cpi.toc.htm

CPI Calculation Machine (Federal Reserve Bank of Minneapolis)
http://woodrow.mpls.frb.fed.us/economy/calc/cpihome.html

"Consumer Price Index" and "Current Consumer Price Data–New releases" are available from the Bureau of Labor Statistics. The most current data comes in the form of "News Releases." In the near future, the news releases will be in hypertext format. The "CPI Calculation Machine" will calculate what a dollar in a given year is worth in 1996 dollars.

County and City Data Books (1988 and 1994)
http://www.lib.virginia.edu/socsci/ccdb

This is the web version of the County and City Data Books on CD-ROM that was distributed to depository libraries. This version allows the user to search county, city or state data for up to 75 variables at a time.

1992 Economic Census (Census Bureau)
http://www.census.gov/econ/www/econ_cen.html

Provides summary of national statistics by SIC code (two or four digits) for mineral industries, construction industries, manufacturers, transportation, communications and utilities, wholesale trade, retail trade, financial, insurance and real estate industries, and service industries (taxable and tax-exempt).

STAT-USA
http://www.stat-usa.gov

Until the end of September 1996 the University of Michigan downloaded data from the Department of Commerce and several other federal agencies and made it available on the Internet on a site called the *Economic Bulletin Board*. Beginning with October 1996, the University of Michigan ceased to download data. The data is now available through STAT-USA. STAT-USA is a fee-based service, but a single password is available to depository libraries at no cost.

Economic Indicators (Census Bureau)
http://www.census.gov/ftp/pub/statab/www/indicator/

Monthly data for standard economic indicators. Data also goes back a few years. Some of the indicators included are consumer price index, gross domestic product, interest rates, civilian labor force and unemployment and the index of leading indicators.

Economic Report of the President (1995-1997)
http://www.access.gpo.gov/su_docs/budget/index.html

Full-text version, including tables. Standard resource for Economics students in need of aggregate time-series data.

Economics Statistics Briefing Room (White House)
http://www.whitehouse.gov/fsbr/esbr.html

Current macroeconomics data presented graphically. Importantly, each statistic has a link to the original table of the web page of the source department or agency.

Poverty (Census Bureau)
http://www.census.gov/ftp/pub/hhes/www/poverty.html

Data and reports on poverty from the Poverty and Health Statistics Branch of the Census Bureau. Includes the definition of poverty (poverty threshold) and data on poverty threshold and historical data going back to 1959.

State Web Pages on the Internet (Council of State Governments)
http://www.csg.org/links/index.html

Potentially, this is a very good site for possible state-level data that may not be found in the federal sites. However, state-level statistical data is not prevalent on most state pages, and some state pages do not include any statistical data. All fifty states now have web pages.

1995 Statistical Abstract of the United States
http://www.census.gov/stat_abstract

1994 Statistical Abstract of the United States
http://www.medaccess.com/census/census_s.htm

The 1995 Statistical Abstract of the United States is a much abridged version of the print edition. If a library user wants the most current data for whatever number, it is better to try the web site of the department or agency that maintains the requested data. A much more complete version of Statistical Abstracts is the site for the 1994 Statistical Abstract of the United States. This Statistical Abstract site lists over 1400 tables from that volume with some tables are missing for copyright reasons. A CD-ROM version of the 1995 and 1994 was given to depository libraries.

Universal Currency Converter
http://www.xe.net/currency

Expedia's Currency Converter (Microsoft)
http://expedia.msn.com/pub/curcnvrt.dll?qscr=alcc

GNN/Koblas Foreign Exchange Converter
http://bin.gnn.com/cgi-bin/gnn/currency

Exchange Rate Service (Policy Analysis Computing and Information Facility in Commerce, University of British Columbia: PACIFIC)
http://pacific.commerce.ubc.ca/xr

Olsen and Associates 164 Currencies Converter (January 1990-Present)
http://www.olsen.ch/cgi-bin/exmenu

The "Universal Currency Converter" and "Expedia's Currency Con-verter" allow the user to input any given amount of one major currency for conversion into another currency. The Koblas site allows the user to choose one major currency, and the foreign exchange rate will be calculated for the rest. The PACIFIC site provides daily foreign exchange rates for and information on 65 major international currencies and also foreign exchange rates for over 200 other currencies; foreign exchange rates are for Canadian and US dollars only. The Olsen site allows the user to get the daily foreign exchange rate for any two of 164 currencies going back to January 1, 1990.

USDA Economics and Statistics (Cornell)
http://usda.mannlib.cornell.edu/usda

A very important data site for those interested in Agricultural Economics. This site is a joint project between the Mann Library of Cornell University and agencies of the USDA: Economic Research Service, National Agricultural Statistics Service and World Agricultural Outlook Board.

Government Information Sharing Project (Oregon State University)
http://govinfo.kerr.orst.edu/

The Government Information Sharing Project seeks to provide a user-friendly interface to raw government data and to make the data available over the Internet. This is a very good effort to fulfill the mandate of the project. The project includes the Economic Census, Census of Agriculture, Equal Employment Opportunity data, county data, import and export data, the School District Data Book, Regional Economic Information Service data, the Consolidated Federal Funds Report and population estimates. Librarians can benefit greatly by more user-friendly interfaces being created for raw government data sets and, moreover, by having the data and interfaces made accessible via the web.

International Data

1994 Country Reports on Economic Policy and Trade Practices (State Department)
gopher://dosfan.lib.uic.edu:70/1D-1%3A5844%3A011994%20Report

This State Department site was intended to provide a "comprehensive and comparative analysis of the economic policies and trade practices of each country with which the United States has an economic or trade relationship." This site provides useful textual analysis broken down by various topics and includes summary numerical trade data.

Penn World Tables (Alan Heston and Robert Summers)
http://cansim.epas.utoronto.ca:5680/pwt/pwt.html

The Penn World Tables began as a table in a well-received and re-spected journal article published in 1991. The tables were created in order to better compare purchasing power parity across countries. Since the original article appeared, the table has grown. It now includes 152 coun-tries and 29 subjects.

1994 International Handbook of Economic Statistics (Central Intelli-gence Agency)
http://www.odci.gov/cia/publications/hes/index.html

To get to the data, click on the "Table of Contents" button at the bottom of the initial welcoming page. Some of the statistical data included goes back to 1970. The source of the data appears to be from other federal government agencies.

Statistical Agencies on the Internet (United States and non-United States)
http://www.science.gmu.edu/csi779/drope/govstats.html

Statistical Agencies on the Internet (International)
http://www.census.gov/main/www/stat-int.html

The first site provides links to the data and press release sections of United States and foreign statistical agencies. Very good site for current data from the handful of foreign governments providing data through the Internet. The second site provides a link to the initial home page of the foreign statistical agencies: many of which do not contain statistical data.

World Economic Window
http://nmg.clever.net/wew/

This is a service of an American company. This graphic site provides very current data on selected Economic statistics using European Union (EU) and Organization for Economic Cooperation and Development (OECD) data. At the top of the page, there are definitions of the terms used and explanations as to why these are important.

WORKING PAPER SITES

BibEc
http://netec.mcc.ac.uk/BibEc.html

WoPEc
http://netec.wustl.edu/~adnetec/WoPEc/WoPEc.html

BibEc lists print working papers by institution, making the search engine crucial. Many of the items listed only include a brief citation and may not include an abstract. In order to receive the working papers, the economists will have to communicate with the author or institution to receive (or, more likely, purchase for a nominal fee) a copy of the working paper. WoPEc is a database for electronic full-text working papers, which can be downloaded.

Economics Research Network (ERN)
http://205.241.57.6/ERN/index.html

Financial Economics Network (FEN)
http://205.241.57.6/FEN/index.html

For American economists, this may emerge as THE site to submit working papers. This site includes a search engine that allows searching by title, author, affiliation, and/or *Journal of Economic Literature (JEL)* classification. Economists electronically submit abstracts of their working papers to ERN or FEN. Economists create a profile, and they then receive notification via e-mail of any new working paper that falls within their profile. The e-mail message provides directions on how to obtain the working paper. ERN and FEN are part of a larger Network project called the Social Science Research Network. This project was initiated by well-respected scholars, giving the site instant momentum, publicity and credibility. Somewhere down the line, fees for some of the services may be charged.

EconWPA (Washington University)
http://econwpa.wustl.edu

Working papers are broken down by 22 *JEL* subject classifications. The user can then look at a title or author list including all working papers listed under the *JEL* subject classifications–the retrieved lists can also be broken down by year. There is also a search engine. Economists can submit their working papers directly to the archive in postscript or Adobe Acrobat format. Readers can download the full-text working papers. In addition, this site provides a free e-mail notification service whereby the economists can select *JEL* subject classifications for which they receive notification when something is submitted.

SITES FOR ECONOMISTS

In this final section, several reference-type sites are listed that are of interest to economists. These sites may help social science librarians assist economists in a variety of ways.

Economics Departments on the Internet (United States)
http://price.bus.okstate.edu/econdept.html-ssi

World-Wide Economics Departments, Faculties and Centres (non-United States)
http://castle.uvic.ca/econ/depts.html

These two sites provide links to Economics Departments and Economics Research Institutes throughout the world.

American Economics Association Directory
http://www.eco.utexas.edu/AEA

Directory of Economists (Sam Houston State University)
gopher://Niord.SHSU.edu/11gopher_root%3a%5b_DATA.ECONDIR%5d

The AEA directory includes only members. Economists can fill in a template at the Sam Houston State University site to be included in its directory. The Sam Houston site also includes a link to the AEA directory.

Economics Listservs
gopher://una.hh.lib.umich.edu/00/inetdirsstacks/acadlist.busecon

Tile.Net Lists: Business
http://tile.net/lists/business.html

Both of these sites list Economics listservs. In the Tile.Net list, the Economics listservs are listed under "Business." The Tile.Net site also provides a convenient template from which a user can easily and quickly subscribe to a listserv. Listservs are an important means by which economists communicate with one another. Issues are discussed, and ideas and data are exchanged.

Resources for Economists on the Internet by William Goffe
gopher://wuecon.wustl.edu:10672/11/econfaq

Resources for Economists on the Internet by William Goffe (hypertext version)
http://econwpa.wustl.edu/EconFAQ/EconFAQ.html

This is considered THE guide to Internet resources for Economics. It is written and maintained by an economist. The gopher version includes many things for which a hypertext cannot be made. Consequently, the hypertext version is considerably shorter and covers fewer resources.

Nobel Laureates in Economics
gopher://Niord.SHSU.edu/00gopher_root%3a%5b_DATA.ECONOMICS.
INFO%5d.NOBELS

This is a simple listing of the winners. No biographical information is provided.

HUMANITIES

Internet Reference Sources in the Performing Arts

Richard AmRhein

SUMMARY. There are an enormous number of web-based Internet resources available in the performing arts. They have been created by hobbyists, amateurs, professionals, and corporations for commercial and recreational purposes. With proper evaluation, a number of sites can be useful in the provision of reference services in libraries. Collected here are Internet sites in the areas of music, dance, film/ cinema, and theater/drama that are useful when answering typical reference questions in these performing arts. *[Article copies available for a fee from The Haworth Document Delivery Service: 1-800-342-9678. E-mail address: getinfo@haworth.com]*

INTRODUCTION

Providing reference services for the performing arts is a multifaceted endeavor. In addition to being areas of academic study for the profession-

Richard AmRhein is Associate Dean for Technical and Automation Services at Southern Illinois University at Carbondale, Carbondale, IL 62901-6632.

[Haworth co-indexing entry note]: "Internet Reference Sources in the Performing Arts." AmRhein, Richard. Co-published simultaneously in *The Reference Librarian* (The Haworth Press, Inc.) No. 57, 1997, pp. 139-146; and: *Reference Sources on the Internet: Off the Shelf and Onto the Web* (ed: Karen R. Diaz) The Haworth Press, Inc., 1997, pp. 139-146. Single or multiple copies of this article are available for a fee from The Haworth Document Delivery Service [1-800-342-9678, 9:00 a.m. - 5:00 p.m. (EST). E-mail address: getinfo@haworth.com].

139

al, and an occupation of love for the amateur, the performing arts are of substantial continuing interest to the population at large. Because of this, professionals, enthusiasts, and corporations have created a vast array of Internet resources devoted to the performing arts in an effort to serve the varying needs of all. Therein lies the problem of providing reference service using Internet resources. Many sites, in an effort to be the biggest or most comprehensive, simply gather everything that they can find with little or no attempt at evaluation. Additionally, there are excellent sites available that restrict themselves to providing regional information, and libraries that wish to include regional arts information in their site should seek them out, for there are many. The collection of sites listed here is by no means comprehensive; these have been chosen because they offer information that is commonly requested in academic and public libraries alike, and because they are organized in a way that makes them efficient in providing reference services.

MUSIC

Research

Maintained by the Eda Kuhn Loeb Music Library at Harvard University, *Internet Resources for Music Scholars (http://www.rism.harvard.edu/MusicLibrary/InternetResources.html)* contains a large number of specialized links for serious research in music. Organized into eleven broad categories, it contains numerous general reference resources, search engines, and online catalogs of other libraries so that the user of this resource will have all that is needed close at hand. In the area of *Ethnomusicology, Folk Music, and World Music (http://www.lib.washington.edu/libinfo/libunits/soc-hum/music/world.html),* the University of Washington has provided a nice collection of resources with links to various related organizations, research sites and e-journals, and extensive links organized by geographic region. Especially useful is the keyword-searchable Ethnomusicology Current Bibliography.

The entire corpus of Latin music theory written during the Middle Ages and the early Renaissance can be found at *TML: Thesaurus Musicarum Latinarum (gopher://iubvm.ucs.indiana.edu/11/tml).* Manuscripts are presented in full-text with accompanying graphics files to represent musical examples. Anyone specifically interested in working with Gregorian Chant will find *The Gregorian Chant Home Page (http://www.music.princeton.edu/chant_html/)* helpful. First established to support graduate coursework taught at Princeton University, it contains numerous links to indexes, manuscript inventories, liturgical resources, and other sites devoted to the study of Gregorian Chant and other related topics.

Doctoral Dissertations In Musicology (http://www.music.indiana.edu/ ddm/), a long-time essential print resource, marks a new phase in its life with this online publication. Development is proceeding in stages, and since mid-1996 new additions to this resource have been included in the online version. Anyone choosing a dissertation topic in music needs to consult this source. *On-line Music and Education Resources (http://www. ed.uiuc.edu/music-ed/on-line.html)* is designed for music teachers of grades K-12. It collects sites from all of the major music education associations including the American Orff-Schulwerk Association and the Kodaly Home Page as well as numerous links to general music and arts sites. Several sites that provide music education software are also included as are many commercial resources that are commonly used by music educators.

Lyrics

Library users often have questions with regard to the lyrics of popular songs. Perhaps the best known and comprehensive site providing this information has been the University of Wisconsin-Parkside Lyrics Archive, but recent concerns regarding copyright of the lyrics have caused this site to be shut down for now. Efforts are under way to work collaboratively with the music industry to reintroduce the site in a mutually agreeable form. This is a site to watch for. Other lyrics databases include *The Digital Tradition Folk Song Database (http://www. deltablues.com/ dbsearch.html)* which contains lyrics for thousands of folk songs with a keyword search engine as well as a list of topics for browsing. *The Cyber Hymnal (http://www.accessone.com/~rwadams/Hymns/hymns.htm)* contains lyrics and information about approximately 200 hymns that are in the public domain, including some audio clips. Around the beginning of December, reference librarians will be happy to find *The Carols of Christmas* at *http://www.osmond.net/chill/christmas/carols.htm.* It is a large collection of lyrics to traditional and popular Christmas Songs, including some humorous ones with many including audio clips. For the serious singer, *The Lied and Song Texts Page (http://www. recmusic.org/ lieder/)* provides many art song and Lieder texts indexed by poet, composer, and title or first line, with many also including literal English translations.

Performing Groups

Formerly known as the Web Wide World of Music, *The Ultimate Band List (http://www.ubl.com/)* is a collection of sites for hundreds of popular music performers and bands, links to popular music radio station sites world-wide, and a fairly comprehensive set of links to record companies. It also includes popular music news, links to music clubs, record stores, schedules for chat site discussions and events, and utilizes a search engine for specific searches and an alphabetic index for browsing. *The All-Music Guide (http://205.186.189.2/amg/music_root.html)* is an enormous database of mainly popular sound recordings and the artists who made them. Fully searchable by album, artist, or song title, this database often includes extensive biographical information for the artists and bands, a full list of theirs recordings, and reviews wherever available.

Performance Rights, Publishers, Copyright

The Harry Fox Agency, Inc. (http://www.nmpa.org/hfa.html) is an information source, clearinghouse, and monitoring service for licensing musical copyrights. It represents more than 16,000 American music publishers and licenses a large percentage of the uses of music in the United States on records, tapes, CDs and imported sound recordings. The site provides information on how to obtain performance rights, and its searchable song list makes it easy to find all of the information needed to do so. The *Music Publishers' Association (http://host.mpa.org/* or *http://www.mpa.org/)* provides an excellent comprehensive listing of contact information for more than 500 music publishers through its Music Publishers Sales Agency List, as well as an index to publisher's imprints.

The *U.S. Copyright Office (http://lcweb.loc.gov/copyright/)* is a source for all pertinent information regarding copyright. Basic information, official circulars and announcements, and links to the full-text of the U.S. copyright law and other related topics are included. Official copyright registration forms can be downloaded directly from the site, but an Adobe Acrobat Reader (http://www.adobe.com/prodindex/acrobat/readstep.html) is required in order to read and print them.

Directories, Dictionaries, Rankings

The *Library of Musical Links (http://www.wco.com/~jrush/music/)* includes a comprehensive set of links to musical newsgroups and excellent links to record companies, sites that focus on particular instruments, and various musical genres and styles. *Billboard Online Charts (http://www. billboard-online.com/charts/)* contain an up-to-date listing of Billboard charts in major music categories. Access to all charts is by subscription only, but the most frequently requested information is available here for free. The *Rap Directory (http://www.sci.kun.nl/thalia/rapdict/)* contains a wide variety of useful information regarding Rap music. An extensive dictionary defines terms used in Rap songs and frequently includes quotes from songs to show context. Also included is a guide to the terminology used to represent places in the songs and a listing of Rap performers.

The *Classical Net Home Page (http://www.classical.net/music/)* is generally useful for basic information about classical music. There is a guide to classical repertoire organized by musical periods and recommendations for sound recordings to listen to or buy. There is an extensive collection of links in its *Classical Music Links* section that lead the user to specific composer information, music societies and organizations, sites about instruments and performing ensembles, commercial links, and much more.

ArtsInfo's Performing Arts Links (http://205.187.62.122:80/artslists/) is a listing of a variety of links to symphony orchestras, opera companies, and singers. Detailed performance information and schedules are often included as well as lists of recordings. The orchestras and opera companies are listed alphabetically and by country. The singers are listed alphabetically and by voice type.

DANCE

Dancin on the WEB (http://artswire.org/Artswire/www/dance/browse. html) includes a comprehensive alphabetical listing of links to dance companies, dance schools (including university programs), and an excellent set of links to sites that are organized by type of dance. *Dance Links (http://www.dancer.com/dance-links/)* is an excellent general source for dance information. In addition to links for dance companies, organizations, and schools, it contains lists of newsgroups, funding resources, and an index of various other dance resource sites from around the world.

Dance Pages (http://www.ens-lyon.fr/~esouche/danse/dance.html) is a French resource principally for ballet information. It lists ballets alphabetically and chronologically including basic information about each of them. Biographical information about dancers and choreographers is included along with excellent information about European ballet companies.

Users who are interested in dance competitions should consult *Colby's Competition Central (http://www.danceronline.com/competition/competition. html)*. It provides contact information for many major dance competitions, and a contest calendar that is searchable by month, place, and name of competition. *The Costume Page (http://members.aol.com/nebula5/costume. html)*, an index of costume and costuming-related links, is very useful for those who study and/or make costumes. It contains a wealth of information about all aspects of costuming, including links on costume history, ethnic styles, sources for costume-making supplies, organizations, and much more. This would be suitable for reference assistance in music and theater as well.

FILM/CINEMA

The *Online Film Dictionary (http://userpage.fu-berlin.de/~oheiabbd/ moviedict_e.html)* provides translations of the most common terms used in film. Users can enter the term they want translated, or browse terms in 14 categories for selected languages. The dictionary currently supports English, Dutch, French, German, Hungarian, Italian, Polish, Serbian, Spanish, Swedish, and Turkish.

It is the goal of the *Internet Movie Database (http://www.imdb.com/)* to collect any and all information associated with movies from around the world. It covers filmographies for all professions in the industry–plot summaries, character names, movie ratings, year of release, running times, movie trivia, quotes, goofs, soundtracks, personal trivia, alternative names, certificates, color information, country of production, genres, production companies, sound mix, reference literature, filming locations, sequel/remake information, release dates, advertising tag lines, detailed technical data, alternative versions, laserdisc availability, languages, reviews, links to official studio pages, fan pages, image and multimedia archives, direct purchase links for movies and associated merchandise, box office grosses, and Academy Award information. Like the Internet Movie Database, *Cinemedia (http://ptd15.afionline.org/CineMedia/)* provides broad coverage for all kinds of movie resources, but rather than providing internal information from a database, this one connects you to external sites for films, directors, organizations, studios, festivals, etc.

Film Festivals (http://www.laig.com/law/entlaw/filmfes.htm) is a comprehensive collection of links to films festivals world-wide. The main listing is organized geographically, but a chronological listing is also available. *Producerlink (http://www.producerlink.com/)* is excellent for quick links to the major film production companies, current box office receipts and ratings, as well as other up-to-date industry data, studio contacts and even job listings.

Clamen's Movie Information Collection (http://www.cs.cmu.edu/

Unofficial/Movies/README.html) provides much general movie information that is available in a variety of other sources, but also includes a list of all films in the U.S. National Film Registry, current Academy Award nomination information as well as past winners and nominees, and other interesting information. *CineWEB (http://www.cineweb.com/)* is useful for those who need information or services in the film industry. It includes an index called *Connections* which is available alphabetically or through a search engine and contains links to hundreds of film services companies. CineWEB also has a *Locations* index which provides information on films being shot on location around the world, and a *Calendar* of film trade shows and their locations worldwide.

THEATER/DRAMA

Playbill Online (http://piano.symgrp.com/playbill) is a commercial site designed to serve anyone who is interested in musicals and plays showing around the country and in a few international cities. It includes a full range of information about show schedules and tours, hotels and shopping, as well as news and books. For reference purposes, Playbill Online has an excellent search engine for quick answers when a user is looking for where a particular show is playing and what shows are coming to a particular city. For users only interested in what's playing on- and off-Broadway, the *On Broadway WWW Information Page (http://artsnet.heinz.cmu.edu:80/ OnBroadway/)* is a quick guide to where, when, and how much performances will cost. It includes some additional features such as year by year listing of Tony Award nominees and winners, the New York Cabaret scene, and summaries of the current and past Broadway seasons.

Users with academic needs will want to look into the *Brief Guide to Theatre and Performance Studies (http://www.stetson.edu/~csata/thr_guid. html)*. Created and maintained by Ken McCoy, Ph.D., Assistant Professor, Communication Studies and Theatre Arts, Stetson University, this is a thoroughly reviewed collection of non-commercial theater resources. A hierarchically organized index leads the user to a wide variety of materials including full-text plays and listings of theater-related listservs and newsgroups. An excellent site for aspiring screenwriters and playwrights is the *Screenwriters & Playwrights Home Page (http://www.teleport.com/ ~cdeemer/scrwriter.html)*. It will lead them to resources that should answer any kind of questions they have about getting into the business. Resources are grouped by topic and the site includes a pull-down menu for quick tips on writing, getting an agent, contests, and other topics.

Theatre Central (http://www.theatre-central.com/) is a well-organized, comprehensive index to a wide variety of theater related sites. The Resources section is the most useful for providing reference assistance. It's divided into broad categories including listings of theater companies, contact people and associations, educational resources, stagecraft, and other resources. Each of these are further divided into sub-categories making desired information easy to find. It is particularly strong in commercial resources. Users seeking definitions for *Theatrical Terms* can find them at *http://www.scsn.net/users/ckeenan/dsunkle/terms.html.*

No guide to Internet resources in theater would be complete without the *Complete Works of William Shakespeare (http://the-tech.mit.edu/Shakespeare/works.html).* Any questions regarding the words of Shakespeare can easily be answered at this site. The full text of his complete works are included and can be searched with a powerful keyword search engine. Also included are familiar Shakespeare quotations, discussion groups, FAQs, and links to other Shakespeare resources.

CONCLUSION

In general, coverage of the performing arts on the World Wide Web is uneven. Some resources, such as the All-Music Guide and the Internet Movie Database, do their best to be as comprehensive as possible and are systematic in their approach to gathering information. Other sites, such as Internet Resources for Music Scholars or the Brief Guide to Theatre and Performance Studies, focus on a specific area and utilize subject specialists to evaluate links for inclusion. These types of resources can be of immense use in providing efficient reference assistance. But many of the sites available on the World Wide Web are not comprehensive, have not been evaluated, and do not even necessarily provide correct information. Because of this, users must place each resource they use in the context of who created it and how it was created.

Architecture:
Reference Sites on the Internet

Jeanne M. Brown

SUMMARY. Key architecture reference sites are highlighted and discussed, grouped into the following areas: directory and biographical information, bibliographical databases, architectural education, product information, databases of buildings, and search engines. *[Article copies available for a fee from The Haworth Document Delivery Service: 1-800-342-9678. E-mail address: getinfo@haworth.com]*

Architects and architecture students must be interested and involved in a variety of fields. Since 1993 I have maintained a guide, *Architecture and Building: Net Resources [http://www.nscee.edu/unlv/Libraries/arch/rsrce/webrsrce/index.html]*, to architecture sites classified into categories such as: computing, lighting, HVAC, products, services, images, energy efficiency, green design, real estate and housing, safety, architectural firms, buildings, building types, standards, universal design, and urban environment. These topical listings link to many sites of information value. In addition I have developed a collection of web architecture reference tools *[http://www.nscee.edu/unlv/Libraries/arch/rsrce/webrsrce/sect5-6.html#6.0]*, which contains all sites mentioned below as well as others. While *Architecture and Building: Net Resources* is a guide to selected sources, two other compilations aim to be comprehensive and both are categorized by subject: the *Web Virtual Library: Architecture [http://www.clr.toronto.edu:1080/*

Jeanne M. Brown is Architecture Studies Librarian, University of Nevada, Las Vegas, Box 45-7001, Las Vegas, NV 89154-7001.

[Haworth co-indexing entry note]: "Architecture: Reference Sites on the Internet." Brown, Jeanne M. Co-published simultaneously in *The Reference Librarian* (The Haworth Press, Inc.) No. 57, 1997, pp. 147-151; and: *Reference Sources on the Internet: Off the Shelf and Onto the Web* (ed: Karen R. Diaz) The Haworth Press, Inc., 1997, pp. 147-151. Single or multiple copies of this article are available for a fee from The Haworth Document Delivery Service [1-800-342-9678, 9:00 a.m. - 5:00 p.m. (EST). E-mail address: getinfo@haworth.com].

VIRTUALLIB/arch.html] and *PAIRC–Planning and Architecture Internet Resource Center [http://www.arch.buffalo.edu/pairc].* Both types of compilations–selected and comprehensive–are important tools for locating architectural information on the net.

Sites that serve a reference function compose a limited subset of the thousands of architecture sites. Well-represented are directories, indexes, bibliographies, library catalogs, university program information, and manufacturers' catalog information. The type of information that is not freely accessible via the web tends to be the more technical practice-oriented information. There is not, thus far, any web equivalent for cost data books. Graphic standards materials have not been posted to the web, nor have American Institute of Architects (AIA) documents and contract forms. Codes are not yet available through the web. Strangely, dictionary and encyclopedia type information is also not readily found for architecture. One exception is the *Perseus Encyclopedia, Architecture Section,* which contains definitions of about 150 terms related to classical architecture *[http://www.perseus.tufts.edu/Secondary/Encyclopedia/encyc. subj.html# Architecture].*

DIRECTORY AND BIOGRAPHICAL INFORMATION

Directories on the web are generally searchable and often provide links to individual "primary" sites of the persons or organizations mentioned in the directory. The American Institute of Architects' *ProFile,* a staple of the print architecture reference collection, is now available in abbreviated format on the web *[http://profile.cmdonl.com/aia/search.html].* This directory of approximately 20,000 U.S. firms is searchable by name, location, key personnel, and architectural specialty. The print *Profile* has more detailed firm profiles, including figures on type of staff and type of buildings making up the firm's business. *Profile* online does not link to web sites. Examples of directories which do are the *On-Line Arts and Crafts Movement Resource Directory [http://www.tango.org/ragtime/Ragtime_ Resources.html]* (searchable and browsable, it constitutes a yellow pages of services and products), *AIA Firms on the Web [http://www.aia.org/ archwww.htm],* and the *ENR* (Engineering News-Record) directory of top 500 design firms *[http://www.enr.com/dbase/dbase3.htm]. AIA Firms on the Web* includes groups with a web presence only; the *On-Line Arts and Crafts Movement Resource Directory and ENR* include those both on and off the web.

Biographical and professional information is a rapidly growing segment of the architecture presence on the web, with many architects and architectural firms setting up web sites, and other sites created to focus on famous architects such as Frank Lloyd Wright. Both the *Virtual Library* and *PAIRC* mentioned above maintain substantial link collections to this category of web pages. Biographical compilations equivalent to biographical dictionaries are infrequent on the web at present, but examples can be found in the *International Archive of Women in Architecture [http://scholar2. lib.vt.edu/spec/iawa/iawa.htm]*, which describes the manuscript collections at Virginia Technical and contains entries (both name and geographically organized) on women who practiced architecture primarily before 1950, and at the *Society of Architectural Historians Web Site [http://www. upenn.edu/sah/aame/bioint.html]* which contains biographical material on American architects 1897-1947 transcribed from the *American Art Annual* by Earle G. Shettleworth, Jr.

BIBLIOGRAPHICAL DATABASES

Bibliographical databases are a substantial and valuable web resource. Such databases include indexes, catalogs and bibliographies. The Getty Information Institute has posted an experimental (and temporary) web version of the *Avery Index to Architectural Periodicals [http://www.ahip. getty.edu/aka/aka_form_pub.html]*, the most comprehensive periodical index for architecture and related fields. The convenience of access prompts its inclusion here despite its temporary net presence. While the index is no longer being updated on the web, it can still be a handy source for verifying an architect's name, generating a partial list of his buildings, or producing a quick list of citations. Other less global indexes are also available, such as Arizona State's *Solar Energy Index [telnet://csi.carl.org,* choose Other Library Systems/Carl Corporation Network Libraries–Western US (Menu 1)/Arizona Libraries/Other ASU Libraries Specialized Collections and Databases] which includes journal articles, patents, technical reports and pamphlets.

Library catalogs especially useful to architecture are Columbia University's *CLIO* catalog *[telnet://columbianet.columbia.edu]* which includes holdings of the Avery Architectural and Fine Arts Library and the University of California's *Melvyl* catalog *[telnet://melvyl.ucop.edu]* which includes UC–Berkeley's Environmental Design Library as well as UCLA and other University of California libraries. Both have strong architecture collections; however, *CLIO* only includes items from 1981 onward. Publishers' catalogs can also be a valuable reference source, such as *Worldwide Books Online [http://www.worldwide.com]*, a searchable catalog of 30,000 (18,000 still in print) titles on art, architecture and photography including international museum and gallery catalogs from 1960 on, and American trade and university press books from 1992 to present.

Bibliographies of varying size and usefulness can be found at many web sites. Two examples of substantive bibliographies in architecture include the bibliography of *Dissertations on American Architectural History 1897-1995* by James M. Goode (indexed by author, institution, subject) posted on the *Society of Architectural Historians Web Site [http://www.upenn.edu/sah/daah/daah1.html]*, and David Eisenberg's *Annotated Bibliography on Straw Bale Construction [http://www.xmission. com/~shea/straw/anbib.html]*.

ARCHITECTURAL EDUCATION

Information on university programs is a frequently asked reference question. Many architecture programs have posted course information on the web. In addition, various associations have compiled linked lists of member schools. Although its site is currently changing hosts and there is no URL to cite, look to the Association of Collegiate Schools of Architecture to provide links to U. S. and Canadian schools with professional architecture programs. The National Architectural Accrediting Board directory *NAAB Accredited Programs in Architecture [http://www.aia.org/schools.htm]* provides online information about accredited programs. Accredited programs in landscape architecture are found at *Landnet*, the site of the American Society of Landscape Architects *[http://www.asla.org/asla/nonmembers/accredited_programs.html]*. Rankings of top architecture programs as reported in *U. S. News and World Report* are also online *[http://www.usnews.com/usnews/edu/beyond/garch.htm]*.

PRODUCT INFORMATION

Product and manufacturer information is widely available on the web. *Sweet's Catalog File,* a multi-volume print source for product information and catalogs, has a web equivalent *[http://www.sweets.com]*. Sweet's allows searching over 6,000 manufacturers by company, keyword, and product area. Although product categorization/indexing is not yet as thorough as the print catalog, Sweet's is a very useful net resource. There are many sites which offer product information in specific areas, such as Oikos' *Resources for Environmental Design Index* (REDI) 1996 *[http://www.oikos.com/redi/index.html]*, a database of 1,700 companies providing green building products (searchable by topic), and the *Landscape Construction Manufacturer Directory [http://pro3.com/LAinfo/]* listing over 500 companies by CSI category.

DATABASES OF BUILDINGS

Databases of buildings are a growing source of quick answer information. One such is the database *archInform [http://www.archINFORM.de]* comprised of 5,000 built and unbuilt projects (primarily 20th century). This database supplies birth and death dates for the architect and a list of projects, and often includes bibliographic citations and net links to pertinent sites (depth of information for each entry is variable, and in German). Projects are listed by architect and by town, and the database is searchable. Searchable image databases, such as *SPIRO* from the University of California Berkeley *[http://www.mip.berkeley.edu/query_forms/browse_spiro_form.html]* provide access to thousands of images. Information on print sources of building illustrations is provided by *Archpics [telnet:// library.cmu.edu],* and often by *SPIRO* as well, along with dates for the architect and the building. The *National Register of Historic Places [telnet://victor.umd.edu]* provides online information through the University of Maryland catalog on buildings significant in American history and architecture including the name and address of the property and the criterion for listing. General search engines such as Lycos and *AltaVista* have also proven useful for searching for specific buildings on the net, although the type of information retrieved is highly variable.

SEARCH ENGINES

Search engines specifically for architecture do exist, but search a limited number of sites. Nonetheless, they may prove useful for searches where the vocabulary is non-specific and items from other fields are likely to be retrieved if general search engines are used. Two architecture-specific search engines are *ADAM* (Art Design Architecture and Media) *[http://adam.ac.uk]* and *BuildingOnline: The Search Engine [http://www. buildingonline.com/blsearch.shtml].* Overall, specific architecture information is still most effectively searched using general search engines, or by browsing compiled guides to Internet sites.

Internet Reference Resources in Language and Literature

Pam Day

Literature and language resources on the Internet are great in number, type, and quality. The number and size of language dictionaries available on the Web has increased dramatically in the past year. Internet literature resources are still found to be lacking for in-depth scholarly research and criticism. Research in this area will need to be supplemented with print resources. Author-related pages and information have expanded, but many are limited to biographical material while the number and quality of full-text literary resources available on the Internet continues to increase. Sites in some fields continue to be developed and maintained by individuals with an interest in the area and lack institutional or organizational affiliation, which may be of concern if an individual is seeking authoritative information sources.

GENERAL LITERATURE SITES

BUBL WWW Subject Tree: Language, Literature, and Linguistics
http://www.bubl.bath.ac.uk/BUBL/Literature.html

Arranged in a hierarchical structure, BUBL provides access to a comprehensive list of annotated literature, language, and linguistics resources.

Pam Day is Internet Reference Librarian, Milner Library, Illinois State University, Normal, IL 61790-8900. E-mail: pam-d@mhsgate.mlb.ilstu.edu

[Haworth co-indexing entry note]: "Internet Reference Resources in Language and Literature." Day, Pam. Co-published simultaneously in *The Reference Librarian* (The Haworth Press, Inc.) No. 57, 1997, pp. 153-159; and: *Reference Sources on the Internet: Off the Shelf and Onto the Web* (ed: Karen R. Diaz) The Haworth Press, Inc., 1997, pp. 153-159. Single or multiple copies of this article are available for a fee from The Haworth Document Delivery Service [1-800-342-9678, 9:00 a.m. - 5:00 p.m. (EST). E-mail address: getinfo@haworth.com].

153

Categories of available resources include English/American, Scottish, German, French, Italian, Spanish, Portuguese, Slavonic, and the Classics.

Internet Classics Archive and The Perseus Project
http://classics.mit.edu/ and *http://www.perseus.tufts.edu/*

Both of these sites are devoted to classical Greek and Roman texts and writers, including Homer, Aristotle, Euripides, Plato, and Sophocles. Both sites provide access to the full-text of classical texts.

Literary Resources on the Net
http://www.english.upenn.edu/~jlynch/Lit/

This site was created to highlight scholarly resources useful to academics in English and American Literature. However, the sixteen categories of literature cover a broad range of literary topics from other national literatures, to classical and biblical literature, to medieval and romantic literature. Each category includes scholarly listservs, calls for papers, lists of course syllabi submitted by university faculty, and general and specific author links. This is one of the most comprehensive general literature sites.

Literature Resources
http://nimrod.mit.edu/depts/humanities/lit/literature.html

This site at MIT is devoted primarily to English and American literature and includes both scholarly and less-academic sites. The homepage is arranged in seven broad categories: full-text collections of literary works; collections devoted to particular periods or genres; collections devoted to specific authors or works; electronic journals; humanities computing centers and electronic text centers; and miscellaneous.

Voice of the Shuttle: Web Page for Humanities Research
http://humanitas.ucsb.edu/

Voice of the Shuttle offers comprehensive collections of humanities resources, with useful collections in the areas of linguistics, literature, the classics, and literary theory.

LANGUAGE DICTIONARIES

Dictionaries and Translators
http://rivendel.com/~ric/resources/dictionary.html

Featuring a comprehensive collection of on-line dictionaries and translators, this site indicates if the on-line dictionary translates both ways and if the dictionary is searchable.

On-line Dictionaries
http://www.bucknell.edu/~rbeard/diction.html

This collection of over 150 on-line dictionaries is arranged by language, and alternatively by language group.

Dictionaries, Thesauri, and Acronyms
http://thorplus.lib.purdue.edu/reference/dict.html

The Virtual Reference Desk at the Libraries of Purdue University features a selective list of on-line dictionaries, including English language, international, technical, acronym, thesauri, and miscellaneous dictionaries. A few of the sources, notably the *Oxford English Dictionary,* are available only to Purdue staff and students.

LANGUAGE RESOURCES

Ethnologue: Languages of the World
http://www.sil.org/ethnologue/ethnologue.html

This is the electronic version of the 12th edition of *Ethnologue,* published in 1992. *Ethnologue* is a catalog of the world's languages browseable by country name, language family, and language name. Useful information is included for each language such as number of speakers, alternate name, dialects, country location, and linguistic affiliation.

Human Languages Page
http://www.june29.com/HLP/

Touting itself as a "comprehensive catalog of language-related Internet resources," this site serves as a collecting point for many language resources both scholarly and popular. The search function is useful as many resources are buried a few layers deep on the site.

Yamada Language Center
http://babel.uoregon.edu/yamada/guides.html

Internet resources for approximately 115 languages are listed here alphabetically, by geographic region, and by language family. The archive includes fonts for many of the languages.

ELECTRONIC TEXT COLLECTIONS

CETH Directory of Electronic Text Centers
http://www.ceth.rutgers.edu/info/ectrdir.html

A directory providing access to the major electronic text centers and their collections, and to the Digital library projects sponsored by the National Science Foundation (NSF), the Department of Defense's Advanced Research Projects Agency (ARPA), and the National Aeronautics and Space Administration (NASA), as part of the inter-agency Digital Library Initiative (DLI).

Digital Text Collections
http://sunsite.berkeley.edu/Collections/othertext.html

This site contains pointers to all of the major on-line text collections, including the SunSITE Digital Collection at Berkeley.

AUTHOR INFORMATION AND CRITICISM

A Celebration of Women Writers
http://www.cs.cmu.edu/People/mmbt/women/writers.html

An alphabetical listing of resources by and about women writers on the Web, this site provides links to on-line editions of an author's works, author pages, bibliographies, and portraits.

Literary Menagerie
http://sunset.backbone.olemiss.edu/~egcash/

Billed as "your resource for links to the best of the best author-based sites on the net," *The Literary Menagerie* offers a nice selection of useful author sites listed alphabetically.

Yahoo!: Authors
http://www.yahoo.com/Arts/Humanities/Literature/Authors/

Yahoo! has developed a comprehensive directory of author pages listed by categories such as mystery, romance, literary fiction, children's, and non-fiction.

POETRY

American Verse Project
http://www.hti.umich.edu/english/amverse/

The American Verse Project, a collaborative project between the University of Michigan Humanities Text Initiative (HTI) and the University of Michigan Press, is an electronic archive of volumes of American poetry prior to 1920.

Contemporary American Poetry Archive
http://shain.lib.conncoll.edu/CAPA/capa.html

An electronic archive of out-of-print American poetry, the *Contemporary American Poetry Archive* currently has available about thirty volumes searchable by keyword.

LitWeb: Poetry
http://www.vmedia.com/shannon/poetry.html

Reserved for classic poetic works and the study of the poetic form, this alphabetical list of poets provides links to pages, poetry, and related information on each poet.

Yahoo!: Poetry
http://www.yahoo.com/Arts/Humanities/Literature/Genres/Poetry/

The poetry section of Yahoo! provides collections of links to poetry resources divided into useful categories such as indices, anthologies, children's, poets, haiku, journals, and countries and cultures.

FOLKLORE AND MYTHOLOGY

Brewer's Dictionary of Phrase and Fable
http://www.bibliomania.com/Reference/PhraseAndFable/

The hypertext edition of Brewer's 1894 edition of *The Dictionary of Phrase and Fable* provides the user with the capability to browse alphabetically, search by headword, or search the full-text of the dictionary.

Children's Literature Web Guide: Folklore, Myth and Legend
http://www.ucalgary.ca/~dkbrown/storfolk.html

Featured at this site are folklore resources emphasizing children's materials in this area.

Encyclopedia Mythica
http://www.pantheon.org/myth/

Useful as a quick reference tool, *Encyclopedia Mythica* covers the areas of folklore, mythology, mysticism, legends superstitions, and festivals. A bibliography of sources used to compile the work is included.

Mythology and Folklore
http://pubweb.acns.nwu.edu/~pib/mythfolk.htm

A comprehensive meta-list of links to resources in folklore and mythology divided into the categories: general folklore and mythology; journals, mailing lists, newsgroups, societies, and university departments; regional folklore; and special topics in folklore and mythology. This site is maintained by an individual for whom this is a general interest.

Tales of Wonder: Folk and Fairy Tales from Around the World
http://www.ece.ucdavis.edu/~darsie/tales.html

This site provides the text of selected folktales from Russia, Siberia, Central Asia, China, Japan, the Middle East, Scandinavia, Scotland, England, Africa, India, and America. Complete bibliographic information is included as the source for each tale.

Yahoo!: Mythology and Folklore
http://www.yahoo.com/Society_and_Culture/Mythology_and_Folklore/

Yahoo! provides links to resources in folklore and mythology with an easy-to-use search engine for locating other Internet folklore resources.

CHILDREN'S LITERATURE

Children's Literature Web Guide
http://www.ucalgary.ca/~dkbrown/index.html

David K. Brown has authored this comprehensive Web guide to Internet resources relating to children's and young adult literature. Children's stories and collections, publishing information, research tools, electronic journals, and resources for parents, teachers, storytellers and writers are all available at this site.

Electronic Resources for Youth Services
http://www.ccn.cs.dal.ca/~aa331/childlit.html

A well-designed and comprehensive site with materials relating to children's literature and youth services. Included at this site are connections to book reviews, associations, listservs and newsgroups, authors, publishers and booksellers, and educational entertainment.

World History Internet Resources

Sarah Landeryou

SUMMARY. The following article provides an overview of Internet resources relevant to reference work in world history. It also provides URLs to select sites representing different uses of the world wide web in presenting information for the subject of World History. *[Article copies available for a fee from The Haworth Document Delivery Service: 1-800-342-9678. E-mail address: getinfo@haworth.com]*

Below is a select group of sites representing what is most useful to librarians and patrons for answering queries and exploring topics in world history. These sites were collected after a thorough review of available Internet resources, and after careful consideration of the site's scope, frequency of updating, the authority of the editor, appearance, organization and, most importantly, its comparability to similar pages so that there is very little duplication. A few sites can provide quick answers to questions about world leaders, wars and treaties and dates, but for the most part World Wide Web resources for world history are limited to directories, links to smatterings of electronic primary sources, and information about countries and regions of the world. For example, there is a site which provides a thorough and impressive directory to archives throughout the world, and others that provide links to primary documents related to a particular country, region or era. Yet one will most likely find world history websites provide the user with pointers to very specific subject sites, i.e., a site devoted entirely to Irish History or Ancient Mediterranean History. While this may not be the fastest and most efficient method for

Sarah Landeryou is Social Sciences Reference Librarian and Bibliographer, Penrose Library, University of Denver, 2150 E. Evans Avenue, Denver, CO 80208.

[Haworth co-indexing entry note]: "World History Internet Resources." Landeryou, Sarah. Co-published simultaneously in *The Reference Librarian* (The Haworth Press, Inc.) No. 57, 1997, pp. 161-166; and: *Reference Sources on the Internet: Off the Shelf and Onto the Web* (ed: Karen R. Diaz) The Haworth Press, Inc., 1997, pp. 161-166. Single or multiple copies of this article are available for a fee from The Haworth Document Delivery Service [1-800-342-9678, 9:00 a.m. - 5:00 p.m. (EST). E-mail address: getinfo@haworth.com].

using the internet for reference work, it is what is currently available. Rather than listing each of these subject specific sites, I have included an entry for the *"Gateway to World History"* which acts as a good starting point for locating these sites. The alternative method for finding these sites is to use one of the World Wide Web search engines like Yahoo! or AltaVista, and enter the query using keywords at the most specific level. Using these search engines or the *Gateway* site can allow users to explore the Web for what may be relevant. However, as with many World Wide Web sites and documents, users should be reminded to evaluate the site, look for an editor, their affiliation, the scope of the page and the frequency of updating to avoid misleading information. While the sites listed below may be helpful in some situations, it still looks like the standard print collection may prove to be irreplaceable for quick queries in world history, but for finding primary sources or up-to-date directories, the World Wide Web may prove to be most effective.

PRIMARY SOURCES

http://www.uidaho.edu/special-collections/Other.Repositories.html

This site called the *Repositories of Primary Sources* is a worldwide directory of archives and manuscript repositories with links to more than 1,700 websites. The site is organized by region and country, is easy to navigate and can be used to locate a particular archive, contact person, the address, phone number and e-mail and a brief description of the collection. Some of the entries also provide links to finding aids when available. The page should be commended for its thoroughness and international content.

http://www.msstate.edu/Archives/History/

Known as the *"Historical Text Archive"* this site is housed at Mississippi State University. It provides information about countries, national histories, maps and some electronic primary documents such as travel accounts and narratives. For ease of use, the information is organized by region, topic or type of resource. In addition, it can be used to quickly locate a brief history, all of which are fully cited with bibliographies. What is interesting about this site is its forward thinking as the site has a long history on the Internet. It began in 1990 as an anonymous FTP site for electronic storage and retrieval to provide original materials by using the Internet.

http://library.byu.edu/~rdh/eurodocs/

Known as *Eurodocs,* this site provides links to primary historical documents from Western Europe. These documents include transcriptions, facsimiles and translations. The site is organized by country or region, and then the document links are presented chronologically. Also included in the site is information on how to cite Internet resources.

FACTS AND FIGURES

http://www.hyperhistory.com/online_n2/History_n2/a.html

This is the beginning of an interesting project of presenting historical facts and figures integrating a timeline and web-based frames. This site, called *HyperHistory Online,* has the potential to be valuable in finding facts, important dates and biographical data. Currently the only segment that is completed is the biographical data. However, if this segment stands as an indication of what may follow, the site should be noteworthy. One can click on a time period, then on a name, and read the biography in the column on the left without losing the timeline because of the use of the frames. In addition the site uses color to code the significance of each person or fact. For example science and technology is coded green, the arts and culture blue on the timeline so that one can place events and people in an immediate framework. The site is organized very well, and also provides some links to other World Wide Web sites for further information.

gopher://gopher.law.cornell.edu/11/foreign

Provides links to electronically available international documents, treaties and constitutions. Because it is text-based, it loads quickly. The information is organized by region or type of document.

http://www.geocities.com/Athens/1058/rulers.html

Includes a list of the heads of state of government, past and present. The leaders are listed chronologically with their term dates, and birth and death dates as well. Also includes data about the leaders of international organizations.

http://www.LIB.UTEXAS.EDU/Libs/PCL/Map_collection/Map_collection.html

A collection of electronic maps which includes historical maps. A pointer leads to the historical maps that are available. These are made available by the General Libraries at the University of Texas at Austin. Note that some of the maps are very large files and may take some time to load.

http://h-net2.msu.edu/~world/

Known as *H-WORLD* this site provides many resources, including archived copies of book reviews that were compiled from moderated history discussion groups, lists of teaching materials, course syllabi and bibliographies. The site includes its own search engine. The overall project is part of the *H-NET Humanities On-Line Initiative* and is supported by Michigan State University and the National Endowment for the Humanities.

AREA STUDIES

Area studies sites provide detailed information about a region and specific countries, including historical data, country studies, images, electronic documents, economic data, contacts in the home country and further links to discussion groups. In some cases these may prove most useful in locating information relating to a particular region or country and its historical development. The following are excellent examples of such sites, and each is organized similarly. Each site can be searched and provides the name of the country as an organizational starting point, and in some cases a particular era or subject, such as history.

Africa
http://www.sas.upenn.edu/African_Studies/AS.html

African Studies WWW (U. Penn) Supported by the African Studies Center at the University of Pennsylvania.

Asia
http://coombs.anu.edu.au/WWWVL-AsianStudies.html

Asian Studies WWW Virtual Library, The Internet Guide to Asian Studies, provided by the Australian National University.

Latin America
http://lanic.utexas.edu

Latin American Information Center, University of Texas at Austin.

Middle East
http://menic.utexas.edu/mes.html

Middle East Network Information Center, The University of Texas at Austin. Service of the Center for Middle Eastern Studies.

Russia and Eastern Europe
http://www.pitt.edu/~cjp/rees

REESWeb: Russian and East European Studies. Sponsored by the Center for Russian and East European Studies of the University of Pittsburgh.

Western Europe
http://www.lib.virginia.edu/wess/index.html

Western European Specialists Section of the Association of College and Research Libraries.

STARTING POINTS

http://library.ccsu.ctstateu.edu/~history/world_history/

The self-proclaimed *"Gateway to World History,"* this site provides links to "collections of resources to support study and teaching of world history." The site is an attempt to bring together world history resources, and can be used as a starting point for web-based research. The links are organized into broad categories: geographical, images, general resources for history and history departments to name a few. Some may find it useful for lengthy browsing and building lists of notable sites. However, one should note that the editorial intent is social progress and a concern for indigenous rights, thus some of the selections may reflect this content more than others.

http://argos.evansville.edu/

This site, the *"Limited Area Search of the Ancient World Internet,"* provides a search engine which will only search websites that were selected by a team of editors to have information pertaining to the "ancient world." One can run a search on a person or topic to retrieve relevant websites, and know that the search engine has an implied meaning or context for the search. Their example is that a search on Plato will only retrieve sites relevant to the person, not to the software product. This site also includes links to other important world history websites, such as the Perseus Project which is a digital library on Rome and Greece and the Labyrinth, a World Wide Web server for medieval studies.

http://www.byuh.edu/coursework/hist201/

This website was formed in relation to the teaching of a course on *"world history to 1500."* The site follows an outline from a syllabus noting significant people, places and events. Clicking on one of these boxes will lead to further links or information on the topic culled from other Internet resources. This site offers a unique presentation for the topic of world history, and can be a quick way to locate websites on a particular time period or place relevant to world history prior to 1500.

Reference Sources
on the Internet in United States History

Stanley D. Nash

SUMMARY. This article is a selective guide to some of the best Internet sites for obtaining reference information in the area of United States History. The categories covered include historical documents, archival directories, bibliographies, book reviews, statistics, discussion groups, biographical information, and online guides to the Internet. *[Article copies available for a fee from The Haworth Document Delivery Service: 1-800-342-9678. E-mail address: getinfo@haworth.com]*

INTRODUCTION

The past several years have witnessed an explosion of Internet historical resources. Texts and text archives have sprung up in large numbers, providing access to the full text of works by historical figures, such as Thomas Jefferson, Benjamin Franklin, Henry David Thoreau, and Abraham Lincoln, as well as a significant number of diaries, speeches, treaties and other documents. With respect to the monographic texts, while they certainly have many useful applications, such as the creation of custom-made anthologies for course instructors, keyword searchability, and access to patrons of libraries which may not own these texts, they are sometimes problematic in that editorship, provenance, and method of scanning and markup are often obscure, leading the critical user to be uncertain of the absolute integrity of the texts. And, since these texts are typically based on

Stanley D. Nash is Head of Reference and U.S. History Bibliographer, Alexander Library, Rutgers University. E-mail: snash@rci.rutgers.edu

[Haworth co-indexing entry note]: "Reference Sources on the Internet in United States History." Nash, Stanley D. Co-published simultaneously in *The Reference Librarian* (The Haworth Press, Inc.) No. 57, 1997, pp. 167-178; and: *Reference Sources on the Internet: Off the Shelf and Onto the Web* (ed: Karen R. Diaz) The Haworth Press, Inc., 1997, pp. 167-178. Single or multiple copies of this article are available for a fee from The Haworth Document Delivery Service [1-800-342-9678, 9:00 a.m. - 5:00 p.m. (EST). E-mail address: getinfo@haworth.com].

167

public-domain publications, they would usually not satisfy the scholar who clearly would prefer the copyright-protected latest definitive edition. In terms of United States History, discrete documents, such as the first *Virginia Charter* or the Constitution of the Confederate States, are probably less a problem with respect to text integrity, and are indeed useful ready reference sources. A very large number of these are available on the Internet.

Perhaps even more useful, at least from the perspective of a reference librarian, and certainly less fraught with the problems described above for digital monographs, are a myriad of other historical tools increasingly emerging on the Net. These include quality listservs (electronic discussion groups), archival and historical societies web pages, directories relevant to historians, online book reviews, biographical information, bibliographies, and sites offering historical statistics.

A good number of high quality history listservs are now available. The ones sponsored by H-Net (see below) are particularly well done and offer historians and librarians the opportunity to communicate the latest ideas and information of concern to historians. Finding the right book to read, the authenticity of a recent historical motion picture, or a short reading list on a subject is now a relatively easy task for those with access to the Internet. The ability to consult with experts was in the past restricted by rather small communication circles, usually closed to the vast majority— the lists have opened this opportunity up to all serious individuals. Similarly, the ability to consult with an historical society or with an archive on where to find fugitive scholarly information has been exponentially enlarged by Internet access to the growing number of historical archives and societies who have created home pages, most of which give a direct e-mail link for those wishing to make inquires. Moreover, many of the archival sites have begun to make available online the full text of finding aids critical to using their collections. A similar communication revolution the Internet offers is the ability to maintain up-to-date accessible and searchable directories of individuals or organizations relevant to the researcher. For example, one site mentioned below permits an enhanced ability to search for information on any individual historian at a university or college department throughout the world.

Book reviews on works dealing with United States History are increasingly becoming available via the Internet. The sites described below which offer reviews are notable because they include fairly in-depth scholarly essays which the editors try to disseminate well ahead of the reviews which appear notoriously late in academic periodicals. Similarly, biographical data is becoming increasingly obtainable on the Net, not only for well-known figures, such as presidents, but also for relatively obscure individuals, such as enlisted personnel in the armed forces.

Two areas which offer great potential for historians, bibliography and statistics, are just beginning to emerge. Full-length high-quality bibliographies, as opposed to reading lists, are rather rare. However, a few excellent ones are out there and it is hoped this will be an area which will attract new efforts in the near future. The same is true of historical statistics; however, the example set by Harvard University in creating interactive databases for the *Census,* 1790-1860 (see below) is indicative of the kind of powerful information resources which can only be generated by computers.

Finally, for librarians and patrons using the Internet to retrieve reference information relating to United States history, it should be pointed out that there are a number of areas better developed than others. Clearly military history, especially the Civil War and to some extent the American Revolution and World War II, are strong areas on the Net. Also, the eighteenth century, Afro-American History, and Women's History are areas for which the Internet is an excellent source of information. And, increasingly, historical information held in government databases, such as census material and legal documents, are finding their way onto the Internet. It is expected that much more is coming. In the meantime, the sites described below illustrate that there is already a tremendous amount of reference information related to the History of the United States on gophers and the World Wide Web.

FINDING HISTORICAL DOCUMENTS

Historic Documents of the United States
http://history.cc.ukans.edu/carrie/docs/docs_us.html

Containing over 280 fundamental primary sources, covering colonial times through President Clinton and including basic documents such as the Maryland Toleration Act of 1649, the Dred Scott decision of 1856, and the various Geneva Conventions, this the is probably the best site on the Internet of this kind. The strongest part of the list of offerings is the texts published before 1789, comprising over one-third of the sources covered. This site is not yet the equal of the standard printed reference source, Henry Steele Commager's *Documents of American History.* The tenth edition of the latter includes 727 sources and is fully indexed. However, it is worth noting that the Kansas Web page already has more listings than Commager for the period up to 1789. An interesting feature of the Kansas site is the inclusion of lyrics for a number of traditional American songs, such as *Yankee Doodle* and the *Battle Hymn of the Republic.*

FedWorld/FLITE Supreme Court Decisions Homepage
http://www.fedworld.gov/supcourt/index.htm

This site offers the full text of 7,407 Supreme Court decisions, covering the years 1937 through 1975, the equivalent of volumes 300 through 422 of *U.S. Reports.* Users may search by case name or by key words from the texts themselves. Links are provided for the Cornell University site which permits access to cases from 1990 onward and to a site containing some 300 major historic cases. For patrons with fragmentary information, this is a great tool for finding Supreme Court cases without having to resort to the sophisticated commercial indexes and digests, which are not available at many libraries, especially in computer format.

Inaugural Addresses of U.S. Presidents
gopher://gopher.cc.columbia.edu:71/11/miscellaneous/cubooks/inau

This is a U.S. government document, digitalized, edited, and proofread under the auspices of Project Bartleby at Columbia University. The full text of addresses from George Washington through George Bush are included.

ARCHIVES AND SPECIAL COLLECTIONS

Repositories of Primary Sources
http://www.uidaho.edu/special-collections/OtherRepositories.html

Offers well over 1,000 links to the web pages of archives and special collections all over the world. The first three categories on the main menu are "Western United States and Canada," "Eastern United States . . . A-M," and "Eastern United States . . . N-Z." While the Web pages vary, many of are the highest quality, including exhaustive finding aids to archival collections, many of which are not published and formerly only available at the site in question. This makes an excellent supplement to the *National Union Catalog of Manuscript Collections* and such standards as the *Directory of Archives and Manuscript Repositories in the United States.* For reference librarians serving advanced researchers, Internet sites such as this one permit them to guide patrons to instant access to much information about a distant collection as well as information concerning hours and policies of various archives. In addition, many of the archival sites include e-mail buttons, which permit instant inquiries about their holdings.

National Archives and Records Administration
http://www.nara.gov/

NARA's web page includes locations and hours of their facilities, links to the Presidential Libraries and other federal records centers, a link to their own catalog, and an extensive inventory of the federal records held by them. In addition, they are a gateway to other United States archives, offering a good number of Internet links to such places. This web page can answer many questions regarding the location and extent of historical federal records.

ACCESS TO BIBLIOGRAPHIES

Martin Luther King Jr. Bibliography
telnet://forsythetn.stanford.edu (for acct type SOCRATES, then type YES, then type SELECT MLK).

While there are many bibliographies to be found on the Internet, few are of this caliber. This site permits access to some 2,700 bibliographic listings of books, documents, and articles related to Dr. King and the civil rights movement. What makes it such an excellent reference tool is that it is at least the equal of any comparable paper bibliography, offering multiple access points and enormous coverage of the subject. This database truly strengthens the reference librarian guiding patrons to a variety of sources in Afro-American History.

American Studies Dissertations, 1986-1995
http://www.georgetown.edu/crossroads/dis

A select but lengthy list of dissertations dealing with American Studies. Indexed by author, each listing comes with an abstract. Hopefully subject or keyword searching will be added at some point. For patrons seeking doctoral dissertations on a multi-disciplinary historical subject, this can be a useful bibliography to survey and can especially helpful to librarians without computer access to *Dissertation Abstracts International.*

Moise's Vietnam War Bibliography
http://hubcap.clemson.edu/~eemoise/bibliography.html

A lengthy and useful bibliography, covering nearly every aspect of the Vietnam War. The only problem is that it does not come with a search engine; however, the menu of categories is very easy to follow. Certainly a good starting point for undergraduate students and above doing papers on the Vietnam War.

FINDING BOOK REVIEWS

H-Net Review Project
http://h-net2.msu.edu/reviews/

H-Net, which is responsible for the best quality history listservs on the Internet, also offers a collection of book reviews solicited by the 140 editors of the various electronic discussion groups they sponsor. Quality control is also achieved though additional scholars acting in an advisory capacity. The goal is to offer quality reviews in a more timely fashion than paper reviewing sources. After connecting to this site the user may find all reviews from all historical areas, searchable by author, title, and reviewer. You may also choose to find reviews, divided by listserv and then searchable by author, title, and reviewer. Thus, for patrons needing to find up-to-date scholarly reviews before they appear in printed academic sources, they may choose from such categories as the Civil War, the West, the South, and Politics. While it is not clear that the goal of timeliness has been fully met, this is clearly an excellent path to sound scholarly reviews in American History.

History Reviews On-Line
http://www.uc.edu/www/history/reviews.htmlx

Begun in 1995, this site is a review journal, offering lengthy scholarly history book reviews as well as reviews of history computer products and sites of interest to historians. Thus far much emphasis has been placed on United States History. In the summer 1996 issue, for example, of the twenty-three items reviewed over half are related directly to U.S. History. Along with the H-Net site listed above librarians may be able to help patrons find quality book reviews with greater ease and speed.

HISTORICAL STATISTICS ON THE INTERNET

Historical Demographic, Economic, and Social Data for the United States, 1790-1860
http://icg.harvard.edu/census/

Produced at Harvard, with the "cooperation and consent of ICPSR (Inter-university Consortium for Political and Social Research)," this site permits easy access to the decennial censuses from 1790 through 1860. The user may choose a census and produce a tailor-made-made chart by choosing among a list of the states and then selecting from a list of variables, such as a number of categories relating to families, ethnic groups, slave holding, and many others. Geographic breakdowns are by state and county. This is a rich source for ready reference queries regarding an enormous amount of information from the decennial censuses. For example, one could quickly offer a patron the number of slave owners in Georgia in the 1850s owning over 200 slaves.

U. S. Census Bureau
http://www.census.gov/

After connecting to this site choose "Subjects A-Z." For many of the subjects given historical series are available, often going back to the 1940s. Some in fact go back even earlier; however, the coverage is predominantly from the mid-twentieth century on. Some very difficult inquiries can be answered from this site regarding such topics as fertility, education, voting and registration, housing, and a variety of other areas treated by the census. Basically, the end result of the search is the reproduction of the printed chart one would find in the actual census. For librarians, who are not expert on the use of the census this is a very valuable reference tool, particularly when trying to ferret out a historical statistic by subject, which is no easy matter in the paper census.

FINDING THE RIGHT ONLINE DISCUSSION GROUP
(LISTSERVS)

H-Net discussion List Home Page Index
http://h-net2.msu.edu/about/lists.html

H-Net, centered at Michigan State University, is the strongest site on the Internet dedicated to computer access to information on history. Among their many activities they sponsor some 75 "lists" and offer much in the way of quality assurance for these discussion groups. By connecting to the home page index the user is able to choose the web pages of over 50 history discussion lists. These offer a description of what they focus on as well as details on how to subscribe. Since the lists offer historical discussions on hot topics in the fields they cover and typically offer job announcements, call for papers, grant opportunities, book reviews, and many other items, reference inquiries about such things can be gleaned from these lists. This is made easier by the fact that most of these list offer a search engine to look for current as well as past discussions and items. Many of the lists, such as H-AmStdy (American Studies), H-CivWar (Civil War), and H-West (History of the United States' West) deal directly with United States History. Also many cover themes which include U. S. history, such as H-Women (Women's History) and H-Ethnic (Ethnic History, including Immigration and Emigration studies). For additional listservs dealing with history or related topics see also *Tilenet (http://tile.net/lists/history2.html)*.

USEFUL DIRECTORIES

WWW-pages of History Departments
http://grid.let.rug.nl/ahc/history.html

Scroll down to United States and you will get to the home page of a multitude of United States university and college history departments. Many of these offer a listing of their faculty and the areas these historians specialize in. Some offer course syllabi and/or course descriptions. Useful site for patrons seeking quick information on history departments they may wish to apply to for graduate work. Also useful for instructors who might wish to sample syllabi for courses they are planning to teach. Less complete for history departments from other countries, other than Canada; however, this may be due to the absence of web pages at the universities and colleges not mentioned.

Scholarly Societies Project
http://www.lib.uwaterloo.ca/society/overview.html

From the University of Waterloo in Canada, this site features connections to the home pages of nearly 1,000 scholarly societies as well as connections to hundreds of related organization web pages. If you click or point to the subject guide you may choose from among some 67 history organization sites, including the American Antiquarian Society, the History of Science Society, the American Jewish History Society and many more, directly related to United States History. This is an excellent tool for referring historians to organizations related to a specific or general inquiry, as well as pinpointing the calendar of events of organizations of interest to historians. And, many of the sites will naturally include e-mail "buttons" for easy and speedy access to these societies for the purpose of making reference inquiries.

American Historical Association
http://web.gmu.edu/chnm/aha/

The most prestigious historical society in the United States now has an extremely useful web page, offering their calendar of events, information on the annual meetings, "Public Policy issues," lists of the AHA's publications, and most striking, a full-text version of *Perspectives,* the Association's newsletter. The newsletter provides many items of importance to historians, including job announcements and award recipients, as well as current issues of interest to historians.

Organization of American Historians
http://www.indiana.edu/~oah/index.html

This site offers a tremendous amount of useful information for historians, including a ten-year index to the OAH *Magazine of History* (1986-1995) and the full-text of the newsletter. The latter covers awards, grants, fellowships, meetings and conferences, and calls for papers–all in great detail.

BIOGRAPHICAL INFORMATION

Civil War Soldiers and Sailors System (CWSS)
http://www.itd.nps.gov/cwss/

A searchable database, via the National Park Service, which eventually will include "basic facts" on servicemen from both sides, as well as information on regiments and 384 "significant" battles. This site already permits the user to search through the database of some 230,000 names of the "United States Colored Troops." For each soldier listed there are links to brief information on the individual and his regiment, as well as over a full page on any major battle that regiment was engaged in. Genealogical reference questions are among the many reference inquiries for which this site will provide rapid answers.

Biography
http://www.biography.com/

A searchable database of some 15,000 one-paragraph biographical sketches courtesy of A&E Television Network. Biographies are from the 1994 *Cambridge Biographical Encyclopedia* and cover historical figures from all over the world; however, there is good coverage of famous North Americans from Pocahontas to Ralph Nader.

Dead Presidents
http://www.csn.net/~mhand/Presidents/

Looking beyond the obvious attempts at humor which is an integral part of this web page, this site does in fact offer a rich variety of information about U. S. presidents. It includes the text of obituaries form the *New York Times* or death notices and a brief biographical sketch ("White House" biographies) for most of the presidents covered, as well as a myriad of links to valuable Internet sites dealing with individual presidents. Links vary but many will provide such items as the text of speeches, timeliness, the presidential libraries homepage, lengthy biographies, and many other items. While not a replacement for such reference tools as Simon & Schuster's four-volume *Encyclopedia of the American Presidency,* this web page does offer an ability to quickly retrieve many facts about some 37 of the Presidents of the United States. A more serious approach to an Internet guide to the presidency may be found at *President (http://sunsite. unc.edu/lia/presidents/pres.html),* which offers links to sites dealing with the presidents, their libraries, and first ladies as well. Unfortunately, the latter appears not to have been updated for some time.

Medal of Honor Citations
http://160.147.68.21:80/cmh-pg/moh1.htm

From the U. S. Army Center for Military History this site offers full paragraph biographies. You may choose the war in question and then use the browser's "find" command to search the text by name, battle, or any key word you wish to enter. A patron searching for medal of honor winner, knowing only the battle could easily retrieve the answer via this database.

GATEWAYS AND GUIDES TO U.S. HISTORY ON THE NET

American Studies Web
http://www.georgetown.edu/crossroads/asw/

Probably the best site for exploring the possibilities of finding American historical sources on the Internet. Offers a breakdown by subject (e.g., history, archives, race, women, economics, etc.) and then lists an enormous number of sites with a descriptive annotation of what each site contains. It is also part of the larger *American Studies Electronic Crossroads,* developed by David Philips in 1994.The latter includes access to many special databases, such as author indexed abstracts of dissertations in American Studies, 1986-1995 (see above) and an index to *American Quarterly* (1975-1995). *Crossroads* is readily connected to by link on the *American Studies Web* main page. The indexes just mentioned may be found by clicking on Reference & Research from the *Crossroads* first page.

American and British History
http://www.libraries.rutgers.edu/rulib/socsci/hist/amhist.html

This gateway web page offers connections to over 80 other gateways which provide access to United States history information, including *Yahoo!,* Yale's American History page, the *Gateway to World History,* the *History Computerization Project,* and the huge site created at the University of Kansas. It also provides connections to many specialized web projects, such as the Library of Congress *American Memory Project,* and projects specializing in such diverse areas as the eighteenth century, Afro-American history, the Civil War, women's suffrage, and the Great Chicago Fire. In addition, access to electronic journals, book reviews, a myriad of specific full-texts, and many reference tools are available from this site.

CMH U.S. Army Center of Military History
http://160.147.68.21:80/cmh-pg/

An excellent gateway to major web sites dealing with military history as well as a reference resource unto itself. Selections on the main menu include listings for books and sources, medal of honor winners, the CMH Publications Catalog, and FAQs about army history. The latter offers information on campaigns, casualties in each war, who was the first female general, and much more. The list of connections to other sites includes the U.S. Army Military Institute (MHI), which in turn offers connection to the Carlisle Barracks Total Library System, a major database on the history of the military. Another gateway to military history to consider is the very thorough *E-Hawk Cadre (http://www.olcommerce.com/cadre/milhist/index. html),* which is an excellent reference source unto itself.

LEISURE STUDIES

Entertainment Resources on the Internet

Allison Cowgill

SUMMARY. This article describes fourteen Internet sites on popular entertainment subjects that provide information on books and book reviews, celebrities, movies, and restaurants. While there are innumerable entertainment-related resources on the Internet, these were selected because they provide a great deal of authoritative information that is easy to find. A brief summary describes the contents of each site. *[Article copies available for a fee from The Haworth Document Delivery Service: 1-800-342-9678. E-mail address: getinfo@ haworth.com]*

The Internet offers an amazing array of sites devoted to ever-popular entertainment topics. Many reference librarians routinely receive questions on books, celebrities, movies, and restaurants. While some answers can be found in print materials, many Internet sites readily bring together

Allison Cowgill is Social Sciences Reference Librarian, Penrose Library, University of Denver, 2150 East Evans Avenue, Denver, CO 80208. E-mail: acowgill@du.edu

[Haworth co-indexing entry note]: "Entertainment Resources on the Internet." Cowgill, Allison. Co-published simultaneously in *The Reference Librarian* (The Haworth Press, Inc.) No. 57, 1997, pp. 179-186; and: *Reference Sources on the Internet: Off the Shelf and Onto the Web* (ed: Karen R. Diaz) The Haworth Press, Inc., 1997, pp. 179-186. Single or multiple copies of this article are available for a fee from The Haworth Document Delivery Service [1-800-342-9678, 9:00 a.m. - 5:00 p.m. (EST). E-mail address: getinfo@haworth.com].

wide varieties of current information not available elsewhere. This very select list of Internet resources contains descriptions for unique sites that are particularly applicable to reference work. They are comprehensive, authoritative, and very easy to use. Reference librarians can quickly instruct users on how to find the information they want. The list is divided into sections on books and book reviews, celebrities, movies, and restaurants; each section has a brief introduction explaining why these sites were chosen. While Internet entertainment resources can be interesting, informative, valuable, and fun to explore, the quality of Web sites varies dramatically. It is important that users understand the necessity of evaluating Internet resources for accuracy and relevance.

BOOKS AND BOOK REVIEWS

Many Internet resources on books and book reviews are quite commercial because they have been created and maintained by publishers and booksellers. While their profit-making motives and efforts to sell books are frequently obvious, the three sites discussed here provide a great deal of easily accessible information on current books, book reviews, and the publishing industry that will be helpful at busy reference desks.

Book lovers of all types will enjoy exploring these databases.

Amazon.com Books! Earth's Biggest Bookstore
Access: http://www.amazon.com

This is the site of the world's largest electronic bookseller and while its intent is to sell books, this database can be very useful for reference work. It contains over one million in-print titles which can be easily searched by basic keywords, authors' names, titles, and subjects. Clear instructions explain how to conduct more refined searches using "and," "not," and "or." The ability to manipulate and combine a variety of elements to identify in-print materials makes this resource particularly valuable. Bibliographic records include prices and availability. The site also contains news items, best seller lists, awards lists, short reviews of recent noteworthy releases, and interviews with authors.

BookWire: The First Place to Look for Book Information
Access: http://www.bookwire.com

This site, sponsored by a group of prominent publishers, calls itself the "most comprehensive guide to book-related resources of the Internet." It offers about "3,500 categorized links to book sites around the world." Clear directions instruct users on how to search the database by author, title or publisher. Also included are links to: "Authors on the Highway" for book tour information; recent reviews from *Publishers Weekly,* the *Hungry Mind Review,* the *Boston Review,* and the *Quarterly Black Review of Books*; best seller lists; calendars of book fairs, conventions and events; and publishing industry news. Its index provides links to numerous Web sites for booksellers, publishers, libraries, and "hundreds of other book-related resources." This site was the winner of the 1995 *Literary Market Place* Technical Achievement Award.

Internet Road Map to Books
Access: http://www.bookport.com/b_welcomehome.html

Called the "home for publishers' Web pages," this site offers numerous links to book review sites such as the *Atlantic Monthly, Book Page,* and *Fiction Addiction.* It provides access to publisher and bookseller Web sites, lists of book fairs, and *Publishers Weekly* best seller lists. A wide variety of reading lists and bibliographies, online editions of books, and information for people involved in the publishing industry are also available.

CELEBRITIES

Reference librarians routinely get questions about people who are well known for all sorts of reasons, and interest in celebrities seems to continually increase. There are innumerable Web sites devoted to famous and not-so-famous individuals from movies, television, and music. Many are done by adoring fans who create online shrines honoring their favorite stars, and their accuracy is frequently questionable. A popular actress like Sandra Bullock, for example, has several sites devoted to her relatively short life and small body of work. This category probably demands the most effort from librarians and users because there can be so many different resources to check for information on specific individuals. The two sites noted here were selected because of their wide scope or breadth; they provide links to a large number of resources that cover a large number of people. Material on particular celebrities can also be found using one of the common Internet search engines, and again, it is important to carefully evaluate the results of searches using the two resources discussed here or using such tools as Yahoo!, InfoSeek or Lycos. Some of the sites discussed in the following section on movies include biographical information on people involved in the film industry.

Mr. Showbiz
Access: http://www.mrshowbiz.com

This site provides over 300 links to celebrity biographies, late-breaking entertainment industry news, and reviews of recent movies. While the entire database can be readily searched by keyword or browsed by people's last names, there are several ways to limit and refine searches. Users can also browse by professions such as actors and actresses, directories, and comedians. Other features include thorough listings of Oscar winners, interviews with stars currently in the news, lists of new film releases, and collections of celebrity quotations.

Yahoo! Top: Entertainment: People
Access: http://yahoo.com/Entertainment/People/

Yahoo! created this subdivision index so users can readily locate information on people in the entertainment industry. While users can look for people's last name by browsing an alphabetical index, it is preferable to do a search for individuals by last names. The number of resulting hits simply depends on the number of sites the search locates, and as noted before, their quality and usefulness can vary dramatically. This resource also includes links to over fifty sites which can help users find information on all sorts of people, inside or outside of the entertainment industry.

MOVIES

The Internet has countless sites devoted to movies. Many major studios have their own sites; Paramount Pictures' site, for example, offers information about the movies, television programs and home videos they produce. Some sites are devoted to individual films and newspaper advertisements frequently include their URLs. Happily, however, a large number of sites contain readily available, authoritative, and timely information on movies, past and present. Selection for this category was the most difficult because so many excellent resources exist; the following sites were specifically chosen because of their usefulness to librarians working at reference desks. Other excellent Web sites, too numerous to highlight here, also provide access to all aspects of this popular topic.

All-Movie Guide: An Online Film and Video Database
Access: http://205.186.189.2/amg/movie_Root.html

This resource provides information on "more than 130,000 films and documentaries" and "contains over 1,000,000 cast and production credits." It also includes over 12,000 biographies of actors, actresses, and directors. The database can be searched by film title, artist, and keyword. An entry for a specific film is very thorough and includes such elements as its rating, a plot synopsis, genre, warnings about excessive violence or sexual activity, and the cast of characters with links to other sites for those individuals. Users can also browse by genre, country of origin, and date of release. It is quite comprehensive historically; for example, there is a list of best films for each decade that begins in the 1920s. The coverage of this exciting and highly recommended site is thorough, and will delight film enthusiasts with its many interesting comparisons and links. Users can, for example, find favorite films and get links to other movies with the same actors, directors, or similar themes.

Cinemachine: The Movie Review Search Engine
Access: http://www.cinemachine.com

The site brings together the full text of recent movie reviews from such diverse sources as the *Chicago Sun Times,* the *Washington Post, Time, Entertainment Weekly, Newsday,* and *Boxoffice Magazine.* Users can simply enter names of specific films; the resulting list of abbreviated article titles are links to the complete text of every reference. Critics' opinions can be wildly divergent and this site offers great opportunities for making interesting comparisons. It is very easy to search and quickly brings together film critiques in a way other print or online sources do not.

CineMedia: The Internet's Largest Film and Media Directory
Access: http://ptd15.afionline.org/CineMedia

This Web index provides "links to over 10,000 sites" related to film and television. The cinema section offers links to films, directors, videos, organizations, studios, and film festivals, theaters and relevant schools. Actors can be searched alphabetically by last name which results in lists of pertinent Web sites. Descriptions of films include the names of major performers, directors, script writers, brief plot synopses, and casts of characters. This resource is particularly valuable for people who are interested in many aspects of the film industry, not just individual movies. Its comprehensiveness makes it an excellent place to begin an Internet search on movies because it provides a real sense of what the Web offers on this high-interest subject.

The Internet Movie Database
Access: http://us.imdb.org

This is one of the Internet's premier movie sites. Billed as the "most comprehensive free source of movie information on the Internet," it currently includes over 75,000 movies and over one million filmography entries, from the early days of cinema to current releases. It covers actors, directors, writers, composers, plot summaries, awards, reviews, and ratings, just to name a few of the categories or subjects available here. While this massive database has clear instructions and provides lots of help, it is the most complex source listed here. While simple searches are easy to do, it is necessary to read the directions and descriptions of its contents to take full advantage of everything this respected resource offers. The effort is definitely rewarded. In addition to information on films, there are "local cinema schedules, movie-related mailing lists, a movie quote of the day," and "pointers to film festivals." Numerous links provide access to other sites which involve all aspects of the film industry.

Roger Ebert on Movies
Access: http://www.suntimes.com/ebert/ebert.html

This site contains full-text reviews by Pulitzer prize winner Roger Ebert, *Chicago Sun Times,* one of America's most influential and respected film critics. The database contains reviews from 1985 to date and is searchable by movie titles, the names of actors, producers, directors, writers, and dates. Movie ratings range from one to four stars. This resource is included here because it is very easy to search, it covers a number of years, and many users are interested in Ebert's perspectives and opinions.

Screen It! Entertainment Reviews for Parents
Access: http://www.screenit.com/movies/srch-mov.htm

This site is an excellent resource for parents who are concerned about the films their children see. Its list of recently released movies can be searched alphabetically by title, by ratings or by genre. Entries for individual films are quite lengthy and include information on their depictions of alcohol/drug use, violence, profanity, and sex and nudity. Brief plot synopses, ratings, appropriateness for children, recommendations for parents, brief critical reviews, and overviews of the analyses are all included. Easy to use and easy to understand, this resource's focus on films and their suitability for children is a very unique resource for adults.

RESTAURANT REVIEWS

Restaurant guides and reviews are widely available on the Internet. It is very easy to find restaurant information for specific cities using standard Internet search engines. The following sites were selected because they offer broad coverage of restaurants nationwide. People who love to travel and love to eat will especially enjoy these databases, and of course, they are particularly useful for individuals who are planning vacations or business trips and armchair travelers.

DineNet: Menus Online
Access: http://www.dinenet.com

This site provides restaurant reviews and menus with prices for Atlanta, Boston, Chicago, Dallas, Houston, Los Angeles, Miami, New Orleans, New York, Philadelphia, San Francisco, and Washington D.C./Baltimore. The database can be searched by restaurant name, location, or kind of cuisine. Updated monthly, this site is very easy to use and the menus' prices are especially helpful for people planning trips to these locales. It also includes basic maps of these cities so users can identify restaurants in specific areas or neighborhoods.

Dining Out on the Web
Access: http://www.ird.net/diningout.html

This database provides access to a large number of relevant Internet restaurant resources, including the North American Restaurant Guide, the Kosher Restaurant Database, and an alphabetical list of United States locations arranged by state and city. It offers links to a wide variety of local resources such as the San Francisco Bay Area Restaurant Guide and the Daytona Beach Diner's Express. There are also many links to restaurant information for other countries such as Austria, Australia, Belgium, Canada, and Japan. This index is an excellent introduction to the number and diversity of Internet sources for restaurant information and reviews.

Zagat Dine
Access: http://pathfinder.com/@@urxB8AUAUYa3cubH/travel/Zagat/
Dine

This site contains restaurant evaluations from the "the results of the 1996 *Zagat Survey of America's Top Restaurants* and the *Zagat Survey of America's Best Meal Deals.*" The database provides authoritative and respected Zagat reviews for restaurants in thirty American cities, including Atlanta, Atlantic City, Baltimore, Boston, Cincinnati, Denver, Houston, Kansas City, New Orleans, Orlando, New York City, Palm Beach, Philadelphia, Salt Lake City, and Washington D.C. These surveys reflect the opinions of "large numbers of local restaurant-goers and diners." After selecting a city, users can search for names of specific restaurants, kinds of cuisine, rankings, popularity, and "top bargains." Individual reviews include brief descriptions, addresses, and telephone numbers. Like the preceding restaurant resources, this is a valuable site for people planning trips, and of course, the armchair traveler.

OTHER ENTERTAINMENT RESOURCES

As noted earlier, there are many, many Internet sites devoted to popular entertainment topics. Suzanne Lafontain has compiled a list of her choices for the best Web entertainment sites. It is included here for those who want a useful, interesting, and entertaining summary list of additional resources which could not be covered here.

Top 10% Entertainment Sites
Access: http://www.pebbs.com/megabites/et.html

This list of Web resources, compiled by Suzanne Lafontaine, covers all aspects of the entertainment industry; there are separate categories for celebrities, movies, music, and television shows. It provides links to a wide variety of sites, some serious and some not so serious. For example, *Wills on the Web, Find a Grave, Famous Movie Star Marriages,* the *Celebrity Chronicle,* the *Hollywood Reporter* and *Teen Movie Critic* are all included. Each reference includes a brief summary describing their contents. This gives researchers a great sense of the variety of entertainment sites the Internet now offers.

Reference on the Internet:
Sports

Bruce Weaver

SUMMARY. This article presents a selective annotated list of sports-related websites for reference use. Current sports news, sports information, directories, and recreation sites are included. *[Article copies available for a fee from The Haworth Document Delivery Service: 1-800-342-9678. E-mail address: getinfo@haworth.com]*

Sports information on the Internet is largely current events and commercial organization intensive. Team pages, league and conference pages, and current news pages abound. When your reference need goes beyond the current and into the past, the Internet pickings are much slimmer. For current information, often updated on a minute-by-minute basis, the Internet can be very useful. It can not only answer the "who won" questions, it can often handle the "who's winning" inquiries.

This directory of sports on the Internet is organized into cream of the crop sites, sports indexes/links, sports media sites, recreation sites, and professional organization sites.

CREAM OF THE CROP

These sites are the best of the best, whether indexes or content-based sites. They provide a good start to a web-based sports reference collection.

Bruce Weaver is Reference Librarian, Eisenhower National Clearinghouse for Mathematics and Science Education, Columbus, OH. He has previously served as a reference and undergraduate librarian at The Ohio State University. E-mail: bweaver@enc.org

[Haworth co-indexing entry note]: "Reference on the Internet: Sports." Weaver, Bruce. Co-published simultaneously in *The Reference Librarian* (The Haworth Press, Inc.) No. 57, 1997, pp. 187-190; and: *Reference Sources on the Internet: Off the Shelf and Onto the Web* (ed: Karen R. Diaz) The Haworth Press, Inc., 1997, pp. 187-190. Single or multiple copies of this article are available for a fee from The Haworth Document Delivery Service [1-800-342-9678, 9:00 a.m. - 5:00 p.m. (EST). E-mail address: getinfo@haworth.com].

WWW Women's Sports Page [http://fiat.gslis.utexas.edu/~lewisa/womsprt. html] is a good place to begin looking for information on women's sports. Well-organized and indexed, this site is comprehensive and has received Magellan and Point top site awards.

Sportsline USA [http://www.sportsline.com/] is a personal favorite because it is very current and comprehensive. Up to the minute news on current professional sports, including online nearly-real-time mockup web views of important games like the World Series, NFL playoffs, or college football's Florida/Florida State matchup, make this site a must for up-to-the minute information. A hybrid free/commercial site, it includes for-fee links to additional information, graphics, online chats, and sports wagering information.

ESPNet SportsZone [http://espnet.sportszone.com/]. Part index and part current news, part free and part for-fee, ESPNet SportZone and SportsLine USA are very closely matched.

World Wide Web of Sports [http://www.tns.lcs.mit.edu/cgi-bin/sports] is an index/link site worthy of mention because of its breadth, depth, and ease of use. Under 100 links on its initial page to individual sports or categories like "TV and Radio" or "University Athletics" make this site very easy to use. Each entry may lead to a few, many, or dozens of sites. This is the place to be to find the rules of croquet!

AFP Sports International [http://www.afp.com/sportsreport/] is an excellent site providing a world view of sports news. Agence France-Presse covers sports worldwide, with stories appearing 4 hours after they are distributed over the wires. Both a frames and a no frames version are available. This author is uncertain of the difference between the Rugby League and the Rugby Union, but both are well-covered here. This site provides a welcome view of sports beyond the United States.

The Sports Network [http://www.sportsnetwork.com/] provides current coverage of major sports news. A good "current scores by sport" section is useful in following a current day's activity. Wagering information is plentiful, though wagering is not endorsed by this author.

SPORTS INDEXES/LINKS

The following sites generally provide a high degree of links to other sites and a low degree of initial content. All have their individual strengths and weaknesses depending on user preferences.

Starting Point™ Sports [http://www.stpt.com/cgi-bin/sports/sports.cgi] is a broadly indexed site providing approximately 20 categories of sports links. Starting Point™ Sports leads to many of the entries in this directory.

Yanoff's List Sports [http://www.spectracom.com/islist/inet3.html#SPORTS] lacks both depth and breadth. Nonetheless, it provides links to sites that might otherwise be missed and is worth perusing when other avenues fail.

Yahoo! Scoreboard [http://sports.yahoo.com/] links to sports by professional organization, providing simple links to professional team websites. It also provides current news information by organization (NBA, NCAA Women's Basketball, etc.).

My Virtual Reference Desk Sports Sites [http://www.refdesk.com/sports. html] is an above-average sports links list. It is listed here not for special or unusual features, but because My Virtual Reference Desk is an exceptional site, and likely already familiar to many reference librarians.

InfoSeek sports guide [http://guide.infoseek.com/Sports?tid=1653&sv=N3] is more layered and cumbersome to use than most. Its relatively few subject links lead to layer upon layer of links, making it difficult to get where you'd like to go.

Power Links Leisure, Sports, and Recreation page [http://www.abacom. com/innomagi/online/l_s_rec/l_s_rec.htm] is a good general index to indexes of sports sites by sport. It also includes a link to general sports resources on the web and selected sports media sites.

Magellan Sports Index [http://www.mckinley.com/browse_bd.cgi?Sports], yet another index to sports sites, includes an effective "ranking" feature that brings up the best sites by topic. Its sparse initial list of 22 topics includes "Miscellaneous," but its ability to display the sites in rank order (number of Magellan "stars") makes it easy to quickly find the best sites on a topic.

MEDIA SITES: NETWORKS AND PERIODICALS

Media site URLs link to major sports media outlets and sports publications. All contain varying degrees of current and historical information.

USA Today Sports Index [http://www.usatoday.com/sports/si.htm]. USA Today's sports sections, offering comprehensive coverage of major sports, often serves as a reference to fantasy sports league players.

SI Online (Sports Illustrated) [http://pathfinder.com/si/] is the online version of *Sports Illustrated* magazine.

Those interested in the points of view of particular sportscasters may be interested in the NBC and CBS sites.

NBC Sports [http://www.nbc.com/sports/].
CBS Sports [http://www.cbs.com/sports].
Fox Sports [http://www.tvguide.com/sports].

RECREATION SITES

Yahoo! recreation [http://www.yahoo.com/Recreation/] is a large and simply-organized site. Links include Cooking@, Drugs@, Games (9,875), Hovercraft (13), Outdoors (2,907), Sports (14,689), and others.

GORP Index page [http://www.gorp.com/gorp/guide.htm]. An outdoor recreation cornucopia, the GORP (Great Outdoor Recreation Pages) index leads to commercial and non-commercial outdoor recreation sites. Travel, equipment, books, activities, and more–indexed and easy-to-use–this site links to more than most outdoor enthusiasts will need.

PROFESSIONAL ORGANIZATIONS

From a very traditional point of view, baseball, basketball, hockey, and football are the major sports. Their organizations' official home page addresses follow without description. These four sites, as well as the home pages of a multitude of other professional sports organizations, can be found via the sports indexes/links previously listed:

National Basketball Association [http://www.nba.com/];
Major League Baseball [http://www.majorleaguebaseball.com/];
National Football League [http://www.nfl.com/];
National Hockey League [http://www.nhl.com/].

Internet Reference Resources
for the Life Sciences

Kathleen A. Clark

SUMMARY. A virtual cornucopia of resources is available for biologists on the Internet. Many have been put up by biologists themselves; others have been mounted by organizations, government agencies or commercial businesses. In some cases, the best or only way to obtain the information is via the Internet (e.g., the gene sequence information from Genbank). Over sixty Internet biological resources are reviewed in this report in which the life sciences have been defined to include all areas of biology, agriculture and veterinary science except those which pertain to the environment or human medicine. *[Article copies available for a fee from The Haworth Document Delivery Service: 1-800-342-9678. E-mail address: getinfo@ haworth.com]*

Biologists have been using the Internet to communicate and share data for many years, so it is no surprise that the Web is rich in biological

Kathleen A. Clark is Assistant Professor of Library Science and Assistant Librarian, Life Sciences Library, Purdue University, 2-400 Lilly Hall of Science, West Lafayette, IN 42907-1323. E-mail: flora@purdue.edu

[Haworth co-indexing entry note]: "Internet Reference Resources for the Life Sciences." Clark, Kathleen A. Co-published simultaneously in *The Reference Librarian* (The Haworth Press, Inc.) No. 57, 1997, pp. 191-202; and: *Reference Sources on the Internet: Off the Shelf and Onto the Web* (ed: Karen R. Diaz) The Haworth Press, Inc., 1997, pp. 191-202. Single or multiple copies of this article are available for a fee from The Haworth Document Delivery Service [1-800-342-9678, 9:00 a.m. - 5:00 p.m. (EST). E-mail address: getinfo@haworth.com].

resources. Many researchers are using the Web to open up their labs and resources to others, including students. Some have put up their picture archives, or are using the Web as part of their teaching effort. Many organizations and government agencies are giving open access to valuable databases. But a word to the wise: as with any reference resource, rely on information from reputable sources; if the credentials of the author are not apparent, send a message of inquiry to the webmaster.

For the purposes of this report, the life sciences include all areas of biology, agriculture and veterinary science except those which pertain to the environment or human medicine. Two other listings of Internet resources for biology (Courtois and Goslen, 1996) and agriculture (Clark, 1996) have recently been published. Reviews of life sciences Internet sites also appear regularly in *Trends in Biochemical Sciences, Trends in Genetics, Trends in Biotechnology, FASEB, Biotechnology, Nature Biotechnology, Nature Medicine,* and other journals. For your convenience, hotlinks to sites mentioned in this paper are available on the Web *(http://omni.cc. purdue.edu/~flora/ref-libr.htm).*

GENERAL BIOLOGICAL COLLECTIONS

Perhaps the best collection of collections on the Web is the *World Wide Web Virtual Library Project (http://www.w3.org/pub/DataSources/bySubject/ Overview.html).* As each section of the WWW-VL is maintained by specialists in the field, topics are generally covered in considerable depth. The life sciences are covered in over 40 "virtual libraries" including: Agriculture; Animal health, well-being and rights; Biochemistry, molecular biology and biophysics; Biodiversity and ecology; Biology departments and institutes; Biological molecules; Biosciences; Biotechnology; Botany; Developmental biology; Environment; Entomology; Evolution; Fish; Forestry; Gardening; Genetics; Herpetology; History of science; Immunology; Instructional resources in biology; Irrigation; Landscape architecture; Medicine; Microbiology and virology; Microscopy; Model organisms; Mycology; Neurobiology; Oceanography; Physiology and biophysics; Remote sensing; Science fairs; Technology and medicine; Veterinary medicine; Vision science; Whale watching; Yeasts; and Zoos. The primary WWW Virtual Library for biology, under which many of these are listed, is *WWW-VL Biosciences (http://golgi.harvard.edu/biopages.html)*; its goal is to index nearly every biological server on the Internet.

California State University's *Biology Web Server (CSU BioWeb) (http://arnica.csustan.edu/index.html)* is a well-designed collection of biological resources. One can search the entire BioWeb by keywords, or browse within disciplines which range from agricultural science, biochemistry, and genetics to mammalogy, ornithology and virology. In addition to the more than 30 disciplines, there are pointers to biological Web-based instructional or multimedia materials, as well as to U.S. government and other comprehensive biological servers. All entries have been briefly annotated.

No list of "lists" would be complete without mentioning *Yahoo! (http://www.yahoo.com)*. Yahoo!'s hierarchical structure makes it easy to zero in on topical areas. For example, starting at the first page, one can select (sequentially): Science/Biology/Ecology/Pollution, finally arriving at annotated references to 18 sites and indirect pointers to 34 additional sites. At each juncture, one is given the opportunity to enter a keyword search of either the entire Yahoo! database, or part of it.

Librarians at the University of California at Riverside, together with many subject specialists, have produced *Infomine: Comprehensive Biological, Agricultural and Medical Internet Resource Collection (http://lib-www. ucr.edu/bioag/)*, which is really a goldmine! Not only is this part of Infomine comprehensive (about 1,500 links), extensively annotated, and capable of full nested and Boolean searching, it is also fully indexed, allowing the user to link easily to "related" records.

DICTIONARIES AND BIOGRAPHIES

BioTech's illustrated, online *Life Sciences Dictionary (http://biotech. chem.indiana.edu/search/dict-search.html)* contains over 4,000 terms associated with biochemistry, biotechnology, botany, cellular biology, chemistry, ecology, genetics, medicine, pharmacology and toxicology. Several institutions worked together on creating the dictionary: Indiana University, Iowa State University (lead institution), the University of Wisconsin, and the University of Minnesota. The dictionary is designed to be useful both for students and researchers. Definitions are often linked to other definitions, and images. One may search for definitions of terms, or search for the term used within definitions, which provides the queried term in the context of a sentence. Partial word searches are allowed. For example, a search for "peroxid," led to a definition for "peroxidase" and 5 other definitions which contained "peroxidase," "peroxisome" or "superoxide."

While many of us have the second edition of the *Dictionary of Cell Biology* (1995, Academic Press) on our shelves, we can now also access it on the Web *(http://www.mblab.gla.ac.uk/~julian/Dict.html)*. The Web version, with over 6,000 definitions, has numerous enhancements over the paper edition, such as hyperlinks from one definition to another. Furthermore, the Web edition, while containing all the information in the second edition, has additional terms destined for publication in the third edition.

The *Glossary of Microbiology (http://www.bio.umass.edu/mdid/glossary/)* contains definitions for over 750 terms from the glossaries of ten microbiology or biochemistry textbooks. One can browse the dictionary or search for entries; words within definitions are linked to other words in the dictionary.

If you have ever been unable to find biographical information on a scientist, the *History of Science, Technology and Medicine Biographical Dictionary* site *(http://www.asap.unimelb.edu.au/hstm/hstm_bio.htm)* is a resource worth bookmarking. Biographies have been collated from over 70 sources on the Internet. One can browse alphabetically, or search by name. Currently there are biographies of nearly one thousand scientists. Frequently links to more than one biography are available; for example, there are five links to Einstein biographies. The browse mode is informative, as it indicates whether a link includes a photo, when the person lived, and the Internet source of the biography. There is also a separate listing of the Internet sources, which is hot-linked, allowing for more browsing.

ONLINE MONOGRAPHS

For class assignments many of our life science majors need to look up basic diagnoses and therapies for various diseases. The *Merck Manual of Diagnosis and Therapy* is a wonderful resource for this, and fortunately, Merck has made it available on the Web *(http://www.merck.com/!!rE_ e31jmmrE_e40XtZ/pubs/mmanual/)*. One can "read" it chapter by chapter, as with a book, or use the online index to hyperlink quickly back and forth to the cited pages. The online version also has separate indexes for the many tables and figures. Unfortunately, hypertext links within articles are very limited.

The *National Academy of Sciences (http://www.nas.edu/)* has made available in its Reading Room the full text of more than 900 of its monographs from the 1980s and 1990s. Most are available as images of scanned pages, but some are ASCII, HTML, PDF or PostScript files. Biological areas include agricultural sciences, marine and maritime studies, natural resources, environmental issues, food and nutrition, and medicine. Also of interest to biologists are books on research issues, scientific leadership, and science ethics.

COMPANY INFORMATION AND CATALOGS

WWW Virtual Library: Biotechnology, General/Products and Services (http://www.cato.com/interweb/cato/biotech/bio-prod.html) lists the Web sites of over 250 companies that market products and services for the life sciences. Also provided is a listing of companies that actually produce (as opposed to just market) pharmaceuticals and biologically active compounds. If the company needed isn't listed, try the *ATCG Molecular Biology Suppliers' Vendor Catalog (http://www.atcg.com/comppage/comppage. htm),* which supplies contact information for nearly 300 companies in the life sciences industry, including their URL and email address, when available.

According to the *American Type Culture Collection (ATCC) (http:// www.atcc.org/),* their mission is to "acquire, authenticate, and maintain reference cultures, related biological materials, and associated data, and to distribute these to qualified scientists in government, industry, and education." As such, they are an indispensable source of biological materials ranging from bacteria, cell lines, fungi, plant tissue cultures, seeds, and viruses, to recombinant clones and vectors. On-line orders may be placed.

SCHOLARLY SOCIETIES AND PUBLICATIONS

Internet links to nearly 1,000 scholarly societies are currently listed on the University of Waterloo's Electronic Library page, *Scholarly Societies Project: Webpages & Gophers of Scholarly Societies (http://www.lib. uwaterloo.ca/society/webpages.html).* Agricultural organizations and associations may be found at *WWW Virtual Library (Agriculture)–Associations and Organizations (http://ipm_www.ncsu.edu/cernag/associations.html),* while an extensive list of biological societies and organizations is located at *Biology Societies and Organizations (http://golgi.harvard.edu/afagen/ depts/orgs.html).*

As the age of electronic journals dawns, publishers are seeking to use and define this new medium in a variety of ways. Some journals, such as *Nature (http://www.nature.com)* and *Science (http://www.sciencemag.org)* are now publishing addenda to their print articles solely on the Web. Publishers are currently deciding whether or not these materials will be freely accessible. Many publishers have put up the table of contents, and in some cases abstracts, of their articles. *WWW Virtual Library Electronic Journals List: Academic and Reviewed Journals (http://www.edoc.com/ ejournal/)* provides an extensive listing of on-line journals in all disciplines. *Journals, Conferences, and Current Awareness Services (Biosciences) (http://golgi.harvard.edu/biopages/journals.html)* points to over 200 biological e-journals and publishers. *BetaCyte (http://www.betacyte. pair.com/journals.html)* currently lists about 200 e-journals in chemistry, biochemistry, and molecular biology, and has conveniently grouped the titles into those which are available in full text, or as abstracts, for free, or with a paid or preconditional registration. Another convenient feature is that one can join a mailing list and receive notification about new additions to the BetaCyte list.

BIBLIOGRAPHIC TOOLS

The full *Medline* (1966 to the present) database is searchable for free, courtesy of NCBI *(http://www4.ncbi.nlm.nih.gov/PubMed/)*. The "advanced search" mode includes full Boolean capabilities, including limiting the search by field. One major limitation is that there in no capability to "explode" MESH terms, such as found with OVID or SilverPlatter access to the Medline database. This site was set up, in part, to allow publishers of e-journals to link dynamically to Medline citations. A subset of *AGRICOLA* (termed the "Journal Article Citation database," and including only 1989 to the present) is available *(http://www.nal.usda.gov/isis/)* but its search engine is not currently very user-friendly.

Although CARL's *UnCover database (http://www.carl.org/uncover)* is not intrinsically a biological resource, it certainly is one biologists (and reference librarians) depend upon to find or verify citations conveniently over the Internet. In addition, I'd like to recommend a subscription to CARL's Reveal service for both librarians and their clients. For a mere $25 per year, one can elect to have the table of contents of up to 50 journals delivered by e-mail as soon as they are entered into the UnCover database. In addition, up to 25 predetermined user search queries can be run weekly against new entries to UnCover, and e-mailed. Online ordering of articles is available.

Frequently patrons are interested in finding the price and availability of books. *Amazon (http://amazon.com),* billed as the largest online bookstore with over a million titles, lists both technical and popular books and in coverage seems similar to *Books in Print*. Besides listing the usual bibliographic and price information, it gives the LC subject headings for each title, which allows the user to link to other books with the same subject headings.

STUMPERS

For help with biological reference "stumpers," try posting your question to one of the *BIOSCI/bionet Usenet* newsgroups. Currently BIOSCI has nearly 100 research discussion groups in such topics as audiology, botanical education, molecular biology, neuroscience, photosynthesis, maize, women in biology, molecular biology of HIV, and free-radicals. As with any newsgroup, you should familiarize yourself with the group before posting. These are research groups, and don't suffer lay-person requests gladly! I once saw a replier tell a poster to check out "that big building on campus. . . . it's called the Library"! On the other hand, when I sought help in finding the correct citation for a book and posted a query to the appropriate subject group, I shortly had three correct citations, one each from Crete, Hong Kong and North Carolina! It turned out that both the author and title of my original citation had been wrong! You may post directly to a group via your Usenet client of choice (look for the groups which start with "bionet"), or go to the *BIOSCI/bionet Web* page *(http://www.bio.net/)*. In addition to forms for posting to the groups, this site maintains a searchable archive of past posts and a database of biological scientists. If you don't find a BIONET newsgroup which seems to match your need, post to one of the groups listed in Diane Kovac's *Directory of Scholarly Electronic Conferences (http://www.n2h2.com/KOVACS)*, which is both browsable and searchable.

After exhausting their local resources, librarians (only) may email the *National Library of Medicine Reference Section (ref@nlm.nih.gov)* for help with medically-related questions (for more information about this service, see *http://www.nlm.nih.gov/services/libraries/reference_special_lib.html)*. NLM's online catalog is also available *(http://www.nlm.nih.gov/databases/locator.html)*. The *National Agricultural Library Reference Desk (agref@nalusda.gov.purdue.edu)* also offers assistance via e-mail (for more details, see *http://www.nal.usda.gov/answers/reference/gen_ref_services.html)*. Access to NAL's library catalog is also available *(http://www.nal.usda.gov/isis/)*.

AGRICULTURE

AgDB: Agriculture-Related Information Systems, Databases, and Datasets (http://www.agnic.org/agdb/erdcalfr.html), generated by the Agriculture Network Information Center (AgNIC), is a comprehensive listing of about 600 agriculture-related databases, datasets, and information systems. One of the unique and very useful features of this resource is that every item has a record attached to it which gives such information as the producer, update frequency, contact information, cost, and a helpful description. It is searchable by AGRICOLA subject category codes *(http://www.agnic.org/cc/index.html)* or keywords. Only databases with primary content are included, not bibliographic databases such as AGRICOLA. Although not all the datasets described are available on the Internet, Web-links have been established to those which are. Among the hundreds of Internet-accessible resources listed: Amazon Plants, Bacterial Nomenclature, Breeds of Livestock, numerous floras (state, country, regional), plant and animal image sites, Poisonous Plants, McCormick Spice Chart, Landscape Insects, Guide to Gardens of the USA, Medicinal Plants of Native America, and Culinary Herb FAQ.

Agrigator (http://www.ifas.ufl.edu/www/agator/htm/ag.htm), from the Institute of Food and Agricultural Sciences at the University of Florida, groups agricultural sites by their source, e.g., international, commercial, U.S. State, U.S. Federal, or marketing services. A comprehensive guide to upcoming agricultural conferences is also maintained. Lists of other agricultural resources may be found at the *WWW Virtual Library–Agriculture (http://ipm_www.ncsu.edu/cernag/)* or Wilfred Drew's *Not Just Cows (http://www.snymor.edu/~drewwe/njc/)*.

For unparalleled access to food nutrient information consult the *USDA Nutrient Database for Standard Reference, Release 11 (http://www.nal. usda.gov/fnic/foodcomp/Data/SR11/)*, produced by the USDA's Nutrient Data Laboratory, Human Nutrition Research Center. A search tool is provided to look up detailed nutrient analyses for over 5,600 different foods; reports are generated on-the-fly, based on the amount of the food specified by the user (e.g., tablespoon, cup, 100 grams, etc.). Data reported include the specific amount of the individual lipids, amino acids, vitamins, minerals, calories, protein, fiber, etc. An option to download the entire flat data files for local use is also provided.

BIOCHEMISTRY AND MOLECULAR BIOLOGY

Pedro's BioMolecular Research Tools (http://www.public.iastate.edu/ ~pedro/research_tools.html) indexes nearly all the Internet-accessible tools necessary for the molecular biologist. Included are molecular biology search and analysis tools, bibliographic and WWW tools, guides, tutorials, and lists of journals and newsletters.

One of the most outstandingly useful and heavily used resources available to molecular biologists via the Internet is *Entrez (http://www3. ncbi.nlm.nih.gov/Entrez/)* from the National Center for Biotechnology Information (NCBI). Entrez provides interlinked access to three large databases: a subset of the National Library of Medicine's MEDLINE database, the NCBI protein database, and the NCBI nucleotide database. Each MEDLINE citation has been compared to all the other MEDLINE citations in the Entrez database using an algorithm that compares the text and MeSH terms found in those citations; the most similar citations, called "neighbors," can then be retrieved. Medline records are also linked to the respective protein or nucleotide records, which have been compiled from a variety of sources, including GenBank, EMBL, DDBJ, PIR, SWISS-PROT, PRF, and PDB. Using the BLAST algorithm, sequences with similarities can be viewed. Recently a structure database, which allows viewing of the 3-dimensional structure of proteins, has also been added to Entrez. Faster, more flexible access to Entrez can be obtained if one downloads the free *Entrez client software (http://www3.ncbi.nlm.nih.gov/ Entrez/nentrez. overview.html)*.

From the ExPASy World Wide Web (WWW) molecular biology server (Geneva University Hospital and the University of Geneva), *ENZYME (http://expasy.hcuge.ch/sprot/enzyme.html)* is a repository of information relative to the nomenclature of enzymes. It is primarily based on the recommendations of the Nomenclature Committee of the International Union of Biochemistry and Molecular Biology (IUBMB) and may be searched by EC number, enzyme class, official name, alternative name, by substrate, product or cofactor. In addition to the aforementioned data, records show the reaction(s) catalyzed, list genetic diseases associated with the enzyme, and provide cross-links to multiple databases such as SWISS-PROT.

Many laboratories are now required to have on hand *Material Safety Data Sheets* for every chemical in the lab. There are several sites for these on the Internet. *Fisher Scientific (http://www.fisher1.com)* provides extensive MSDS for both inorganic and organic chemicals, including safety, hazard, first aid, safe handling and storage, personal protection, physical and chemical properties, stability, toxicology, and regulatory information for Fisher's chemicals. A search engine is provided to allow for quick access to the required information. If the compound of interest isn't found at Fisher's site, try the University System of Georgia's *Right to Know* page *(http://www.ps.uga.edu/rtk/)*, which lists other MSDS Internet sites, including sites which specialize in agri-chemicals, pharmaceuticals or office supplies (e.g., Xerox toner).

EDUCATION AND RESEARCH

Access Excellence (http://www.gene.com/ae/), sponsored by the biotechnology industry pioneer, Genentech, is a great resource to point biology education majors toward. Here high school biology teachers share protocols for labs that work, exchange teaching ideas, and can read up on current hot science news. On the other hand, for a look at what materials faculty are putting on the Web for collegiate-level courses (in all disciplines) take a look at the *World Lecture Hall (http://www.utexas.edu/ world/lecture/index.html).*

As part of a complete literature search, I often recommend to graduate students that they search several of the *grants-awarded databases.* This way they can find out if someone else is already doing the same project as they are planning to do, or they may find persons with whom to collaborate. Searching these databases also has the advantage of letting the students see the breadth and quality of research which is being funded. Besides identifying the principle investigator and institution, many records in these databases will give abstracts, literature cited, the funding level, and progress reports for the supported grant applications. Over 100 universities are part of the *Community of Science* and have excellent access to these databases at *http://cos.gdb.org.* Others may access them on the Internet at the following sites:

- U. S. Department of Agriculture's *CRIS database: http://cristel.nal. usda.gov:8080/*
- *National Science Foundation (NSF) database: http://www.nsf.gov/ verity/srchawd.htm*
- Department of Health and Human Services (NIH, FDA, CDC, etc.) *CRISP database: gopher://gopher.nih.gov:70/11/res/crisp*

ORGANISM-BASED RESOURCES

Mammal Species of the World (http://www.nmnh.si.edu/msw/) contains information on the 4,629 currently recognized species of mammals, in a taxonomic hierarchy that includes order, family, subfamily, and genus. The information, which was compiled under the auspices of the American Society of Mammalogists, was taken from the book of the same title (1993). Searchable by common or scientific name, each record provides information about the species' author, distribution, original name, common name, scientific name, references, type locality, and specimens located at the Smithsonian Institute.

PLANTS (http://plants.usda.gov/plants/qurymenu.html) contains an up-to-date list of the approximately 45,000 individual plant taxa, both vascular and nonvascular, known to occur as native or naturalized within the boundaries of the United States, including its territories. PLANTS was created to replace the *National List of Scientific Names* published by the National Resources Conservation Service (formerly the Soil Conservation

Service). The aim of the database is to provide anyone who is interested in plants with a common, standardized vocabulary. One may search by common name, scientific name, family, or genus; limit by state; sort by scientific name or common name; or search for threatened, endangered or wetland species. For each species the following is provided: synonyms, distribution map information, references, wetlands information, growth habit, origin, perennial or annual status and family name.

One of the most comprehensive gardening resources on the Web is the *Time Life Gardening Library (http://pathfinder.com/@@m52R* PFR4gIAQCWD/vg/TimeLife/)*, which includes the *Time Life Electronic Encyclopedia,* with photos and information for growing plants from over 1,400 genera, and *The House Plant Pavilion,* with information on identifying and caring for house plants. Gardeners should also check out the *WWW Virtual Library on Gardening (http://www.gardenweb.com/vl/).*

Presented by the Department of Animal Science at Oklahoma State University, the illustrated *Breeds of Livestock (http://www.ansi.okstate. edu/breeds/)* provides information about breeds of livestock throughout the world. It is an especially rich source of information on cattle, sheep, goats, horses and swine, but also includes information on buffaloes, camels, donkeys, llamas, yaks, and poultry. For each breed an essay on the use, characteristics, origin, and distribution of the breed has been written by a specialist.

The World Conservation Monitoring Centre has made available the *Endangered Plants and Animals* databases which are used to generate the "Red Lists" of threatened and endangered plants (Europe) and animals (world) at *http://www.wcmc.org.uk:80/species/data/.* In the plants database, one can generate lists of species for specific countries, or search for specific families, species or common names; in addition, one can qualify the search as to the level of endangerment. The animals database has the additional capacity of searching by class or order. For U. S. endangered plants and animals, check the *Endangered Species Program (http://www. fws.gov/~r9endspp/endspp.html),* maintained by the U. S. Fish and Wildlife Service, Division of Endangered Species. This site also provides online access to the *Endangered Species Bulletin* and the *Endangered Species Act.*

For virtually all types of animal-related information (health care, organizations, discussion groups, government regulations, and veterinary education), go to *NetVet Veterinary Resources & The Electronic Zoo (http://netvet.wustl.edu/welcome.htm).* The author, veterinary professor Dr. Ken Boschert, has also collected homepages for nearly every conceivable type and breed of pet! *The Electronic Zoo* includes information on hundreds of animals, from cats and dogs, to invertebrates, rodents and zoo animals.

MISCELLANEOUS SITES

A resource which is not specifically biological, but which is very handy to have available online to look up food regulations, endangered species information, etc., is the *Code of Federal Regulations (http://law.house. gov/cfr.htm)*. Similarly, *GPO Access (http://thorplus.lib.purdue.edu:8100/ gpo/)* is useful for obtaining the full text of the *Federal Register,* Congressional records, bills and reports, or to refer to the *United States Government Manual.*

There are several excellent *unit of measurement converters* available on the Web. For example, see *http://www.mplik.ru/~sg/transl/index.html* or *http://www.eardc.swt.edu/cgi-bin/ucon/ucon.pl.*

Field biologists and holiday-seekers alike will profit from having a look at *L.L. Bean's Parksearch (http://www.llbean.com:80/parksearch/)*. This site not only provides information about park addresses, phone numbers, picnic facilities, campgrounds, visitor centers, and fees for nearly 1,500 parks in the U. S., but fact-filled summaries indicate whether the park has spots for paddling, cross-country skiing, camping, fishing, biking, hunting, hiking, swimming, rock climbing and many other popular outdoor sports and activities. Search by name, activity or state.

BIBLIOGRAPHY

Clark, Kathleen A. "Internet resources for agriculture." *College and Research Library News* 57 (June 1996): 359-363.
Courtois, Martin P. and Alan H. Goslen. "Internet resources in biology." *College and Research Library News* 57 (July/August 1996): 431-435.

Ready Reference Web Sites
in Earth and Physical Sciences

Edward Lener
Flora G. Shrode

SUMMARY. This article presents a selection of web-based reference resources in the earth and physical sciences, focusing in particular on geology, chemistry, physics, astronomy, and weather. Such a compilation is designed to be of use in meeting a wide range of informational needs in these areas. Sites chosen by the authors are those likely to be of broad interest. In addition, most or all of the contents of the resources listed are available for free. *[Article copies available for a fee from The Haworth Document Delivery Service: 1-800-342-9678. E-mail address: getinfo@haworth.com]*

For most scientists, having quick access to current and accurate information is of vital importance in their daily work. The rapidly growing wealth of information available over the Internet can now make it possible for them to fill a substantial amount of these needs electronically. Provided, that is, that they know where to look! As librarians, we have the opportunity to provide a valuable service for our respective user communities by locating resources which meet their informational needs and

Edward Lener is Collegiate Librarian for the Sciences, User Services Department, University Libraries, Virginia Tech, P.O. Box 90001, Blacksburg, VA 24062. Flora G. Shrode is Reference and Collections Coordinator for Science and Technology, Hodges Library, University of Tennessee, Knoxville, TN 37996-1000.

[Haworth co-indexing entry note]: "Ready Reference Web Sites in Earth and Physical Sciences." Lener, Edward and Flora G. Shrode. Co-published simultaneously in *The Reference Librarian* (The Haworth Press, Inc.) No. 57, 1997, pp. 203-213; and: *Reference Sources on the Internet: Off the Shelf and Onto the Web* (ed: Karen R. Diaz) The Haworth Press, Inc., 1997, pp. 203-213. Single or multiple copies of this article are available for a fee from The Haworth Document Delivery Service [1-800-342-9678, 9:00 a.m. - 5:00 p.m. (EST). E-mail address: getinfo@haworth.com].

203

organizing them into a user-friendly format. We should also be willing to take an active role in making our users aware of these resources and, whenever necessary, teach them the skills needed to access them.

There is now such a wide range of information available in electronic form that it would be impossible for any one article to cover all of the many sources in existence except in the narrowest of subject areas. The focus of this article is on selected web-based reference resources likely to be of broad interest in the earth and physical sciences. This includes geology, chemistry, physics, astronomy, and weather. The majority of the sites listed are available for free. While commercial sites are becoming more commonplace on the Internet, it is surprising how much useful information is still available at no cost. Government, of course, has played an important role in this regard as have several of the major professional societies. But many others, including individuals, have continued to make important contributions as well through their efforts to compile and prepare information for digital access.

Any web pages libraries develop will, of course, require periodic maintenance to ensure that links are still current. It is also very helpful to highlight any new resources which have been added. Ideally, pages should contain an e-mail address or other contact information so that users can report any difficulties they encounter or can suggest additional sites. The selection of resources in this article and others in this issue should provide a starting point in developing subject oriented web page(s) for the sciences. General resources for the sciences are listed first, followed by subject specific links. Other collections of links such as *Yahoo! (http://www.yahoo.com/Science/)*, *EI Net Galaxy (http://galaxy.einet.net/galaxy/Science.html)*, or *WWW Virtual Library (http://www.w3.org/pub/DataSources/bySubject/Overview2.html)* can also prove extremely helpful in this regard.

GENERAL SCIENCE RESOURCES

Community of Science
http://cos.gdb.org/

The Community of Science web server maintains several easy-to-search databases about scientific expertise, inventions, and facilities. Most popular, though, may be their database of funding opportunities for scientific research. Please note, however, that some features are available only to member institutions.

Mad Scientist Network
http://medinfo.wustl.edu/~ysp/MSN/

This graphically dynamic site will especially appeal to younger users. Over 300 scientists in a wide range of disciplines have signed up to answer questions related to everything from why the sky is blue to quantum physics. Archive files are organized by subject and are keyword searchable.

Scholarly Societies Project
http://www.lib.uwaterloo.ca/society/overview.html

Professional societies are often one of the best sources for a wide range of subject-specific information. Anyone who has tried to compile a list of sites by discipline will appreciate this wonderful resource available through the University of Waterloo. The page for earth science societies alone contains 83 different links. Also featured are hypertext links to full text serial publications and meeting/conference announcements.

ScienceOnline
http://www.sciencemag.org/science/

The premier journal of the American Association for the Advancement of Science (AAAS) is now available over the web. The site features full-text with graphics of all issues from June 1995 to present with author and subject indexes. Access to the search capability (author, keywords in titles or abstracts, or keywords anywhere) and tables of contents for the current and back issues of *Science* is available at no cost. AAAS members (and those whose institutions are members, including librarians) can have access to the full-text of articles. Everything is arranged in a highly intuitive way, but be aware that load times may be slow.

National Science Foundation
http://www.nsf.gov/

The primary role of the National Science Foundation is to promote the progress of science and engineering. Of particular interest, of course, is their research grants program. Not surprisingly, their web site contains extensive information about the grants which the agency awards and the proposal submission process.

U.S. Environmental Protection Agency
http://www.epa.gov/

The well-designed web site of the Environmental Protection Agency offers resources on regulations, publications, contracts, grants, and fellowships. The section on "You and Your Environment" provides collections of resources oriented to the needs of different user groups from teachers, to scientists, to business and industry.

U.S. Department of Energy
http://www.doe.gov/

Along with lots of press releases, mission statements, and "lessons learned," this site does provides many useful links to all of the major national laboratories and other energy-related facilities across the nation. There is also a searchable bibliographic database of DOE reports from January 1994 to present.

GEOLOGICAL SCIENCES

United States Geological Survey
http://www.usgs.gov/

The United States Geological Survey has recently assumed many of the duties of the former U.S. Bureau of Mines as well as those of the National Biological Service, thereby broadening its role as provider of information in the earth sciences. The main USGS web site contains links on geology, mapping, natural hazards, and water resources.

Geographic Names Information System
http://www-nmd.usgs.gov/www/gnis/

A service of the USGS, this site contains location information on almost two million geographic features in the United States. Each record lists the state, county, and geographic coordinates along with a reference to the topographic map on which the feature appears. When using the database it is interesting to note how often multiple entries share the same name in different regions.

National Earthquake Information Center
http://wwwneic.cr.usgs.gov/

Based in Golden, Colorado the National Earthquake Information Center serves as the major source of information from the USGS on earthquakes and seismicity. Information on recent seismic activity with location maps is conveniently provided as a separate category.

National Geophysical Data Center
http://www.ngdc.noaa.gov/ngdc.html

Part of the Geophysical On-Line Data (GOLD) program, this site provides a wealth of geophysical data on magnetics, gravity, heat flow, marine geology, and solar-terrestrial physics. While much of the information presented is highly technical, the "Science for Society" page provides users with an easy-to-understand interface for links on natural hazards, resource management, climate modeling, ocean mapping, and other agency activities.

Electronic Volcano
http://www.dartmouth.edu/~volcano

Mountains of information are provided here on volcanoes around the world including catalogs and maps of active volcanic sites along with links to related literature.

Mineral Gallery
http://mineral.galleries.com/

While put out by a commercial firm, much of the best information at this site is available for free. Minerals can be searched by name or by class, and entries include both descriptive information and a photograph. There are also several specialized listings of gemstones, birth stones, etc.

UC Museum of Paleontology
http://www.ucmp.berkeley.edu/

Located on the campus of the University of California at Berkeley, the museum has put together an impressive on-line collection of paleontological resources. Particularly interesting are the *"Geological Time Machine"* *(http://www.ucmp.berkeley.edu/help/timeform.html)* which allows you to get an informational overview related to specific geologic time periods and the *"Taxon Web Lift"* *(http://www.ucmp.berkeley.edu/help/taxaform.html)* which allows users to search the exhibits by taxa. (For convenience, both scientific and common names are generally provided.)

CHEMISTRY

ACS ChemCenter
http://www.ChemCenter.org/

This comparatively new site from the American Chemical society serves as a useful starting point for a wide range of chemistry-related information. A number of educational and professional links are provided including information on job opportunities, upcoming conferences, and links to ACS electronic publications. Note that some features may require registration or be available only on a fee basis.

Nobel Prize Winners in Chemistry
http://www.almaz.com/nobel/Chemistry.html

The Nobel Prize Internet Archive offers this useful compilation of prize winners in Chemistry arranged in reverse chronological order going back to 1901. An alphabetical listing is also available.

ChemFinder
http://chemfinder.camsoft.com/

This site makes it much easier to locate information on the Internet about specific chemical compounds. Searching can be done by chemical name, formula, structure, or CAS Registry Number. Sites dealing with a wide range of topics such as toxicology, pesticides, medications, physical property data, and chemical regulations are indexed.

Periodic Table of the Elements
http://www.shef.ac.uk/uni/academic/A-C/chem/web-elements/
web-elements-home.html

Through the power of hypertext links, the familiar periodic table now offers a wealth of information at your fingertips. Clicking on any of the elements brings up a host of detailed information on atomic radii, reduction potentials, and other helpful data.

NIST Chemistry WebBook
http://webbook.nist.gov/

Finding thermodynamic data can often be difficult, especially in a smaller library which may lack some of the familiar printed reference works. The Chemistry WebBook from the National Institute of Standards and Technology helps to get around this problem. It provides data on enthalpy of formation, heat capacity, and entropy complete with literature references for over 5,000 compounds.

Materials Safety Data Sheets (MSDS)
http://www.phys.ksu.edu/~tipping/msds.html

It is essential to have quick access to up-to-date chemical safety information. This site leads to several other web sites which offer MSDS information. Typically, the sites are searchable by chemical name, manufacturer name, and CAS registry number. Often links are provided to MSDS web pages of individual manufacturers as well to other sites featuring chemical hazard information.

ChemConnect
http://www.chemconnect.com/home.htm

This site offers a worldwide directory of chemical manufacturers and distributors. It also features a chemical trading exchange where users may post messages concerning chemicals wanted or available for sale.

Jobs in Chemistry
http://chemistry.mond.org/

In addition to a searchable database of chemistry related jobs, this site from *Chemistry Today* offers an e-mail job alerting service as well as an informative guide to chemistry job hunting on the Internet.

PHYSICS

The Internet Pilot to Physics
http://www.tp.umu.se/TIPTOP/

This massive collection of physics resources serves as an invaluable meta-index to Internet resources in the field. The site links to calendars of conferences, news releases, job announcements, as well as to *Physics Around the World (http://www.physics.mcgill.ca/physics-services/physics_ services.html)*, a searchable guide to physics resources in areas of education, companies, reference tools, institutions and organizations, electronic publications, exhibitions, and more.

NIST Physical Reference Data
http://physics.nist.gov/PhysRefData/contents.html

Databases useful for finding physical constants, units, and conversion factors are provided from this site. *"Fundamental Physical Constants"* *(http://physlab.nist.gov/PhysRefData/codata86/codata86.html)* gives values of the basic constants and conversion factors of physics and chemistry. The *"Fundamental Constants Bibliographic Database"* *(http://physics. nist.gov/PhysRefData/fundconst/html/cover.html)* is a searchable index to publications relevant to the fundamental constants and precision measurement published since the mid 1980s. Some earlier papers of particular interest are also included.

Nobel Prize Winners in Physics
http://www.almaz.com/nobel/physics.html

Like its counterpart for Chemistry, this site from the Nobel Prize Internet Archive offers a useful compilation of prize winners in Physics arranged in reverse chronological order going back to 1901. An alphabetical listing is also available.

Physics Lecture Demonstrations
http://www.mip.berkeley.edu/physics/physics.html

The Lecture Demonstration staff at University of California, Berkeley's Physics Department created this site to provide on-line access to the department's collection of demonstrations available to professors teaching undergraduate physics courses. Demonstrations are described and presented with diagrams teachers can use to carry out the procedures in their own classroom or lab. Some of the items in the database are summaries of films available only to UC Berkeley teachers. The demonstrations are arranged by topical area (mechanics, optics, electricity, and others), and an index is also provided.

LANL E-Print Archive
http://xxx.lanl.gov/

Electronic media, particularly preprints, play an important role in the communication of new ideas in physics. This site from the Los Alamos

National Laboratory provides an automated archive and distribution service for electronic preprints in physics. A thorough help directory is provided and will likely be needed by first time users. Other useful physics preprint archives include the *Stanford Linear Accelerator Center (SLAC)* high energy physics preprint archive *(http://www-spires.slac.stanford. edu./FIND/hep)* and the *CERN preprint server (http://preprints.cern.ch/).*

ASTRONOMY

The Nine Planets
http://seds.lpl.arizona.edu/nineplanets/nineplanets/nineplanets.html

As stated on its opening page, "The Nine Planets is an overview of the history, mythology, and current scientific knowledge of each of the planets and moons in our solar system." It is intended for a general audience with minimal technical background. A glossary provides explanations of many astronomical terms and proper names. Each page has text and images; some have sounds and movies; and most provide references to additional related information.

Astronomy and Space Science on the Internet
http://fly.hiwaay.net/~cwbol/astro.html

A comprehensive Web site which points to all types of astronomy-related resources on the Internet for finding data, software, images, current sky news, and other information about astronomy and astronomers. This site is an excellent example of how individuals who are very knowledgeable about a given field can make significant contributions to the Internet.

AstroWeb: Astronomical Internet Resources
http://www.stsci.edu//net-resources.html

This service was established by the *AstroWeb Consortium (http://fits. cv.nrao.edu/www/astroweb.html)* and is maintained at servers in participating institutions. The AstroWeb database is searchable using a WAIS index at the site. One version of the *AstroWeb* resource list is maintained by the *Space Telescope Science Institute* and is arranged by category *(http://www.stsci.edu/astroweb/astroweb-categories.html),* and is probably the most useful.

NASA SpaceLink
http://spacelink.msfc.nasa.gov/home.index.html

This electronic aeronautics and space resource is designed to provide current educational information to teachers and students throughout the

United States. The site presents an overview and descriptions of NASA's organization and many of its projects. Files containing classroom activity guides and software can be downloaded. Videos and schedules for NASA television are also available. A "Hot Topics" area provides shortcuts to links on items of current interest such as shuttle missions, the international space station, Mars exploration, the Galileo spacecraft, and the Hubble telescope. Also of interest is the *NASA Observatorium (http://observe. ivv.nasa.gov)* which features an entertaining and educational look at selected earth and space data.

WEATHER

NOAA Network Information Center
http://www.nnic.noaa.gov/

The United States National Oceanic and Atmospheric Administration provides access to many of its offices and services from this homepage. The *Netcast* service *(http://netcast.noaa.gov/cgi-bin/page?pg=netcast)* offers weather forecasts for the United States searchable by location name and state, three-letter city codes, or five-digit zip codes.

National Climatic Data Center
http://www.ncdc.noaa.gov/

Claiming to be the world's largest active archive of weather data, this site offers downloadable information and links for climatic and weather data, radar and satellite images, severe weather, NCDC publications and software, global climate, agriculture and weather, and solar data. The site also provides information about and links to the World Data Center A, for Meteorology.

WeatherNet
http://cirrus.sprl.umich.edu/wxnet/

Developed by the Weather Underground at the University of Michigan, this site offers links to over 250 weather-related sites for WWW, FTP, Gopher, Telnet, and newsgroups along with forecasts, images, weather statistics, and radio and television weather services.

Lighthouse
http://the-tech.mit.edu/Weather/

Also from the University of Michigan's Weather Underground, Lighthouse offers National Weather Service information searchable by region, city name, and airport code. Travel weather conditions from around the world are available as are regional weather images.

WEATHER from CNN Interactive
http://www.cnn.com/WEATHER

This site is especially useful for weather information outside of the United States. Temperature, forecast, and satellite maps are organized by continent. Top weather news stories are presented, and weather information is updated every twelve hours.

The Old Farmer's Almanac
http://www.almanac.com/index.html

Like the familiar print source, one primary feature of the web site is weather forecasts. Long-range forecasts are available for regions of the U.S. and Canada. Five-day forecasts are available for 800 cities in the U.S. and around the world. Weather predictions provided at this site are determined using a secret formula devised in 1792 by Robert B. Thomas, founder of the Almanac, together with calculations based on scientific information about solar activity, sunspot cycles, and weather records.

Health and Medicine

Eric H. Schnell

SUMMARY. The Internet provides librarians with unprecedented access to time sensitive informational resources. The time critical nature of many health and medicine reference requests makes such access important to the health practitioner, educator, researcher, and the consumer. This paper then provides an annotated listing of various Internet sites, many that are starting points for exploration of specific health subject areas. Special considerations for locating and selecting health and medicine resources are also provided. *[Article copies available for a fee from The Haworth Document Delivery Service: 1-800-342-9678. E-mail address: getinfo@haworth.com]*

Librarians responding to health and medical reference questions often rely upon using materials that, because of publication lag, are outdated. In other disciplines this lag time is not as much as a concern, however, the urgent and frequently critical nature of many medically oriented reference questions require current information delivered in a timely manner. The Internet can provide librarians with unprecedented access to time sensitive information. With this unprecedented availability of health and medicine resources through the Internet, librarians must begin to think about using Internet resources on a regular basis when answering reference questions.

Reference resources now exist which are of interest to the health practitioner, educator, researcher, and the consumer. The content of these mate-

Eric H. Schnell is Head, Automation Services, Prior Health Sciences Library, The Ohio State University, 376 W. 10th Avenue, Columbus, OH 43210. E-mail: schnell.9@osu.edu

[Haworth co-indexing entry note]: "Health and Medicine." Schnell, Eric H. Co-published simultaneously in *The Reference Librarian* (The Haworth Press, Inc.) No. 57, 1997, pp. 215-222; and: *Reference Sources on the Internet: Off the Shelf and Onto the Web* (ed: Karen R. Diaz) The Haworth Press, Inc., 1997, pp. 215-222. Single or multiple copies of this article are available for a fee from The Haworth Document Delivery Service [1-800-342-9678, 9:00 a.m. - 5:00 p.m. (EST). E-mail address: getinfo@haworth.com].

rials includes clinical practice guidelines, radiology images, grant data-bases, and treatment options. This paper then provides an annotated listing of various Internet sites, many that are starting points for exploration of specific health subject areas. It begins by providing special considerations that need to be kept in mind when locating and selecting health and medicine resources. The resources listed are divided into four sections, each containing a brief introductory paragraph. Finally, when this paper mentions the Internet it is really referring to the World Wide Web. The Web has become the most popular method of accessing and viewing Internet resources.

SPECIAL CONSIDERATIONS

The nature of health information requests requires the librarian to be critical when selecting Internet resources to present to patrons. In many ways, the process of selecting Internet resources is no different from traditional print resources. Criteria such as quality of content, appropriate-ness, and authority still applies. When selecting health oriented resources on the Internet it is particularly important to look at the source of the document. Keep in mind that anyone with access to the Internet can publish a resource and make it look authoritative. Is the resource published by a reputable individual or organization? Is the author a physician or undergraduate student? Does the organization providing the resource have any known bias that could influence the information?

Most of the health and medicine resources currently available are de-veloped and maintained by private organizations, educational institutions, government agencies, and individuals. Although the number of electronic resources continues to grow, few traditional ready reference materials are being developed by publishers for access on the Internet. Many publishers will not be making resources available until they develop new models to recover the costs associated with resource development. Even then, most traditional biomedically oriented reference resources will likely become available only on a paid subscription or pay-per-use basis. Librarians must keep these resources in mind when developing and allocating their ac-quisitions budgets.

As with any subject or discipline, the novice Internet health sciences librarian may feel locating useful resources can be a frustrating task. The first place to begin a search is by using a search index or directory listing. However, keep in mind that searching for unknown resources in this manner can often be hit or miss. The best strategy to use when using indexes and directories is to use more obscure terms rather than more general or generic ones. For example, using "Zollinger-Ellison Syndrome" will yield more specific results than searching for the general "endocrine tumors." When looking for a concept that is very obscure try to use as many terms, synonyms, and word combinations the search field will allow.

Finally, the fastest growing area of health information on the Internet is the availability of multimedia-based resources. Since most health and medicine disciplines have a visual orientation, the Internet makes an excellent medium for distributing media information to patrons. Soon, the best resources in health and medicine will utilize the Internet's multimedia potential. Librarians selecting such resources need to use criteria and techniques more often used by media librarians rather than those used for selecting traditional print materials.

META DIRECTORIES

The large number of health and medicine subject areas is making it increasingly difficult for any single list to index all possible materials. To make health and medicine resources easier to locate, there are a growing number of sites that have organized resources utilizing a variety of strategies and methods. These sites, often called meta directories, have pre-selected Internet resources and sites based on an established criterion. Meta Directories help to weed out materials that have content useful for answering reference questions.

Hardin Meta Directory of Internet Health Sources
[http://www.arcade.uiowa.edu/hardin-www/md.html]

This site provides pointers to the most complete and frequently cited resource lists. It does not list specific resources. This meta directory is organized using an alphabetical listing of 35 subject areas and can also be searched using a comprehensive site index. Also referred to as Hardin MD, this directory listing is maintained at the Hardin Health Sciences Library at the University of Iowa.

HealthWeb [http://hsinfo.ghsl.nwu.edu/healthweb/]

This resource list is a project developed by the health sciences libraries of the Universities that make up the Big Ten Athletic Conference. Each library involved with HealthWeb has been assigned a small number of subject areas they are responsible for maintaining. All resources added to HealthWeb are reviewed by a librarian, annotated, and organized depending on the discipline.

Medical Matrix: A Guide to Internet Clinical Medicine Resources *[http://www.slackinc.com/matrix/]*

Initially, this guide was a text file distributed using FTP and required printing before the librarian could look up a resource. The Web-based version is much more practical to use and is updated continuously. All the resources listed are selected, ranked, peer-reviewed, and annotated. The content includes full-text patient care resources, medical news, electronic journals, and continuing medical education resources.

READY REFERENCE

The number of sites considered to be ready reference is almost unlimited. In essence, the entire Internet can be viewed as a ready reference collection. Standard reference resources such as online phone directories, dictionaries, and encyclopedias are available. Unfortunately, many standard reference resources will most likely appear on the Internet only on a subscription basis.

AMA Physician Select *[http://www.ama-assn.org/cgi-bin/aps-redir/]*

This resource is compiled and published by the American Medical Association (AMA) as a source of demographic and professional information on individual physicians in the United States. Providing demographic and professional information, it is intended to allow patrons quick access to information on physicians treating themselves or their families.

ICD-9 *[http://www-informatics.ucdmc.ucdavis.edu/icd9/refs.htm]*

This is an online version of the medical coding utility the International Classification of Diseases, 9th edition. In addition to the ICD-9 codes, this resource also includes V-codes and DRG codes. This version can be searched either by using keywords of the code description or by a code number.

The Merck Manual of Diagnosis and Therapy
[http://www.merck.com/!!rIkrg3k5NrIkrg3k5N/pubs/mmanual/]

The Merck Manual is one of the most widely used medical texts in the world. Written by over 300 experts, it covers all but the most obscure disorders. It describes symptoms, common clinical procedures, laboratory tests, and virtually all the disorders that a general internist might encounter. Current therapy is presented for each disorder. The online version of the Manual is the sixteenth edition from 1992.

FEDERAL GOVERNMENT

Information generated by the federal government has become readily available on the Internet. Resources such as the text of recent health care legislation can be accessed hours after passage. Many government compiled health statistics are published first on the Internet and then distributed on paper. This immediate access to timely government information is critical to the health care professional. Knowing how to locate it on the Internet is important for the health sciences librarian.

Center for Disease Control and Prevention (CDC)
[http://www.cdc.gov/]

The CDC provides access to information relating to infectious diseases, health risks, and prevention guidelines. This site also includes online access to several CDC publications including *Emerging Infectious Diseases* and the *Morbidity and Morality Weekly Report*. It provides connectivity to 11 centers, institutes and offices including The National Center for Health Statistics.

GPO Gate
[http://www.gpo.ucop.edu/]

GPO Gate is designed to provide easy access to laws, regulations, reports, and other data provided through GPO Access. GPO Access is a group of databases containing the full text of selected information published by the United States Government. Among the resources available are the Federal Register, the Congressional Record, Congressional Bills, United States Code, Economic Indicators and GAO Reports.

National Institutes of Health (NIH)
[http://www.nih.gov]

In addition to providing access to all the Institutes and Offices, this site contains a selection of some NIH health resources such as CancerNet, AIDS information, clinical alerts, and the Women's Health Initiative. This resource contains grant and contract information on NIH's extramural research and training programs including NIH's funding opportunities, grant policy, on-line library catalogs and journals. It also contains research training information, NIH research labs, and computer and network support for NIH scientists.

National Library of Medicine (NLM)
[http://www.nlm.nih.gov]

NLM provides access to over 40 databases, including Internet access to Medline for those with Grateful Med accounts, through this Web site. Online versions of all NLM publications including fact sheets, reports, ordering information are available. Access is provided to the various NLM research programs such as the Lister Hill National Center for Biomedical Communications and National Center for Biotechnology Information (GenBank).

CLINICAL AND EDUCATIONAL RESOURCES

The number of resources on the Internet used as reference resources in a clinical setting and for education is growing every day. Most of the resources of interest to the clinician have been developed by research institutes, organizations which have obtained grant support, or the federal government itself. Many of the educational resources have been developed by educators for use in courses they are teaching. The following is a small sample of the types of clinical and educational resources available on the Internet.

CancerNet and the Physician's Data Query (PDQ)
[http://wwwicic.nci.nih.gov]

Updated monthly, the National Cancer Institute's (NCI) CancerNet provides access to the most current information on cancer. Information statements from NCI's Physician's Data Query (PDQ) comprehensive cancer database contains peer-reviewed statements on treatment, supportive care, screening, and prevention. PDQ also includes a registry of clinical trials from around the world. All of the information on CancerNet is continually reviewed and revised by oncology experts and is based on the latest research in the field.

National Center for Biotechnology Information
[http://www.ncbi.nlm.nih.gov/]

The National Center for Biotechnology Information (NCBI) provides access to many research databases which are of interest to the clinical researcher. Databases available from this site include Entrez, GenBank, and the Human Genome Project. Access to the *Online Mendelian Inheritance in Man,* a catalog of human genes and genetic disorders which contains textual information, pictures, and other reference resources are also available.

OncoLink
[http://cancer.med.upenn.edu/]

The primary goal of this resource is to disseminate information relevant to the field of oncology and the rapid collection of information pertinent to the specialty. In addition, the intent of Oncolink is to educate health care personnel, patients, and families. All the resources and research published on OncoLink are peer-reviewed by an editorial board.

The Virtual Hospital
[http://indy.radiology.uiowa.edu/VirtualHospital.html]

The Virtual Hospital is a very extensive site offering information for patients, health care providers, educators, and librarians. It provides extensive coverage of health related subjects. This site is being developed by the Electric Differential Multimedia Laboratory, Department of Radiology, University of Iowa College of Medicine, using an award from the National Library of Medicine.

The Visible Human Project
[http://www.nlm.nih.gov/research/visible/visible_human.html]

This site contains anatomically detailed, three-dimensional representations of the male and female human body including transverse CAT, MRI and cryosection images at one millimeter intervals. The Male data set consists of 1,871 images and is 15 gigabytes in size. The Visible Human Female data set has the same characteristics as the male cadaver with one exception. The anatomical images were scanned at 0.33 mm intervals instead of one mm intervals. This has resulted in over 5,000 anatomical images and about 40 gigabytes in size. All the images and data can be repurposed for educational uses.

Reference on the Internet:
Environment

Bruce Weaver

SUMMARY. This article presents a selective annotated list of environment-related websites for reference use. The term "environment" has been considered both broadly and traditionally in compiling this list of useful content-based and linking sites. *[Article copies available for a fee from The Haworth Document Delivery Service: 1-800-342-9678. E-mail address: getinfo@haworth.com]*

I encountered one of my favorite reference questions of my library career as an Undergraduate Librarian at The Ohio State University. More plea for help than a question, it sounded something like this: "I have to do a paper on the environment, but you don't have anything about it!" My response was that the broad topic "environment" might require a bit of focus, but that after focusing the topic, we'd be able to tap the large amount of environmental information available in nearly any collection.

As vast as the topic "environment" is, I've attempted in this article to cover it in its broadest sense–the same sense a student needing to write a paper of the environment would have. It's a large topic on the internet, and I've tried to identify the broadest and most useful reference sites for environmental inquiries. The most effective sites for this broad topic tend to be lists of links instead of content-based sites.

Bruce Weaver is Reference Librarian, Eisenhower National Clearinghouse for Mathematics and Science Education in Columbus, OH. He has previously served as a reference and undergraduate librarian at The Ohio State University. E-mail: bweaver@enc.org

[Haworth co-indexing entry note]: "Reference on the Internet: Environment." Weaver, Bruce. Co-published simultaneously in *The Reference Librarian* (The Haworth Press, Inc.) No. 57, 1997, pp. 223-226; and: *Reference Sources on the Internet: Off the Shelf and Onto the Web* (ed: Karen R. Diaz) The Haworth Press, Inc., 1997, pp. 223-226. Single or multiple copies of this article are available for a fee from The Haworth Document Delivery Service [1-800-342-9678, 9:00 a.m. - 5:00 p.m. (EST). E-mail address: getinfo@haworth.com].

Entries are organized into three groups: the current cream of the crop; environment indexes/links (sites that link to others); and work sites (sites higher in content with fewer links). Because all websites include both content and links, degree of content vs. links was my criteria in placing a site in the "exploration" or "work" categories. Cream of the crop sites are those which I'd regret doing without for environmental reference on the Internet.

CREAM OF THE CROP

U.S. Environmental Protection Agency [http://www.epa.gov/]. This content-intensive site links to Envirofacts, Enviroene, and a prodigious amount of U.S. Government environmental information. Its initial page appears deceptively simple, in fact much mousing-around is required to become comfortable at this site. Its breadth of coverage merits inclusion as a best site, but be warned that current investigation and financial data will not be included.

Envirolink [http://www.envirolink.org/]. Envirolink opens with a pre-home page that allows selection of "more" or "less" graphics. Advertising itself as " the largest online environmental information resource on the planet," it is one of the premier environmental sites on the web. Envirolink has garnered 24 awards as of this writing. Home page links include the Envirolink Library, the One World magazine site, Environews, and a site search engine. The site's large size and scope require many layers of navigation, but if an environmentalist could choose only one link, this might be it.

Enviroene [http://es.inel.gov/]. Part of the EPA's home page, this site deserves its own mention because of its ease of use in leading to government documents and newsletters. Links to the Federal Register, Executive orders, and articles about new laws effecting various groups are easy to find at this site.

Ecoweb [http://ecosys.drdr.virginia.edu/EcoWeb.html]. EcoWeb has been honored with 5 awards including Magellan 3-star and Point top 5%. Its "exploration" links lead to many sites of interests to activists. EcoWeb was also featured in the June 1996 *E!* Magazine.

Environmental Sites on the Internet [http://www.lib.kth.se/~lg/envsite. htm]. This site announces on its opening page "In June 1996 selected as The Best Comprehensive Environmental Directory, by CESSE (Centre for Economic and Social Studies for the Environment), Brussels, Belgium." International in scope, this site's best feature is an easily-viewed and searchable alphabetic index to topical sites. Index entries are as general as

"Environmental Information Sources" or "Local Environment" and as specific as "Oestrogenic Chemicals" or "Electric Vehicles."

WWW Virtual Library Environment [http://ecosys.drdr.virginia.edu/ Environment.html]. According to the page, "the Virtual Library–Environment page has also been recognized as one of Awesome Universal t@p 500 Web Sites." Its "List O' Lists" is both comprehensive and searchable.

The Virtual Library of Ecology, Biodiversity, and the Environment [http://conbio.rice.edu/vl/] is a very easy-to-use and well-organized site. A hierarchical one-page topic list provides an excellent snapshot of the site's coverage. A "browse links" option provides a list of links organized by topic. This site provides links to endangered species, habitat, sustainability, pollution, and human population sites.

ENVIRONMENT INDEXES/LINKS

List of WWW Sites of Interest to Ecologists [http://www.biol.uregina. ca/liu/bio/Ecology.html] is a North American mirror of *[http://biomserv. univ-lyon1.fr/Ecology-WWW.html].* Organized alphabetically by title of link, this list of hundreds of ecology-related links is regularly updated. Utility is limited by its lack of subject organization, but it offers a wealth of current links. Its strength lies in its number of links, not ease of use.

Magellan Environment Directory [http://www.mckinley.com/browse_ bd.cgi?Environment] provides a reviewed list, by topic, of environmental sites. The topic links Activism, Alternative Energy, Career & Employment, Conservation & Ecology, Habitats & Wildlife, Law & Policy, Miscellaneous, News, Organizations, Pollution, Recycling & Waste, and Resources all provide lists of Magellan-reviewed sites from 4-star to no-star order.

Infoseek Guide [http://guide.infoseek.com/Science/Environment?tid= 1378&sv=N3]. Infoseek's guide to the Internet links 25 topics (as of this writing) to a plethora of environmental sources. "Soil Erosion" provides 195 links, "Watchdog groups" leads to a geographic list, the "North America" section providing 17 links. A good place for explore links to broad topics or to refine a question.

Yanoff's List Environment [http://www.spectracom.com/islist/index.html# ENVIRONMENT] provides links to EcoNet, EcoWeb, EE-Link, Environment Virtual Library, EnviroWeb, Environmental Science & Engineering, and the Natural Resources Defense Council.

My Virtual Reference Desk ENVIRONMENT search [http://www.refdesk. com/cgi-bin/refsrch.cgi/search/me?environment]. This URL executes a search for the word "environment" at one of this author's favorite reference sites,

My Virtual Reference Desk (MVRD). As of this writing, it returned links to 24 sites, including EnviroWeb, EcoWeb, Planet Earth, U.S. Environmental Protection Agency, The Earth Times (international online environmental newspaper) and The New Environmentalist (online newsletter).

Yahoo! Society and Culture Environment and Nature directory [http:// www.yahoo.com/society_and_culture/environment_and_nature/index.html]. This Yahoo! index can be slow, but is a very easy-to-use guide to internet environmental resources. Index entries are not rated. A "Today's News" section provides current news stories by topic from multiple sources.

MVRD Environment and Nature [http://www.refdesk.com/nature.html]. This second listing for the MVRD site is for the "Environment and Nature" section, not the search engine previously listed. While the links offered include some duplication, the high level of overall utility of this site merits a second mention. Listed links include some of the URLs mentioned in this article.

WORK SITES: SITES TO DIG INTO

EcoMall [http://www.ecomall.com/] is an excellent site with links to investments, news, restaurants, renewable, solar, quotes, and activism. Truly a mall in the for-profit sense, EcoMall is both an excellent directory of product information as well as a link to non-profit sites.

IDG EcoNet [http://www.igc.org/igc/econet/] includes links to environmental jobs, current news stories, very current issue coverage by topic, action alerts, and a link to The Frugal Living Pages. Activists would find this site quite useful.

Solstice [http://solstice.crest.org/] is a sustainable living, energy efficiency, and renewable energy site. A hybrid non-profit/for profit site, Solstice provides a good starting point for sustainable living and energy topics.

Welcome to EnviroFacts [http://www.epa.gov/enviro/html/ef_home.html] offers a wealth of searchable EPA databases. Because of its excellent link to related websites, this site is a good first stop for environmental information. Like Enviroene, sensitive current investigation and financial data is not included.

Index

"A Business Researcher's Interests" (http://www.brint.com), 87

A Celebration of Women Writers (http://www.cs.cmu.edu/People/mmbt/women/writers.html), 156

A Guide to Job Resources by US Region (http://www.wm.edu/csrv/career/stualum/jregion.html), 25

Academic Position Network (http://www.umn.edu/apn/), 22

Access Excellence (http://www.gene.com/ae/), 199-200

ACS ChemCenter (http://www.ChemCenter.org/), 208

ADAM (Art Design Architecture and Media; http://adam.ac.uk), 151

Administration on Aging and the Aging Network (http://www.aoa.dhhs.gov/aoa/pages/aoa.html), 72

Adobe Acrobat Reader (http://www.adobe.com/prodindex/acrobat/readstep.html), 142

Advertising, sold by WWW search tools, 6

Advertising sites, 90

AffActWeb: the American Association for Affirmative Action (http://www.fga.com/aaaa/), 120

Affirmative action site, 120

AFP Sports International (http://www.afp.com/sportsreport/), 188

African American and African studies, gay/lesbian/bisexual resources, 106-107

African American and African studies sites, 99-102

African Studies WWW (http://www.sas.upenn.edu/African_Studies/AS.html), 164

African Studies WWW (http://www.sas.upenn.edu/African_studies/AS.html), 99

African Studies WWW (U. Penn; http://www.sas.upenn.edu/African_Studies/AS.html), 54

African Web Links: An Annotated Resource List (http://www.sas.upenn.edu/African_Studies/Home_Page/WWW_Links.html), 100-101

AgDB: Agriculture-Related Information Systems, Databases, and Datasets (http://www.agnic.org/agdb/erdcalfr.html), 197

Agent, defined, 8

agref@nalusda.gov.purdue.edu, 197

Agribusiness, 90-91

AGRICOLA (http://www.nal.usda.gov/isis/), 196

Agricultural Economics Virtual Library (http://www.ttu.edu/~aecovl/), 90-91

Agriculture sites, 197-198

Agrigator (http://www.ifas.ufl.edu/www/agator/htm/ag.htm), 198

AIA Firms on the Web (http://www.aia.org/archwww.htm), 148

Alcoholism, sites for, 73

All-Movie Guide: An Online Film and Video Database (http://205.

186.189.2/amg/movie_Root.
html), 183
AllPolitics (http://www.allpolitics.
com), 117
AllPolitics: Vote 96 (http://allpolitics.
com/elections/), 114-115
AltaVista (http://www.altavista.com),
9-10,11f
AMA Physician Select (http://
www.ama-assn.org/cgi-bin/
aps-redir/), 218-219
Amazing Environmental
Organization Directory
(http://www.webdirectory.
com/), 120
Amazon (http://amazon.com), 196
Amazon.com Books! Earth's Biggest
Bookstore (http://www.
amazon.com), 180
American and British History (http://
www.libraries.rutgers.edu/
rulib/socsci/hist/amhist.
html), 177
American Business Information, Inc.
(http://www.abii.com),
89-90
American Civil Liberties Union:
Immigrants' Rights (http://
www.aclu.org/issues/
immigrant/hmir.html), 121
American Civil Liberties Union:
Religious Freedom (http://
www.aclu.org/issues/
religion/hmrf.html), 122
American Economics Association
Directory (http://www.eco.
utexas.edu/AEA), 136
American Historical Association
(http://web.gmu.edu/chnm/
aha/), 175
American Institute of Architects'
ProFile (http://profile.
cmdonl.com/aia/search.
html), 148
American Psychological Society

(http://psych.hanover.edu/
aps/), 64
American Society of Landscape
Architects (http://www.asla.
org/asla/nonmembers/
accredited_programs.html),
150
American Stock Exchange (http://
www.amex.com), 80
American Studies Dissertations,
1986-1995 (http://www.
georgetown.edu/crossroads/
dis), 171-172
American Studies Web (http://www.
georgetown.edu/crossroads/
asw/), 177
American Type Culture Collection
(ATCC) (http://www.atcc.
org/), 195
American Verse Project (http://www.
hti.umich.edu/english/
amverse/), 157
America's Job Bank (http://www.ajb.
dni.us/), 22
Annotated Bibliography on Straw
Bale Construction (http://
www.xmission.com/~shea/
straw/anbib.html), 150
archInform (http://www.
archINFORM.de), 151
Architecture and Building: Net
Resources (http://www.
nscee.edu/unlv/Libraries/
arch/rsrce/webrsrce/index.
html), 147
Architecture sites, 147-151
bibliographical databases, 149-150
biographical information, 148-149
databases of buildings, 151
directories, 148-149
education, 150
product information, 150-151
search engines, 151
Argos search engine (http://argos.
evansville.edu), 7

Argus Clearinghouse (http://www.
   clearinghouse.net), 17
ArtsInfo's Performing Arts Links
   (http://205.187.62.122:80/
   artslists/), 143
Asian American Resources (http://
   www.mit.edu/afs/athena.
   mit.edu/user/i/r/irie/www/
   aar.html), 102
Asian and Asian American studies
   sites, 102-103
Asian Studies WWW Virtual Library
   (http://coombs.anu.edu.au/
   WWWVL-AsianStudies.
   html), 54
Asian Studies WWW Virtual Library
   (http://coombs.anu.edu.au/
   WWWVL-AsianStudies.
   html), 103
Asian Studies WWW Virtual
   Library, The Internet Guide
   to Asian Studies (http://
   coombs.anu.edu.au/
   WWWVL-AsianStudies.
   html), 164
Ask ERIC (http://ericir.syr.edu/),
   57-58
Association of Southeast Asian
   Nations (http://www.asean.
   or.id/), 54
Astronomy and Space Science on the
   Internet (http://fly.hiwaay.
   net/~cwbol/astro.html), 211
Astronomy sites, 211-212
AstroWeb: Astronomical Internet
   Resources (http://www.
   stsci.edu/net-resources.
   html), 211
AstroWeb Consortium (http://fits.cv.
   nrao.edu/www/astroweb.
   html), 211
ATCG Molecular Biology Suppliers'
   Vendor Catalog (http://
   www.atcg.com/comppage/
   comppage.htm), 195

AT&T Business Network (http://
   www.bnet.att.com), 86-87
Author information and criticism
   site, 156-157
Avery Index to Architectural
   Periodicals (http://www.
   ahip.getty.edu/aka/aka_
   form_pub.html), 149

Bartley, C., 75
Basic Facts About Patents and Basic
   Facts About Registering a
   Trademark, 46
Best Jobs U.S.A. (http://www.
   bestjobsusa.com/), 27-28
Best Jobs U.S.A. (http://www.
   bestjobsusa.com/), 23
BetaCyte (http://www.betacyte.
   pair.com/journals.html),
   195-196
BibEc (http://netec.mcc.ac.uk/BibEc.
   html), 135
Big Yellow (http://s18.bigyellow.
   com), 89
Billboard Online Charts (http://www.
   billboard-online.com/
   charts/), 143
Biochemistry sites, 198-199
Biography (http://www.biography.
   com/), 176
Biology Societies and Organizations
   (http://golgi.harvard.edu/
   afagen/depts/orgs.html),
   195
Biology Web Server (CSU BioWeb;
   http://arnica.csustan.edu/
   index.html), 192-193
BIOSCI/bionet Web (http://www.bio.
   net/), 197
Bisexual/gay/lesbian sites, 106-107
Black/African Related Resources
   (Art McGee's List; http://
   www.sas.upenn.edu/African_
   Studies/Home_Page/mcgee.
   html), 100

Blue Web'n Applications Library
  (http://www.kn.pacbell.com/
  wired/bluewebn/), 59-60
Bonds, 82-83
Bonds Online (http://www.bonds-
  online.com), 82-83
Book review sites, 180-181
Book sites, 180-181
BookWire: The First Place to Look
  for Book Information
  (http://www.bookwire.
  com), 180-181
Brewer's Dictionary of Phrase and
  Fable (http://www.
  bibliomania.com/Reference/
  PhraseAndFable/), 158
Brief Guide to Theatre and
  Performance Studies (http://
  www.stetson.edu/~csata/
  thr_guid.html), 145
Brown, D.K., 159
BUBL WWW Subject Tree:
  Language, Literature, and
  Linguistics (http://www.
  bubl.bath.ac.uk/BUBL/
  Literature.html), 153-154
BuildingOnline (http://
  buildingonline.com/
  blsearch.shtml), 151
Bureau of Labor Statistics (BLS),
  links to, 36
Buros Institute of Mental Measure-
  ments (http://www.unl.edu/
  buros/home.html), 66
Business and Economics Numeric
  Data (http://www.clark.net/
  pub/lschank/web/ecostats.
  html), 129
Business schools, 92
Business sites, 85-92
  nonprofit, 92

Campaign finance, 116
Campaign sites, 114-116

CancerNet and the Physician's Data
  Query (PDQ;http://
  wwwicic.nci.nih.gov),
  220-221
Candidates sites, 114-116
Career magazine (http://www.
  careermag.com/), 23-24
Career Mosaic (http://www.
  careermosaic.com/cm), 24
Career sites, 21-30
  career fairs, 27-28
  indexes, 22-27
  megalists, 29-30
  newsgroups, 30
  relocation services, 29
  resume services, 29
CareerPath (http://www.careerpath.
  com/), 23
Catapult (http://www.jobweb.org/
  catapult/catapult.htm), 24
CBS News: Campaign '96 (http://
  www.cbsnews.com/
  campaign96/home/), 115
CBS Sports (http://www.cbs.com/
  sports), 189
Celebrity sites, 181-182
Census Bureau (http://www.census.
  gov/), 129-130
Center for Disease control and
  Prevention (CDC; http://
  www.cdc.gov/), 219
Central Intelligence Agency (CIA;
  http://www.odci.gov/cia), 38
CETH Directory of Electronic Text
  Centers (http://www.ceth.
  rutgers.edu/info/ectrdir.
  html), 156
Chamber Mall (http://www.
  uschamber.org/mall), 90
Chambers of commerce, 90
ChemConnect (http://www.
  chemconnect.com/home.
  htm), 209
ChemFinder (http://chemfinder.
  camsoft.com/), 208

Chemistry sites, 208-209
Chicago Board of Trade (http://www.
cbot.com), 81
Chicano! (http://www.pbs.org/
chicano/), 103
Child & Adolescent Development:
Mental Health Net (http://
cmhcsys.com/guide/pro03.
htm), 72
Children's literature sites, 159
Children's Literature Web Guide
(http://www.ucalgary.ca/
~dkbrown/index.html), 159
Children's Literature Web Guide:
Folklore, Myth and Legend
(http://www.ucalgary.ca/
~dkbrown/storfolk.html),
158
Christian Resources on the Web
(http://www.students.uiuc.
edu/~s-schim/christian/
christian.html), 122
Christian Resources on the Web:
Christian Life: Sexuality
(http://www.students.uiuc.
edu/~s-schim/christian/life.
html#sex), 121
CIBER (Center for International
Business Education and
Research; http://ciber.bus.
msu.edu/busres.htm), 94
Cinemachine: The Movie Review
Search Engine (http://www.
cinemachine.com), 183
Cinema/film sites, 144-145
Cinemedia (http://ptd15.afionline.
org/CineMedia/), 144
CineMedia: The Internet's Largest
Film and Media Directory
(http://ptd15.afionline.org/
CineMedia), 183-184
CineWEB (http://www.cineweb.
com/), 145
Civil War Soldiers and Sailors
System (CWSS; http://

www.itd.nps.gov/cwss/),
175-176
Clamen's Movie Information
Collection (http://www.cs.
cmu.edu/Unofficial/Movies/
README.html), 144-145
Classical Net Home Page (http://
www.classical.net/music/),
143
CLIO catalog (telnet://columbianet.
columbia.edu), 149
CLNet HomePage (http://clnet.
ucr.edu), 103-104
CMH U.S. Army Center of Military
History (http://160.147.68.
21:80/cmh-pg/), 177-178
Code of Federal Regulations (http://
law.house.gov/cfr.htm), 202
Cognitive and Psychological Science
on the Internet (http://www-
psych.stanford.edu/cogsci/),
67
Colby's Competition Central
(http://www.danceronline.
com/competition/
competition.html), 143-144
College and University Home
Pages–Alphabetical Listing
(http://www.mit. edu:8001/
people/cdemello/
univ.html), 61
College and University Home Pages–
Geographic Listing (http://
www.mit.edu:8001/people/
cdemello/geog.html), 61
College Board Online (http://www.
collegeboard.org/), 58-59
Colleges, hotlist directories on, 61
Commercial sites, 2-3
Community of Science (http://cos.
gdb.org), 200
Community of Science (http://cos.
gdb.org/), 204
Community organizing/activism,
sites for, 73-74

Company directories and
   homepages, 87-88
Company information sites, 85-92
   agribusiness, 90-91
   business schools, 92
   chambers of commerce, 90
   company directories and
      homepages, 87-88
   cost of living, 92
   definitions, 87
   government, 91-92
   marketing and advertising, 90
   meta-sites, 86-87
   nonprofit business, 92
   telephone directories, 89-90
Complete Works of William
   Shakespeare (http://the-
   tech.mit.edu/Shakespeare/
   works.html), 146
Congressional Quarterly Vote Watch
   (http://pathfinder.com/CQ/),
   117-118
Consulate sites, 95
Consumer market, general, served by
   World Wide Web (WWW)
   search toolsYellow Pages
   model, 6-7
Consumer Price Index (Bureau of
   Labor Statistics; http://
   stats.bls.gov/cg-bin/
   surveymost?cu), 130
Contemporary American Poetry
   Archive (http://shain.lib.
   conncoll.edu/CAPA/capa.
   html), 157
Cool Works (http://www.coolworks.
   com/showme/), 24
Cost of living sites, 92
Country information, 53
Country studies (http://lcweb2.locgov/
   frd/cs/cshome.html), 53
County and City Data Books (1988
   and 1994; http://www.lib.
   virginia.edu/socsci/ccdb),
   130

CPI Calculation Machine (Federal
   Reserve Bank of
   Minneapolis; http://woodrow.
   mpls.frb.fed.us/economy/
   calc/cpihome.html), 130
Crawler, defined, 8
Crime and victimization, sites for, 74
Crummell, A., 102
Currency converter site (http://
   www.olsen.ch/cgi-bin/
   exmenu), 96
Current Consumer Price Data–News
   Releases (Bureau of Labor
   Statistics; http://stats.bls.
   gov/news/release/cpi.toc.
   htm), 130
Current Index to Journals in
   Education (CIJE), 56

Dance Links (http://www.dancer.
   com/dance-links/), 143
Dance sites, 143-144
DancePages (http://www.ens-lyon.fr/
   ~esouche/danse/dance.html),
   143
Dancin on the WEB (http://artswire.
   org/Artswire/www/dance/
   browse.html), 143
DAX (http://www.exchange.de/fwb/
   indices.html), 81
Dead Presidents (http://www.csn.net/
   ~mhand/Presidents/), 176
Decisions of the United States
   Supreme Court: A Service
   of the Legal Information
   Institute, Cornell
   (http://www.law.cornell.
   edu/supct/), 41
DejaNews (http://www.dejanews.
   com/forms/dnq.html), 30
DeMello, C., 56
Democratic Party Online (http://
   www.democrats.org), 114
Department of Agriculture (http://
   www.usda.gov), 34

Department of Commerce (http://
www.doc.gov), 34
Department of Defense (http://www.
dtic.dla.mil/defenselink),
34-35
Department of Education (http://
www.ed.gov), 35
Department of Education (http://
www.ed.gov/), 57-58
Department of Energy (http://www.
doe.gov), 35
Department of Health and Human
Services (http://www.os.
dhhs.gov), 35
Department of Housing and Urban
Development (http://www.
hud.gov), 35-36
Department of Justice (http://www.
usdoj.gov), 36
Department of Labor (http://www.
dol.gov), 36
Department of State (http://www.
state.gov), 37
Department of the Interior (http://
www.doi.gov), 36
Department of the Treasury (http://
www.ustreas.gov), 37
Department of Transportation (http://
www.dot.gov), 37
Department of Veterans Affairs
(http://www.va.gov), 37
Dictionaries, Thesauri, and
Acronyms (http://thorplus.
lib.purdue.edu/reference/
dict.html), 155
Dictionaries and Translators (http://
rivendel.com/~ric/resources/
dictionary.html), 155
Dictionary of Cell Biology (http://
www.mblab.gla.ac.uk/
~julian/Dict.html), 193
Dictionary of Financial Terms
(http://www.tiaa-cref.org/
dict.html), 79
Digest of Education Statistics, 56

Digital Text Collections (http://
sunsite.berkeley.edu/
Collections/othertext.html),
156
DineNet: Menus Online (http://
www.dinenet.com), 185
Dining Out on the Web (http://www.
ird.net/diningout.html), 185
Directories, WWW-based, 13-15
Directory of Economists (Sam
Houston State University;
gopher://Niord.SHSU.edu/
11gopher_root%3a%5b_
DATA.ECONDIR%5d), 136
Directory of Scholarly Electronic
Conferences (http://www.
n2h2.com/KOVACS), 197
Doctoral Dissertations in Musicology
(http://www.music.indiana.
edu/ddm/), 141
Douglass, F., 102
Drama/theater sites, 145-146
Drew, W., 198
Dun & Bradstreet (http://www.
companiesonline.com),
87-88

Earth science sites, 203-213
EcoMall (http://www.ecomall.com/),
226
Economic Democracy Information
Network (EDIN; gopher://
garnet.berkeley.edu:1250/
1/), 73-74
Economic Indicators (Census
Bureau; http://www.census.
gov/ftp/pub/statab/www/
indicator/), 131
Economic issues sites, 127-137
economists sites, 136-137
international data, 133-134
statistical web sites, 128-134
working paper sites, 135-136
Economic Report of the President
(1995-1997; http://www.

access.gpo.gov/su_docs/
    budget/index.html), 131
Economics Departments on the
    Internet (http://price.bus.
    okstate.edu/econdept.
    html-ssi), 136
Economics Electronic Data Sources
    (http://www.libraries.rutgers.
    edu/rulib/socsci/econ/econ.
    html#menu4.1), 129
Economics Listservs (gopher://una.
    hh.lib.umich.edu/00/
    inetdirsstacks/acadlist.
    busecon), 136
Economics Research Network (ERN;
    http://205.241.57.6/ERN/
    index.html), 135
Economics Statistics Briefing Room
    (White House; http://www.
    whitehouse.gov/fsbr/esbr.
    html), 131
Economists sites, 136-137
EconWPA (Washington University;
    http://econwpa.wustl.edu),
    135-136
Ecoweb (http://ecosys.drdr.virginia.
    edu/EcoWeb.html), 224
EDGAR (Electronic Data Gathering,
    Analysis, and Retrieval
    system), 79-80
Edsearch: Education Statistics on
    Disk, 58
Education sites, 55-61
    classified lists, 59-61
    companies and organizations, 58-59
    federal or federally-funded web
        sites, 57-58
    hotlist directories of K-12 schools,
        colleges, and universities, 61
    hotlists, 59-61
Education World (http://www.
    education-world.com/), 60
E-Hawk Cadre (http://www.
    olcommerce.com/cadre/
    milhist/index.html), 178

Eisenberg, D., 150
Election results sites, 114-116
Electronic Embassy (http://www.
    embassy.org), 53
Electronic Resources for Youth
    Services (http://www.ccn.
    cs.dal.ca/~aa331/childlit.
    html), 159
Electronic Volcano (http://www.
    dartmouth.edu/~volcano),
    207
Embassy sites, 95
Emory Colossal List of Career
    Links (http://www.emory.
    edu/CAREER/Links.
    html), 29
Employment sites, 21-30
    career fairs, 27-28
    indexes, 22-27
    megalists, 29-30
    newsgroups, 30
    relocation services, 29
    resume services, 29
Encyclopedia Britannica: American
    Presidential Elections,
    1789-1996 (http://elections.
    eb.com/), 115
Encyclopedia Mythica (http://www.
    pantheon.org/myth/), 158
Endangered Plants and Animals
    (http://www.wcmc.org.uk:
    80/species/data/), 201
Endangered Species Program (http://
    www.fws.gov/~r9endspp/
    endspp.html), 201
ENR (Engineering News-Record;
    http://www.enr.com/dbase/
    dbase3.htm), 148
Entertainment sites, 179-186
    books and book reviews, 180-181
    celebrities, 181-182
    movies, 182-185
    restaurant reviews, 185-186
Entrez (http://www3.ncbi.nlm.nih.
    gov/Entrez/), 198-199

Entrez client software (http://www3.
ncbi.nlm.nih.gov/Entrez/
nentrez.overview.html), 199
Enviroene (http://es.inel.gov/), 224
Envirolink (http://www.envirolink.
org/), 224
Environment site, 120
Environmental Protection Agency
(http://www.epa.gov), 38
Environmental sites, 223-226
cream of the crop, 224-225
indexes/links, 225-226
work sites, 226
Environmental Sites on the Internet
(http://www.lib.kth.se/~lg/
envsite.htm), 224-225
ENZYME (http://expasy.hcuge.ch/
sprot/enzyme.html), 199
ERIC/AE Test Locator (http://
ericae2.educ.cua.edu/testcol.
htm), 65-66
ESPNet (http://espnet.sportszone.
com/), 188
Ethnic studies sites, 97-105
African American and African
studies, 99-102
Asian and Asian American
studies, 102-103
Latino/Chicano studies, 103-105
Native American studies, 105
Ethnologue: Languages of the World
(http://www.sil.org/
ethnologue/ethnologue.
html), 155
Ethnomusicology, Folk Music, and
World Music (http://www.
lib.washington.edu/libinfo/
libunits/soc-hum/music/
world.html), 140
Eurodocs (http://library.byu.edu/~rdh/
eurodocs/), 163
European Home Page (http://s700.
uminho.pt/europa.html), 54
Exchange Rate Service (Policy
Analysis Computing and

Information Facility in
Commerce, University of
British Columbia:
PACIFIC; http://pacific.
commerce.ubc.ca/xr), 132
Excite Review Service (http://www.
excite.com), 18
Expedia's Currency Converter
(http://expedia.msn.com/
pub/curcnvrt.dll?qscr=alcc),
132

Family Law Advisor (http://www.
divorcenet.com/), 72
Fatigue Resource Directory, 37
FECInfo (http://www.tray.com/
fecinfo), 116
Federal Yellow Book: Who's Who In
Federal Departments and
Agencies, 32
FedWorld Federal Jobs (http://www.
fedworld.gov/jobs/jobsearch.
html), 25
FedWorld/FLITE Supreme Court
Decisions (http://www.
fedworld.gov/supcourt/), 41
FedWorld/FLITE Supreme Court
Decisions Homepage
(http://www.fedworld.gov/
supcourt/index.htm), 170
Felipe's Things Latino (http://
edb518ea.edb.utexas.edu/
html/latinos.html), 104
FeMiNa (http://www.femina.com/
femina/culture), 108
FeMiNa–Lesbians and Bisexuals
(http://www.femina.com/
femina/lesbians), 106
Feminist Activist Resources on the
Net (http://www.igc.apc.
org/women/feminist.html),
123
Feminist Internet Gateway (http://
www.feminist.org/gateway/
master2.html), 108

Film Festivals (http://www.laig.com/
law/entlaw/filmfes.htm),
144
Film/cinema sites, 144-145
Finance sites, 77-83
annual reports, 79-80
bonds, 82-83
definitions, 78-79
exchanges, 80-81
meta-sites, 78
mutual funds, 82
stock and mutual fund quotes, 79
stock indexes, 81
taxes, 82
Financial Economics Network (FEN;
http://205.241.57.6/FEN/
index.html), 135
Financial Times (http://www.usa.
ft.com), 79
Firefly Online (http://www.firefly.
com), 7
Firearms sites, 120-121
First-search, 6
Fisher Scientific (http://www.fisher1.
com), 199
Folklore sites, 158
Fox Sports (http://www.tvguide.com/
sports), 189
Fundamental Constants Bibliographic
Database (http://physics.nist.
gov/PhysRefData/fundconst/
html/cover.html), 210
Fundamental Physical Constants
(http://physlab.nist.gov/
PhysRefData/codata86/
codata86.html), 210

Galaxy (http://www.tradewave.com),
14
Gateway to World History (http://
library.ccsu.ctstateu.edu/
~history/world_history/), 165
Gateway web sites, for social
problems, 70-71

GATT (General Agreement on
Tariffs and Trade; http://itl.
irv.uit.no/trade_law/nav/
freetrade.html), 96
Gay/lesbian issues sites, 121
Gay/lesbian/bisexual sites, 106-107
Gender studies sites, 106-109
men's issues, 107-108
women's studies, 108-109
General business sites, 85-92
agribusiness, 90-91
business schools, 92
chambers of commerce, 90
company directories and
homepages, 87-88
cost of living, 92
definitions, 87
government, 91-92
marketing and advertising, 90
meta-sites, 86-87
nonprofit business, 92
telephone directories, 89-90
Geographic Names Information
System (http://www-nmd.
usgs.gov/www/gnis/), 206
Geographical, Cultural and
People-Related Links
(http://www.cs.uidaho.edu/
~connie/interests-geography.
html), 54
Geography sites, 51-54
country information, 53
gazeteers, 52-53
international organizations, 53-54
maps, 52-53
web guides for, 54
Geological sciences sites, 206-207
Geological Time Machine (http://
www.ucmp.berkeley.edu/
help/timeform.html), 207
GEOnet Names Server (http://164.
214.2.59/gns/html/index.
html), 53
Global Agribusiness Information
Network (GAIN; http://

www.milcom.com/fintrac/
home.html), 91
Glossary of Microbiology (http://
www.bio.umass.edu/mdid/
glossary/), 194
GNN/Koblas Foreign Exchange
Converter (http://bin.gnn.
com/cgi-bin/gnn/currency),
132
Goffe, W., 137
Goode, J.M., 150
gopher://dosfan.lib.uic.edu:70/1D-
1%3A5844%3A011994%20
Report, 133-134
gopher://garnet.berkeley.edu:1250/1/,
73-74
gopher://gopher.cc.columbia.edu:71/
11/miscellaneous/cubooks/
inau, 170
gopher://gopher/law.cornell.edu/11/
foreign, 163
gopher://iubvm.ucs.indiana.edu/11/
tml, 140
gopher://Niord.SHSU.edu/00gopher_
root%3a%5b_DATA.
ECONOMICS.INFO%5d.
NOBELS, 137
gopher://Niord.SHSU.edu/
11gopher_root%3a%5b_
DATA.ECONDIR%5d, 136
gopher://una.hh.lib.umich.edu/00/
inetdirsstacks/acadlist.
busecon, 136
gopher://wuecon.wustl.edu:10672/11/
econfaq, 137
Gore, A., 55
GORP Index page (http://www.gorp.
com/gorp/guide.htm), 190
Government business sites, 91-92
Government Information Sharing
Project (Oregon State
University; http://govinfo.
kerr.orst.edu/), 133
Government Printing Office (GPO)
Electronic Information

Access Enhancement Act
(1993), 32
Government publications
librarians working with, sites for,
41-42
virtual reference collection of,
31-43
executive branch, 33-38
judicial branch, 41
legislative branch, 38-41,
39c-40c
web sites for government
publications librarians,
41-42
Government sites, health and
medicine, 219-220
GPO Access (http://www.access.gpo.
gov), 41
GPO Gate (http://www.gpo.ucop.
edu/), 219
Green, N., 48
Grief and Bereavement/Growth
House Inc. (http://www.
growthhouse.org/death.
html), 73

Hardin Meta Directory of Internet
Health Sources (http://
www.arcade.uiowa.edu/
hardin-www/md.html), 217
Health and Medicine sites, 215-222
clinical, 220-222
educational, 220-222
federal government, 219-220
meta directories, 217-218
ready reference, 218-219
special considerations, 216-217
HealthWeb (http://hsinfo.ghsl.nwu.
edu/healthweb/), 217-218
Helping Your Child, 58
Heston, A., 134
Historic Documents of the United
States (http://history.cc.
ukans.edu/carrie/docs/
docs_us.html), 169-170

Historical Demographic, Economic, and Social Data for the United States, 1790-1860 (http://icg.harvard.edu/census/), 173

Historical Text Archive (http://www.msstate.edu/Archives/History/), 162

History of Science, Technology and Medicine Biographical Dictionary (http://www.asap.unimelb.edu.au/hstm/hstm_bio.htm), 194

History Reviews On-line (http://www.uc.edu/www/history/reviews/htmlx), 172-173

H-Net discussion List Home Page Index (http://h-net2.msu.edu/about/lists.html), 174

H-Net Review Project (http://h-net2.msu.edu/reviews/), 172

Homelessness, sites for, 74

Hoover (http://www.hoovers.com), 88

HotBot (http://www.hotbot.com), 10, 11f

HotList of K-12 Internet School Sites–USA (http://rrnet.com/~gleason/k12.html), 61

http://adam.ac.uk, 151

http://allpolitics.com/elections/, 114-115

http://amazon.com, 196

http://argos.evansville.edu, 7

http://argos.evansville.edu/, 165-166

http://arnica.csustan.edu/index.html, 192-193

http://artsnet.heinz.cmu.edu:80/OnBroadway/, 145

http://artswire.org/Artswire/www/dance/browse.html, 143

http://babel.uoregon.edu/yamada/guides.html, 156

http://bin.gnn.com/cgi-bin/gnn/currency, 132

http://biotech.chem.indiana.edu/search/dict-search.html, 193

http://biz.yahoo.com, 86

http://buildingonline.com/blsearch.shtml, 151

http://cancer.med.upenn.edu/, 221

http://cansim.epas.utoronto.ca:5680/pwt/pwt.html, 134

http://castle.uvic.ca/econ/depts.html, 136

http://chamber-of-commerce.com:80, 90

http://chemfinder.camsoft.com/, 208

http://chemistry.mond.org/, 209

http://ciber.bus.msu.edu/busres.htm, 94

http://cirrus.sprl.umich.edu/wxnet/, 212

http://classics.mit.edu/, 154

http://clnet.ucr.edu, 103-104

http://cmhcsys.com/guide/pro03.htm, 72

http://conbio.rice.edu/vl/, 225

http://coombs.anu.edu.au/WWWVL-Asian Studies.html, 54,164

http://coombs.anu.edu.au/WWWVL-AsianStudies.html, 103

http://cos.gdb.org, 200

http://cos.gdb.org/, 204

http://drseuss.lib.uidaho.edu:80/govdoc/otherdep.html, 42

http://econwpa.wustl.edu, 135-136

http://econwpa.wustl.edu/EconFAQ/EconFAQ.html, 137

http://ecosys.drdr.virginia.edu/EcoWeb.html, 224

http://ecosys.drdr.virginia.edu/Environment.html, 225

http://edb518ea.edb.utexas.edu/html/latinos.html, 104

http://elections.eb.com/, 115

http://ericae2.educ.cua.edu/testcol.htm, 65-66

http://ericir.syr.edu/, 57

http://es.inel.gov/, 224

http://espnet.sportszone.com/, 188
http://expasy.hcuge.ch/sprot/enzyme.
    html, 199
http://expedia.msn.com/pub/curcnvrt.
    dll?qscr=alcc, 132
http://fiat.gslis.utexas.edu/~lewisa/
    womsprt.html, 188
http://fits.cv.nrao.edu/www/astroweb.
    html, 211
http://fly.hiwaay.net/~cwbol/astro.
    html, 211
http://golgi.harvard.edu/afagen/depts/
    orgs.html, 195
http://golgi.harvard.edu/biopages/
    journals.html, 195
http://golgi.harvard.edu/biopages.
    html, 192
http://govinfo.kerr.orst.edu/, 133
http://grid.let.rug.nl/ahc/history.html,
    174
http://guide.infoseek.com/Science/
    Environment?tid=1378&
    sv=N3, 225
http://guide.infoseek.com/Sports?
    tid=1653&sv=N3, 189
http://hanksville.phast.umass.edu/
    misc/NAresources.html,
    105
http://history.cc.ukans.edu/carrie/
    docs/docs_us.html, 169-170
http://h-net2.msu.edu/about/lists.
    html, 174
http://h-net2.msu.edu/reviews/, 172
http://h-net2.msu.edu/~world/, 164
http://host.mpa.org/, 142
http://hsinfo.ghsl.nwu.edu/
    healthweb/, 217-218
http://http.bsd.uchicago.edu/~r-tell/
    swlinks.html, 71
http://hubcap.clemson.edu/~eemoise/
    bibliography.html, 172
http://humanitas.ucsb.edu/, 154
http://icg.harvard.edu/census/, 173
http://iepntl.itaiep.doc.gov/nafta/
    nafta2.htm, 96

http://indy.radiology.uiowa.edu/
    VirtualHospital.html, 221
http://info.lanic.utexas.edu, 104-105
http://info-sys.home.vix.com/men,
    107-108
http://ipm_www.ncsu.edu/cernag/,
    198
http://ipm_www.ncsu.edu/cernag/
    associations.html, 195
http://itl.irv.uit.no/trade_law/nav/
    freetrade.html, 95-96
http://lanic.utexas.edu, 164
http://lanic.utexas.edu/las.html, 54
http://law.house.gov/cfr.htm, 202
http://lcweb2.locgov/frd/cs/cshome.
    html, 53
http://lcweb.loc.gov/copyright/, 142
http://libertynet.org/~edcivic/welfref.
    html, 122-123
http://library.byu.edu/~rdh/eurodocs/,
    163
http://library.ccsu.ctstateu.edu/
    ~history/world_history/, 165
http://lib-www.ucr.edu/bioag/, 193
http://loki.sonoma.edu:80/psychology/
    psychart.html, 65
http://medinfo.wustl.edu/~ysp/MSN/,
    205
http://members.aol.com/nebula5/
    costume.html, 144
http://members.gnn.com/user/
    megapsych.htm, 67
http://menic.utexas.edu/mes.html,
    54,165
http://metacrawler.cs.washington.edu,
    15-16
http://mineral.galleries.com/, 207
http://mitpress.mit.edu/SNDE/WWW/
    journal/index.html, 128
http://nch.ari.net/, 74
http://netcast.noaa.gov/cgi-bin/
    page?pg=netcast, 212
http://netec.mcc.ac.uk/BibEc.html, 135
http://netec.wustl.edu/~adnetec/WoPEc/
    WoPEc.html, 135

http://netvet.wustl.edu/welcome.htm, 201-202

http://networth.galt.com/www/home/equity/irr, 88

http://nimrod.mit.edu/depts/humanities/lit/literature.html, 154

http://nmg.clever.net/wew/, 134

http://odphp2.osophs.dhhs.gov/consumer.htm, 70

http://omni.cc.purdue.edu/flora/ref-libr.htm, 192

http://160.147.68.21:80/cmh-pg/moh1.htm, 176-177

http://160.147.68.21:80/cmh-pg/, 177-178

http://164.214.2.59/gns/html/index.html, 53

http://168.203.8.8/plweb-cgi/iops1.pl, 117

http://199.45.66.207/, 65

http://pacific.commerce.ubc.ca/xr, 132

http://patent.womplex.ibm.com/, 48

http://pathfinder.com/CQ/, 117-118

http://pathfinder.com/@@m52R*PFR4gIAQCWD/vg/TimeLife/, 201

http://pathfinder.com/si/, 189

http://pathfinder.com/travel/maps/index.html, 52

http://pathfinder.com/@@urxB8AUAUYa3cubH/travel/Zagat/Dine, 186

http://physics.nist.gov/PhysRefData/contents.html, 210

http://physics.nist.gov/PhysRefData/fundconst/html/cover.html, 210

http://physlab.nist.gov/PhysRefData/codata86/codata86.html, 210

http://piano.symgrp.com/playbill, 145

http://plants.usda.gov/plants.qurymenu.html, 200-201

http://point.lycos.com/, 18

http://price.bus.okstate.edu/econdept.html-ssi, 136

http://pro3.com/LAinfo/, 151

http://profile.cmdonl.com/aia/search.html, 148

http://psych.hanover.edu/aps/, 64

http://psy.ucsd.edu/otherpsy.html, 64

http://ptd15.afionline.org/CineMedia/, 144

http://ptd15.afionline.org/CineMedia, 183-184

http://pubweb.acns.nwu.edu/~pib/mythfolk.htm, 158

http://qrd.tcp.com/qrd/, 121

http://rivendel.com/~ric/resources/dictionary.html, 155

http://rrnet.com/~gleason/k12.html, 61

http://s18.bigyellow.com, 89

http://s700.uminho.pt/europa.html, 54

http://scholar2.lib.vt.edu/spec/iawa/iawa.htm, 149

http://seds.lpl.arizona.edu/nineplanets/nineplanets/nineplanets.html, 211

http://serendip.brynmawr.edu/Mind/Table.html, 65

http://shain.lib.conncoll.edu/CAPA/capa.html, 157

http://solstice.crest.org/, 226

http://spacelink.msfc.nasa.gov/home.index.html, 211-212

http://sports.yahoo.com/, 189

http://stats.bls.gov/cg-bin/surveymost?cu, 130

http://stats.bls.gov/news/release/cpi.toc.htm, 130

http://sunset.backbone.olemiss.edu/~egcash/, 156

http://sunsite.berkeley.edu/Collections/othertext.html, 156

http://sunsite.unc.edu/lia/presidents/pres.html, 176

http://the-tech.mit.edu/Shakespeare/works.html, 146

http://the-tech.mit.edu/Weather/,
212-213
http://thomas.loc.gov, 38,41
http://thomas.loc.gov/cgi-bin/
bdquwey/z?d104:HR03734:,
74
http://thorplus.lib.purdue.edu/
reference/dict.html, 155
http://tile.net/lists/business.html, 136
http://tile.net/lists/history2.html, 174
http://205.186.189.2/amg/
movie_Root.html, 183
http://205.186.189.2/amg/music_root.
html, 142
http://205.187.62.122:80/artslists/,
143
http://205.241.57.6/ERN/index.html,
135
http://205.241.57.6/FEN/index.html,
135
http://ultra.infoseek.com/, 10-12,11f
http://usda.mannlib.cornell.edu/usda,
133
http://usda.mannlib.cornell.edu/usda.
html, 91
http://userpage.fu-berlin.de/~oheiabbd
/moviedict_e.html, 144
http://users.aol.com/McClendon/
socialwk.html, 71
http://us.imdb.org, 184
http://webbook.nist.gov/, 208-209
http://web.gmu.edu/chnm/aha/, 175
http://web.idirect.com/~tiger/supersit.
htm, 86
http://woodrow.mpls.frb.fed.us/
economy/calc/cpihome.
html, 130
http://www.1mhv.net/acorn/Acorn.
html, 29
http://www3.ncbi.nlm.nih.gov/
Entrez/, 198-199
http://www3.ncbi.nlm.nih.gov/Entrez/
nentrez.overview.html, 199
http://www4.ncbi.nlm.nih.gov/
PubMed/, 196

http://www.aaln.org/vcl/electronics/
etc/acad/womstud.html,
109
http://www.abacom.com/innomagi/
online/l_s_rec/l_s_rec.htm,
189
http://www.abii.com, 89-90
http://www.access.gpo.gov, 38,41,42
http://www.access.gpo.gov/su_docs/
budget/index.html, 131
http://www.accessone.com/~rwadams/
Hymns/hymns.htm, 141
http://www.aclu.org/issues/immigrant/
hmir.html, 121
http://www.aclu.org/issues/religion/
hmrf.html, 122
http://www.adobe.com/prodindex/
acrobat/readstep.html, 142
http://www.afp.com/sportsreport/, 188
http://www.agnic.org/agdb/erdcalfr.
html, 197
http://www.agnic.org/cc/index.html,
197
http://www.ahip.getty.edu/aka/
aka_form_pub.html, 149
http://www.aia.org/archwww.htm, 148
http://www.aia.org/schools.htm, 150
http://www.ajb.dni.us/, 22
http://www.allpolitics.com, 117
http://www.almanac.com/index.html,
213
http://www.almaz.com/nobel/
Chemistry.html, 208
http://www.almaz.com/nobel/physics.
html, 210
http://www.altavista.com, 9-10,11f
http://www.ama-assn.org/cgi-bin/
aps-redir/, 218-219
http://www.amazon.com, 180
http://www.amex.com, 80
http://www.aoa.dhhs.gov/aoa/pages/
aoa.html, 72
http://www.apa.org/, 64
http://www.apa.org/science/stu.html,
64

http://www.arcade.uiowa.edu/
    hardin-www/md.html, 217
http://www.arch.buffalo.edu/pairc, 148
http://www.archINFORM.de, 151
http://www.asap.unimelb.edu.au/
    hstm/hstm_bio.htm, 194
http://www.asean.or.id/, 54
http://www.asla.org/asla/nonmembers/
    accredited_programs.html,
    150
http://www.atcc.org/, 195
http://www.atcg.com/comppage/
    comppage.htm, 195
http://www.basenet.net/~eagle/eagle.
    html, 123
http://www.bestjobsusa.com/, 27-28
http://www.bestjobsusa.com/, 23
http://www.betacyte.pair.com/
    journals.html, 195-196
http://www.bibliomania.com/Reference/
    PhraseAndFable/, 158
http://www.billboard-online.com/
    charts/, 143
http://www.biography.com/, 176
http://www.biol.uregina.ca/liu/bio/
    Ecology.html, 225
http://www.bio.net/, 197
http://www.bio.umass.edu/mdid/
    glossary/, 194
http://www.bizweb.com, 88
http://www.bloomberg.com/markets,
    81
http://www.bnet.att.com, 86-87
http://www.bonds-online.com, 82-83
http://www.bookport.com/
    b_welcomehome.html, 181
http://www.bookwire.com, 180-181
http://www.brint.com, 87
http://www.bubl.bath.ac.uk/BUBL/
    Literature.html, 153-154
http://www.bucknell.edu/~rbeard/
    diction.html, 155
http://www.business.gov, 91
http://www.byuh.edu/coursework/
    hist201/, 166

http://www.cais.com/agm/main/
    index.html, 119-120
http://www.capecod.net/schrockguide/,
    60
http://www.careerexpo.com/pub/
    westech/, 28
http://www.careermag.com/, 23-24
http://www.careermosaic.com/cm, 24
http://www.careerpath.com/, 23
http://www.carl.org/uncover, 196
http://www.cato.com/interweb/cato/
    biotech/bio-prod.html,
    194-195
http://www.cbot.com, 81
http://www.cbs.com/sports, 189
http://www.cbsnews.com/
    campaign96/home/, 115
http://www.ccn.cs.dal.ca/~aa331/
    childlit.html, 159
http://www.cdc.gov/, 219
http://www.census.gov/, 129-130
http://www.census.gov, 34
http://www.census.gov/, 173
http://www.census.gov/cgi-bin/
    gazetteer, 52
http://www.census.gov/econ/www/
    econ_cen.html, 130-131
http://www.census.gov/ftp/pub/hhes/w
    ww/poverty.html, 131-132
http://www.census.gov/ftp/pub/statab/
    www/indicator/, 131
http://www.census.gov/main/stat-int.
    html, 134
http://www.census.gov/stat_abstract,
    132
http://www.ceth.rutgers.edu/info/
    ectrdir.html, 156
http://www.ChemCenter.org/, 208
http://www.chemconnect.com/home.
    htm, 209
http://www.cinemachine.com, 183
http://www.cineweb.com/, 145
http://www.clark.net/pub/jeffd/, 118
http://www.clark.net/pub/lschank/
    web/country.html, 54

http://www.clark.net/pub/lschank/
web/ecostats.html, 129
http://www.clark.net/pub/pwalker/
home.html, 92
http://www.classical.net/music/, 143
http://www.clearinghouse.net, 17
http://www.clr.toronto.edu:1080/
VIRTUALLIB/arch.html,
147-148
http://www.cmhc.com/webpsych/, 66
http://www.cnn.com/WEATHER,
213
http://www.collegeboard.org/, 58-59
http://www.colorado.edu/libraries/
govpubs, 42
http://www.colostate.edu/Depts/
SocWork/webstuff.html, 71
http://www.companiesonline.com,
87-88
http://www.coolworks.com/showme/,
24
http://www.corrections.com/index.
html, 74
http://www.cris.com/~Serranyc, 95
http://www.cs.cmu.edu/~jdg/funds.
html, 82
http://www.cs.cmu.edu/People/mmbt/
women/writers.html, 156
http://www.cs.cmu.edu/Unofficial/
Movies/README.html,
144-145
http://www.cs.colstate.edu/~dreiling/
smartform.html, 16
http://www.csg.org/links/index.html,
132
http://www.csmonitor.com, 117
http://www.csn.net/~mhand/President
s/, 176
http://www.cs.uidaho.edu/~connie/
interests-geography.html,
54
http://www.cs.utk.edu/~bartley/
saInfoPage.html, 75
http://www.dancer.com/dance-links/,
143

http://www.danceronline.com/
competition/competition.
html, 143-144
http://www.dartmouth.edu/~volcano,
207
http://www.dejanews.com/forms/dnq.
html, 30
http://www.deltablues.com/dbsearch.
html, 141
http://www.democrats.org, 114
http://www.designlab.ukans.edu/
profusion/, 16-17
http://www.dinenet.com, 185
http://www.dis.strath.ac.uk/business,
94
http://www.divorcenet.com/, 72
http://www.doc.gov, 34
http://www.doe.gov, 35
http://www.doe.gov/, 206
http://www.doi.gov, 36
http://www.dol.gov, 36
http://www.dot.gov, 37
http://www.dtic.dla.mil/defenselink,
34-35
http://www.eardc.swt.edu/cgi-bin/
ucon/ucon.pl, 202
http://www.ece.ucdavis.edu/~darsie/
tales.html, 158
http://www.ecomall.com/, 226
http://www.eco.utexas.edu/AEA, 136
http://www.ed.gov, 35
http://www.ed.gov/, 57-58
http://www.edoc.com/ejournal/, 195
http://www.education-world.com/, 60
http://www.ed.uiuc.edu/music-ed/
on-line.html, 141
http://www.embassy.org, 53
http://www.emory.edu/CAREER/
Links.html, 29
http://www.english.upenn.edu/
~jlynch/Lit/, 154
http://www.enr.com/dbase/dbase3.
htm, 148
http://www.ens-lyon.fr/~esouche/
danse/dance.html, 143

http://www.envirolink.org/, 224
http://www.epa.gov/enviro/html/
    ef_home.html, 226
http://www.epa.gov, 38
http://www.epa.gov/, 206,224
http://www.exchange.de/fwb/indices.
    html, 81
http://www.excite.com, 18
http://www.fedworld.gov/jobs/
    jobsearch.html, 25
http://www.fedworld.gov/supcourt/, 41
http://www.fedworld.gov/supcourt/
    index.htm, 170
http://www.femina.com/femina/
    culture, 108
http://www.femina.com/femina/
    lesbians, 106
http://www.feminist.org/gateway/
    master2.html, 108
http://www.fga.com/aaaa/, 120
http://www.fisher1.com, 199
http://www.firefly.com, 7
http://www.foto.com/nccjobfair/, 28
http://www.fws.gov/~r9endspp/endspp.
    html, 201
http://www.gardenweb.com/vl/, 201
http://www.gasou.edu/psychweb/, 66
http://www.gene.com/ae/, 199-200
http://www.geocities.com/Athens/
    1058/rulers.html, 163
http://www.georgetown.edu/
    crossroads/asw/, 177
http://www.georgetown.edu/
    crossroads/dis, 171-172
http://www.glweb.com/
    RainbowQuery/Categories/
    Reference.html, 106
http://www.gorp.com/gorp/guide.htm,
    190
http://www.gpo.ucop.edu/, 219
http://www.growthhouse.org/death.
    html, 73
http://www.gwbssw.wustl.edu/
    %7Egwbhome/websites.
    html, 70-71

http://www.health.org/, 73
http://www.homefair.com/homefair/
    cmr/salcalc.html, 29,92
http://www.hoovers.com, 88
http://www.hotbot.com, 10,11f
http://www.hti.umich.edu/english/
    amverse/, 157
http://www.hud.gov, 35-36
http://www.hyperhistory.com/
    online_n2/History_n2/a.
    html, 163
http://wwwicic.nci.nih.gov, 220-221
http://www.ifas.ufl.edu/www/agator/
    htm/ag.htm, 198
http://www.igc.apc.org/acon/, 102
http://www.igc.apc.org/women/
    feminist.html, 123
http://www.igc.org/igc/econet/, 226
http://www.igc.org/igc/labornet/index.
    html, 121-122
http://www.igc.org/igc/members/
    index.html, 119
http://www.imdb.com/, 144
http://www.indiana.edu/~oah/index.
    html, 175
http://www.infoqueer.org/queer/qis,
    106
http://www-informatics.ucdmc.
    ucdavis.edu/icd9/refs.htm,
    218
http://www.ird.net/diningout.html,
    185
http://www.irs.ustreas.gov, 82
http://www.itd.nps.gov/cwss/,
    175-176
http://www.job-hunt.org/, 30
http://www.jobtrak.com/, 25-26
http://www.jobtrak.com/jobguide, 27
http://www.jobweb.org/catapult/
    catapult.htm, 24
http://www.june29.com/HLP/, 155-156
http://www.kn.pacbell.com/wired/
    bluewebn/, 59-60
http://www.laig.com/law/entlaw/
    filmfes.htm, 144

http://www.latimes.com/HOME/ NEWS/POLITICS/, 117

http://www.law.cornell.edu/supct/, 41

http://www.lendman.com/, 28

http://www.lesbian.org/, 106

http://www.lib.kth.se/~lg/envsite.htm, 224-225

http://www.libraries.rutgers.edu/rulib/ socsci/econ/econ.html# menu4.1, 129

http://www.libraries.rutgers.edu/rulib /socsci/hist/amhist.html, 177

http://www.lib.utexas.edu/Libs/PCL/ Map_collection/ Map_collection.html, 52

http://www.lib.umich.edu/chdocs/ employment/, 30

http://www.lib.umich.edu/libhome/ Documents.center/doclibs. html, 42

http://www.lib.umich.edu/libhome/ Documents.center/frames/ statsfr.html, 129

http://www.lib.utexas.edu:80/Libs/ ENG/PTUT/og.html, 48

http://www.lib.utexas.edu/Libs/Eng/ PTUT/ptut.html, 48

http://www.LIB.UTEXAS.EDU/Libs/ PCL/Map_collection/Map_ collection.html, 163-164

http://www.lib.uwaterloo.ca/society/ overview.html, 175,205

http://www.lib.uwaterloo.ca/society/ webpages.html, 195

http://www.lib.virginia.edu/socsci/ ccdb, 130

http://www.lib.virginia.edu/wess/ index.html, 165

http://www.lib.washington.edu/libinfo/ libunits/soc-hum/music/ world.html, 140

http://www.llbean.com:80/parksearch/, 202

http://www.lycos.com, 11f,12,13-14

http://www.majorleaguebaseball.com/, 190

http://www.maxwell.syr.edu/ nativeweb, 105

http://www.mblab.gla.ac.uk/~julian/ Dict.html, 193

http://www.mckinley.com/browse_bd. cgi?Enivronment, 225

http://www.mckinley.com/browse_bd. cgi?Sports, 189

http://www.medaccess.com/census/ census_s.htm, 132

http://www.merck.com/!!rlkrg3k5 Nrlkrg3k5N/pubs/mmanual/, 219

http://www.merck.com/ !!rE_e31jmmrE_e40XtZ/ pubs/mmanual/, 194

http://www.mexconnect.com, 95

http://www.milcom.com/fintrac/home. html, 91

http://www.mip.berkeley.edu/physics/ physics.html, 210

http://www.mip.berkeley.edu/ query_forms/browse_spiro_ form.html, 151

http://www.mit.edu:8001/people/ cdemello/geog.html, 61

http://www.mit.edu:8001/people/ cdemello/univ.html, 61

http://www.mit.edu/afs/athena.mit. edu/user/i/r/irie/www/aar. html, 102

http://www.monster.com/, 26

http://www.mpa.org/, 142

http://www.mplik.ru/~sg/transl/index .html, 202

http://www.mrshowbiz.com, 182

http://www.msstate.edu/Archives/ History/, 162

http://www.music.indiana.edu/ddm/, 141

http://www.music.princeton.edu/ chant_html/, 140-141

http://www.n2h2.com/KOVACS, 197

http://www.nafta.net/global, 95
http://www.nal.usda.gov/answers/
    reference/gen_ref_services.
    html, 197
http://www.nal.usda.gov/fnic/
    foodcomp/Data/SR11/, 198
http://www.nal.usda.gov/isis/, 196
http://www.nara.gov/, 171
http://www.nasdaq.com, 80
http://www.nas.edu/, 194
http://www.nationalgeographic.com/
    ngs/maps/cartographic.html,
    52
http://www.nature.com, 195
http://www.nba.com/, 190
http://www.nbc.com/sports/, 189
http://www.ncbi.nlm.nih.gov/, 221
http://www.ncdc.noaa.gov/, 212
http://www.ncemch.georgetown.edu/,
    72
http://wwwneic.cr.usgs.gov/,
    206-207
http://www.nfl.com, 190
http://www.ngdc.noaa.gov/ngdc.html,
    207
http://www.nhl.com/, 190
http://www.nih.gov, 220
http://www.nlm.nih.gov, 220
http://www.nlm.nih.gov/research/
    visible/visible_human.html,
    221-222
http://www.nlm.nih.gov/services/
    libraries/reference_special_
    lib.html, 197
http://www-nmd.usgs.gov/www/gnis/,
    52-53,206
http://www.nmnh.si.edu/msw/, 200
http://www.nmpa.org/hfa.html, 142
http://www.nnic.noaa.gov/, 212
http://www.nova.edu/Inter-Links/
    health/psy/psychlist.html, 65
http://www.npl.org/research/chss/grd/
    resguides/women3.htm,
    108-109

http://www.nscee.edu/unlv/Libraries/
    arch/rsrce/webrsrce/index.
    html, 147
http://www.nscee.edu/unlv/Libraries/
    arch/rsrce/webrsrce/sect5-6.
    html#6.0, 147
http://www.nsf.gov/, 205
http://www.ny.frb.org/pihome/
    svg_bnds/sb_val.html,
    82-83
http://www.nyse.com, 80
http://www.oas.org/, 54
http://www.occ.com/, 26
http://www.odci.gov/cia, 38
http://www.odci.gov/cia/publications/
    95fact/index.html, 53
http://www.odci.gov/cia/publications/
    hes/index.html, 134
http://www.oikos.com/redi/index.
    html, 150-151
http://www.olcommerce.com/cadre/
    milhist/index.html, 178
http://www.olsen.ch/cgi-bin/exmenu,
    96,132-133
http://www.onelook.com/browse.html,
    87
http://www.opentext.com, 11f, 12-13
http://www.os.dhhs.gov, 35
http://www.osmond.net/chill/
    christmas/carols.htm, 141
http://www.pantheon.org/myth/, 158
http://www.pbs.org/chicano/, 103
http://www.pebbs.com/megabites/et.
    html, 186
http://www.perseus.tufts.edu/, 154
http://www.perseus.tufts.edu/
    Secondary/Encyclopedia/
    encyc.subj.html#
    Architecture, 148
http://www.petersons.com/, 59
http://www.pfaw.org/aboutrr.htm, 122
http://www.pfaw.org/relig.htm, 122
http://www.physics.mcgill.ca/
    physics-services/physics_
    services.html, 209-210

http://www.phys.ksu.edu/~tipping/msds.html, 209

http://www.pitt.edu/~cjp/rees, 165

http://www.pitt.edu/~cjp/rees.html, 54

http://www.pitt.edu/~ian/resource/statist.htm, 54

http://www.politicalindex.com/, 113

http://www.politicalindex.com/sect8.htm, 114

http://www.politicalindex.com/sect10.htm#9, 120

http://www.politicsnow.com, 117

http://www.politicsnow.com/campaign/, 115-116

http://www.ppfa.org/ppfa/resource.html, 75

http://www.prars.com, 80

http://www.producerlink.com/, 144

http://www.prolife.org/ultimate/, 119-120

http://www.ps.uga.edu/rtk/, 199

http://www-psych.stanford.edu/cogsci/, 67

http://www.public.iastate.edu/~pedro/research_tools.html, 198

http://www.qrd.org/QRD/, 107

http://www.recmusic.org/lieder, 141

http://www.refdesk.com/cgi-bin/refsrch.cgi/search/me?environment, 225-226

http://www.refdesk.com/nature.html, 226

http://www.refdesk.com/sports.html, 189

http://www.revcan.ca, 82

http://www.rightweb.com/links.shtml, 118

http://www.rism.harvard.edu/MusicLibrary/InternetResources.html, 140

http://www.rnc.org, 114

http://www.sas.upenn.edu/African_Studies/Home_Page/WWW_Links.html, 100-101

http://www.sas.upenn.edu/African_Studies/AS.html, 54,164

http://www.sas.upenn.edu/African_studies/AS.html, 99

http://www.sas.upenn.edu/African_Studies/Home_Page/mcgee.html, 100

http://www.sbaonline.sba.gov, 91-92

http://www.science.gmu.edu/csi779/drope/govstats.html, 134

http://www.sciencemag.org, 195

http://www.sciencemag.org/science/, 205

http://www.sci.kun.nl/thalia/rapdict/, 143

http://www.screenit.com/movies/srch-mov.htm, 184-185

http://www.scsn.net/users/ckeenan/dsunkle/terms.html, 146

http://www.seas.gwu.edu/nsarchive/, 41-42

http://www.sec.gov, 79-80

http://www.shef.ac.uk/uni/academic/A-C/chem/web-elements/web-elements-home.html, 208

http://www.sil.org/ethnologue/ethnologue.html, 155

http://www.slackinc.com/matrix/, 218

http://www.spectracom.com/islist/index.html#ENVIRONMENT, 225

http://www.spectracom.com/islist/inet3.html#SPORTS, 189

http://www.sportsline.com/, 188

http://www.sportsnetwork.com/, 188

http://www.ssa.gov, 38

http://www.ssc.wisc.edu/irp/, 74

http://www.state.gov/www/about_state/business/business_tools.html, 95

http://www.state.gov, 37
http://www.state.gov/www/
    background_notes/, 53
http://www.stat-usa.gov, 87,94,131
http://www.stetson.edu/~csata/
    thr_guid.html, 145
http://www.stockinfo.standardpoor.
    com/idxinfo.htm, 81
http://www.stockmaster.com, 79
http://www.stpt.com/cgi-bin/sports/
    sports.cgi, 188-189
http://www.streeteye.com, 7
http://www.stsci.edu/astroweb/
    astroweb-categories.html,
    211
http://www.stsci.edu/net-resources.
    html, 211
http://www.students.uiuc.edu/
    ~s-schim/christian/christian.
    html, 122
http://www.students.uiuc.edu/~s-schim/
    christian/life.html#sex, 121
http://www.suntimes.com/ebert/ebert.
    html, 184
http://www.sweets.com, 150
http://www.switchboard.com, 89
http://www.snymor.edu/~drewwe/njc/,
    198
http://www.tango.org/ragtime/
    Ragtime_Resources.html,
    148
http://www.teleport.com/~cdeemer/
    scrwriter.html, 145
http://www.theatre-central.com/,
    145-146
http://www.tiaa-cref.org/dict.html, 79
http://www.tns.lcs.mit.edu/cgi-bin/
    sports, 188
http://www.tp.umu.se/TIPTOP/, 209
http://www.tradewave.com, 14
http://www.tray.com/fecinfo, 116
http://www.tse.or.jp, 81
http://www.ttu.edu/~aecovl/, 90-91
http://www.turnleft.com/issues.
    html#gun, 121

http://www.turnleft.com/liberal.html,
    118-119
http://www.tvguide.com/sports, 189
http://www.ualr.edu/~coedept/index.
    html, 60-61
http://www.ubl.com/, 142
http://www.ubp.com, 101-102
http://www.ucalgary.ca/~dkbrown/
    index.html, 159
http://www.ucalgary.ca/~dkbrown/
    storfolk.html, 158
http://www.uc.edu/www/history/
    reviews/htmlx, 172-173
http://www.ucmp.berkeley.edu/, 207
http://www.ucmp.berkeley.edu/help/
    taxaform.html, 207
http://www.ucmp.berkeley.edu/help/
    timeform.html, 207
http://www.uidaho.edu/
    special-collections/
    OtherRepositories.html,
    170-171
http://www.uidaho.edu/special-
    collections/Other.
    Repositories.html, 162
http://www.umn.edu/apn/, 22
http://www.uncc.edu/lis/library/
    reference/intbus/vibehome.
    htm, 94
http://www.unipissing.ca/psyc/
    psycsite.htm, 66-67
http://www.unl.edu/buros/home.html,
    66
http://www.un.org/, 54
http://www.upenn.edu/sah/aame/
    bioint.html, 149
http://www.upenn.edu/sah/daah/
    daah1.html, 150
http://www.usa.ft.com, 79
http://www.usatoday.com/sports/si.
    htm, 189
http://www.usbc.org/, 121
http://www.uschamber.org/mall, 90
http://www.uscourts.gov/, 41
http://www.usda.gov, 34

http://www.usdoj.gov, 36
http://www.usgs.gov/, 206
http://www.usnews.com/usnews/edu/
beyond/garch.htm, 150
http://www.uspto.gov, 46
http://www.ustreas.gov, 37
http://www.utexas.edu/coc/adv/world,
90
http://www.utexas.edu/world/lecture/
index.html, 61,200
http://www.va.gov, 37
http://www.vmedia.com/shannon/
poetry.html, 157
http://www.vote-smart.org/, 116
http://www.vote-smart.org/congress/
congress.html#votes, 118
http://www.w3.org/pub/DataSources/
bySubject/Overview.html,
192
http://www.washingtonpost.com/,
117
http://www.wcmc.org.uk:80/species/
data/, 201
http://www.wco.com/~jrush/music/,
142-143
http://www.webdirectory.com/, 120
http://www.webfinance.net, 78
http://www.webinvestors.com, 78
http://www.wesleyan.edu/psyc/
psyc260/ranking.htm, 64
http://www.whitehouse.gov, 33-34
http://www.whitehouse.gov/fsbr/esbr.
html, 131
http://www.wiso.uni-augsburg.de/
sozio/hartmann/psycho/
journals.html, 65
http://www.wm.edu/csrv/career/
stualum/jregion.html, 25
http://www.worldwide.com,
149-150
http://www.wsrn.com, 78
http://www.xe.net/currency, 132
http://www.xmission.com/~shea/straw
/anbib.html, 150
http://www.yahoo.com, 14-15,193

http://www.yahoo.com/Arts/
Humanities/Literature/
Authors/, 157
http://www.yahoo.com/Arts/
Humanities/Literature/
Genres/Poetry/, 157
http://www.yahoo.com/Business_
and_Economy/Business_
Schools/, 92
http://www.yahoo.com/Government/
Politics/Political_Issues/
Welfare_Reform/, 74
http://www.yahoo.com/Politics/, 113
http://www.yahoo.com/Recreation/,
190
http://www.yahoo.com/Science/
Geography/Maps/, 52
http://www.yahoo.com/Social_
Science/Social_Work/, 71
http://www.yahoo.com/society_and_
culture/environment_and_
nature/index.html, 226
http://www.yahoo.com/Society_and_
Culture/Mythology_and_
Folklore/, 158
http://www.yahoo.com/Society_and_
Culture/Poverty/, 74
http://www.yahoo.com/text/
Government/Politics/
Political_Issues/Welfare_
Reform/, 123
http://www.yahoo.com/text/Society_
and_Culture/Affirmative_
Action/, 120
http://www.yellownet.com, 89
http://xxx.lanl.gov/, 210-211
http://yahoo.com/Entertainment/
People/, 182
http://yp.gte.net, 89
Human Languages Page (http://www.
june29.com/HLP/),
155-156
Human services/social sciences
solution sites, 69-75
gateway web sites, 70-71

lifespan resources, 71-73
special interest organizations, 73-75
H-WORLD (http://h-net2.msu.edu/
~world/), 164
Hymnal (http://www.accessone.com/
~rwadams/Hymns/hymns.
htm), 141
HyperHistory Online (http://www.
hyperhistory.com/online_n2/
History_n2/a.html), 163

IANWeb (http://www.pitt.edu/~ian/
resource/statist.htm), 54
IBM Patent Server Home Page
(http://patent.womplex.ibm.
com/), 48
ICD-9 (http://www-informatics.
ucdmc.ucdavis.edu/icd9/refs.
htm), 218
IDG EcoNet (http://www.igc.org/igc/
econet/), 226
IGC LaborNet
(http://www.igc.org/igc/
labornet/index.html),
121-122
Immigration sites, 121
Import/Export Directory (http://www.
cris.com/~Serranyc), 95
Inaugural Addresses of U.S. Presidents
(gopher://gopher.cc.columbia.
edu:71/11/miscellaneous/
cubooks/inau), 170
Incumbent voting sites, 117-118
Index(es), as career and employment
resources, 22-27
Index of Native American Resources
on the Internet (http://
hanksville.phast.umass.edu/
misc/NAresources.html), 105
Index to Patent Classification, 48
Indexer(s), as search engine, 8
Individual pages, on Internet, 3
Infomine: Comprehensive
Biological, Agricultural,
and Medical Internet
Resource Collection
(http://lib-www.ucr.
edu/bioag/), 193
Infoqueer (http://www.infoqueer.org/
queer/qis), 106
Information for Students (http://
www.apa.org/science/stu.
html), 64
Information providers, on Internet, 2
Infoseek Guide (http://guide.
infoseek.com/Science/
Environment?tid=1378&
sv=N3), 225
InfoSeek sports guide (http://guide.
infoseek.com/Sports?tid=
1653&sv=N3), 189
InfoSeek Ultra (http://ultra.infoseek.
com/), 10-12,11f
Institute for Global Communications:
Members Directory
(http://www.igc.org/igc/
members/index.html), 119
Institute for Research on Poverty
(IRP) at the University of
Wisconsin-Madison (http://
www.ssc.wisc.edu/irp/), 74
Interface, as search engine, 8-9
International and Area Studies (http://
www.clark.net/pub/lschank/
web/country.html), 54
International Archive of Women in
Architecture (http://
scholar2.lib.vt.edu/spec/
iawa/iawa.htm), 149
International Chamber of Commerce
(http://chamber-of-
commerce.com:80), 90
International data sites, 133-134
International organizations, 53-54
International studies sites, 51-54
country information, 53
gazeteers, 52-53
international organizations, 53-54
web guides for, 54

International travel sites, 93-96
    currency exchange, 96
    directories, 95
    embassies and consulates, 95
    meta-sites, 94
    NAFTA/GATT/Maastricht
        treaties, 95-96
Internet
    architecture sites, 147-151
    business sites, 85-92
    career and employment sites,
        21-30
    company information sites, 85-92
    economic issues sites, 127-137
    education sites, 55-61
    entertainment sites, 179-186
    environmental sites, 223-226
    ethnic studies sites, 97-105
    finance sites, 77-83
    gender studies sites, 106-109
    general business sites, 85-92
    geography sites, 51-54
    government publications sites,
        31-43
    health and medicine sites, 215-222
    human services/social sciences
        solution sites, 69-75
    information providers on, 2
    international studies sites, 51-54
    international travel sites, 93-96
    investment sites, 77-83
    language sites, 153-159
    legislative tools on, comparison
        of, 39c-40c
    literature sites, 153-159
    patent sites on, 45-48
    performing arts sites, 139-146
    political information sites, 111-123
    psychology sites, 63-67
    references librarians using, issues
        facing, 1-2
    resources on, overview of, 1-3
    social problem solution sites,
        69-75
    sports sites, 187-190

United States History sites,
        167-178
    world history sites, 161-166
Internet Classics Archive (http://
        classics.mit.edu/), 154
Internet Mental Hand The Perseus
        Project ealth (http://199.
        45.66.207/), 65
Internet Movie Database (http://
        www.imdb.com/), 144
Internet Resources for Music
        Scholars (http://www.rism.
        harvard.edu/MusicLibrary/
        InternetResources.html),
        140
Internet Road Map to Books (http://
        www.bookport.com/b_
        welcomehome.html), 181
Investment sites, 77-83
    annual reports, 79-80
    bonds, 82-83
    exchanges, 80-81
    meta-sites, 78
    mutual funds, 82
    stock and mutual fund quotes, 79
    stock indexes, 81
    taxes, 82
IRS (http://www.irs.ustreas.gov), 82

Job Search and Employment
        Opportunities: Best Bets
        from the Net (http://www.
        lib.umich.edu/chdocs/
        employment/), 30
JobHunt: On-line Job Mega-List
        (http://www.job-hunt.org/),
        30
Jobs in Chemistry (http://chemistry.
        mond.org/), 209
JobTrak (http://www.jobtrak.com/),
        25-26
Journals, Conferences, and Current
        Awareness Services (http://
        golgi.harvard.edu/biopages/
        journals. html), 195

K-12 schools, hotlist directories on,
61
Kathy Schrock's Guide for Educators
(http://www.capecod.net/
schrockguide/), 60
Kimmel, S., 2

Labor sites, 121-122
Landscape Construction Manufacturer
Directory (http://pro3.com/
LAinfo/), 151
Language sites, 153-159
author information and criticism,
156-157
dictionaries, 155
electronic text collections, 156
folklore, 158
LANL E-Print Archive (http://xxx.
lanl.gov/), 210-211
Latin American Information Center,
University of Texas at
Austin (http://lanic.utexas.
edu), 164
Latin American Network Information
Center (LANIC; http://info.
lanic.utexas.edu), 104-105
Latin American Studies (http://lanic.
utexas.edu/las.html), 54
Latino/Chicano studies sites, 103-105
Lebedev, A., 7
Left/liberal political issues site,
118-119
Lesbian Links (http://www.lesbian.
org/), 106
Lesbian/gay issues sites, 121
Lesbian/gay/bisexual sites, 106-107
Library of Musical Links (http://
www.wco.com/~jrush/
music/), 142-143
Life Sciences Dictionary (http://
biotech.chem.indiana.edu/
search/dict-search.html), 193
Life sciences sites, 191-202
agriculture, 197-198
biblioigraphic tools, 196

biochemistry, 198-199
company information and
catalogs, 194-195
dictionaries and biographies,
193-194
education and research, 199-200
general biological collections,
192-193
molecular biology, 198-199
online monographs, 194
organism-based resources, 200-202
scholarly societies and
publications, 195-196
stumpers, 196-197
Lifespan resources, for social
problems, 71-73
Lighthouse (http://the-tech.mit.edu/
Weather/), 212-213
Limited Area Search of the Ancient
World Internet (http://argos.
evansville.edu/), 165-166
Links to Psychological Journals
(http://www.wiso.uni-
augsburg.de/sozio/hartmann/
psycho/journals.html), 65
List of WWW Sites of Interest to
Ecologists (http://www.
biol.uregina.ca/liu/bio/
Ecology.html), 225
Listing of U.S. Psychology PhD
Programs (http://www.
wesleyan.edu/psyc/psyc260/
ranking.htm), 64
Literary Menagerie (http://sunset.
backbone.olemiss.edu/
~egcash/), 156
Literary Resources on the Net (http://
www.english.upenn.edu/
~jlynch/Lit/), 154
Literature Resources (http://nimrod.
mit.edu/depts/humanities/lit/
literature.html), 154
Literature sites, 153-159
children's, 159
mythology, 158

poetry, 157
resources, 155-156
Lit/Web: Poetry (http://www.vmedia.
    com/shannon/poetry.html),
    157
L.L. Bean's Parksearch (http://www.
    llbean.com:80/parksearch/),
    202
Los Angeles Times: Politics and
    Polls (http://www.latimes.
    com/HOME/NEWS/
    POLITICS/), 117
Lycos A2Z (http://www.lycos.com),
    13-14
Lycos Search Engine (http://www.
    lycos.com), 11f,12

Maastricht Treaty on European
    Union (http://itl.irv.uit.no/
    trade_law/nav/freetrade.
    html), 96
Mad Scientist Network (http://
    medinfo.wustl.edu/~ysp/
    MSN/), 205
Magellan Environment Directory
    (http://www.mckinley.com/br
    owse_bd.cgi?Environment),
    225
Magellan Maps (http://pathfinder.
    com/travel/maps/index.html),
    52
Magellan Sports Index (http://www.
    mckinley.com/browse_bd.
    cgi?Sports), 189
Mailing Lists Related to Psychology
    (http://www.nova.edu/
    Inter-Links/health/psy/
    psychlist.html), 65
Major League Baseball (http://www.
    majorleaguebaseball.com/),
    190
Mammal Species of the World
    (http:// www.nmnh.si.edu/
    msw/), 200

Maps sites, 52-53
Marketing sites, 90
Martin Luther King Jr. Bibliography
    (telnet://forsythetn.stanford.
    edu), 171
Materials Safety Data Sheets
    (MSDS; http://www.phys.
    ksu.edu/~tipping/msds.
    html), 209
McMillan, G., 2
Medal of Honor Citations (http://
    160. 147.68.21:80/
    cmh-pg/moh1. htm),
    176-177
Medical Matrix: A Guide to Internet
    Clinical Medicine
    Resources (http://www.
    slackinc.com/matrix/),
    218
Medicine sites, 215-222. *See also*
    Health and Medicine sites
Medline (http://www4.ncbi.nlm.
    nih.gov/PubMed/), 196
MegaPsych (http://members.gnn.
    com/user/megapsych.htm),
    67
Melvyl catalog (telnet://melvyl.ucop.
    edu), 149
Men's studies sites, 107-108
Merck Manual of Diagnosis and
    Therapy (http://www.
    merck.com/!!rE_
    e31jmmrE_e40XtZ/pubs/
    mmanual/), 194
Metacrawler (http://metacrawler.
    cs.washington.edu), 15-16
Metasearch engines, WWW-based,
    15-17
Mexico Connect (http://www.
    mexconnect.com), 95
Middle East Network Information
    Center, The University of
    Texas at Austin (http://
    menic.utexas.edu/mes.html),
    165

Middle Eastern Studies (http://menic. utexas.edu/mes.html), 54

Mind and Body–Rene Descartes to William James (http:// serendip.brynmawr.edu/ Mind/Table.html), 65

Mineral Gallery (http://mineral. galleries.com/), 207

Moise's Vietnam War Bibliography (http://hubcap.clemson.edu/ ~eemoise/bibliography. html), 172

Molecular biology sites, 198-199

Monster Board (http://www.monster. com/), 26

Movies sites, 182-185

Mr. Showbiz (http://www. mrshowbiz.com), 182

Music
    lyrics-related, 141
    performance rights–related, 142
    performing groups–related, 142
    publisher-related, 142
    research-related, 140-141

Music sites, 140-143

Mutual Fund Company Directory (http://www.cs.cmu.edu/ ~jdg/funds.html), 82

Mutual fund quotes, 79

Mutual funds, 82

MVRD Environment and Nature (http://www.refdesk.com/ nature.html), 226

My Virtual Reference Desk ENVIRONMENT search (http://www.refdesk.com/ cgi-bin/refsrch.cgi/search/ me?environment), 225-226

My Virtual Reference Desk Sports Sites (http://www.refdesk. com/sports.html), 189

Mythology and Folklore (http:// pubweb.acns.nwu.edu/~pib/ mythfolk.htm), 158

Mythology sites, 158

NAAB Accredited Programs in Architecture (http://www. aia.org/schools.htm), 150

NAFTA (North American Free Trade Agreement; http://itl.irv.uit. no/trade_law/nav/freetrade. html), 95-96

NAFTA Register (http://www.nafta. net/global), 95

NASA SpaceLink (http://spacelink. msfc.nasa.gov/home.index. html), 211-212

NASDAQ (http://www.nasdaq.com), 80

National Academy of Sciences (http://www.nas.edu/), 194

National Agricultural Library Reference Desk (agref@ nalusda.gov.purdue.edu), 197

National Archives and Records Administration (http:// www.nara.gov/), 171

National Basketball Association (http://www.nba.com/), 190

National Career Centers USA, Inc. (http://www.foto.com/ nccjobfair/), 28

National Cemetery System, 37

National Center for Biotechnology Information (http://www. ncbi.nlm.nih.gov/), 221

National Center for Education in Maternal and Child Health (http://www.ncemch. georgetown.edu/), 72

National Clearing house for Alcohol & Drug Information (http:// www.health.org/), 73

National Climatic Data Center (http:// www.ncdc.noaa.gov/), 212

National Coalition for the Homeless (NCH; http://nch.ari.net/), 74

National Earthquake Information Center (http://wwwneic.cr.usgs.gov/), 206-207

National Football League (http://www.nfl.com/), 190

National Geographic Map Machine (http://www.nationalgeographic.com/ngs/maps/cartographic.html), 52

National Geophysical Data Center (http://www.ngdc.noaa.gov/ngdc.html), 207

National Hockey League (http://www.nhl.com/), 190

National Institutes of Health (NIH; http://www.nih.gov), 220

National Library of Medicine (NLM; http://www.nlm.nih.gov), 220

National Library of Medicine Reference Section (ref@nlm.nih.gov), 197

National Political Index (http://www.politicalindex.com/), 113

National Political Index: National Political Parties (http://www.politicalindex.com/sect8.htm), 114

National Political Index: Political Activist Groups: Firearms (http://www.politicalindex.com/sect10.htm#9), 120

National Register of Historic Places (telnet://victor.umd.edu), 151

National Science Foundation (http://www.nsf.gov/), 205

National Security Archive (http://www.seas.gwu.edu/nsarchive/), 41-42

Native American studies sites, 105

Native Web (http://www.maxwell.syr.edu/nativeweb), 105

Nature (http://www.nature.com), 195

NBC sports (http://www.nbc.com/sports/), 189

Netcast service (http://netcast.noaa.gov/cgi-bin/page?pg=netcast), 212

NetVet Veterinary Resources & The Electronic Zoo (http://netvet.wustl.edu/welcome.htm), 201-202

Network sites, 189

New York Stock Exchange (http://www.nyse.com), 80

Newsgroups, 30

1992 Economic Census (Census Bureau; http://www.census.gov/econ/www/econ_cen.html), 130-131

1994 Country Reports on Economic Policy and Trade Practices (State Department; gopher://dosfan.lib.uic.edu:70/1D-1%3A5844%3A011994%20Report), 133-134

1994 International Handbook of Economics Statistics (Central Intelligence Agency; http://www.odci.gov/cia/publications/hes/index.html), 134

1994 Statistical Abstract of the United States (http://www.medaccess.com/census/census_s.htm), 132

1995 Statistical Abstract of the United States (http://www.census.gov/stat_abstract), 132

NIST Chemistry WebBook (http://webbook.nist.gov/), 208-209

NIST Physical Reference Data (http://physics.nist.gov/PhysRefData/contents.html), 210

NOAA Network Information Center (http://www.nnic.noaa.gov/), 212

Nobel Laureates in Economics (gopher://Niord.SHSU.edu/ 00gopher_root%3a%5b_ DATA.ECONOMICS. INFO%5d.NOBELS), 137
Nobel Prize Winners in Chemistry (http://www.almaz.com/ nobel/Chemistry.html), 208
Nobel Prize Winners in Physics (http://www.almaz.com/ nobel/physics.html), 210
Nonprofit business sites, 92
Not Just Cows (http://www.snymor. edu/~drewwe/njc/), 198
Notess, G., 15

Occupational Outlook Handbook, 36
Olsen and Associates 164 Currencies Converter (January 1990- Present; http://www.olsen. ch/cgi-bin/exmenu), 132-133
On Broadway WWW Information Page (http://artsnet.heinz. cmu.edu:80/OnBroadway/), 145
OncoLink (http://cancer.med.upenn. edu/), 221
Onelook (http://www.onelook. com/browse.html), 87
On-Line Arts and Crafts Movement Resource Directory (http:// www.tango.org/ragtime/ Ragtime_Resources.html), 148
Online Career Center (http://www. occ.com/), 26
On-line Dictionaries (http://www. bucknell.edu/~rbeard/diction. html), 155
Online Film Dictionary (http:// userpage.fu-berlin.de/ ~oheiabbd/moviedict_e. html), 144

On-line Music and Education Resources (http://www.ed. uiuc.edu/music-ed/on-line. html), 141
Open Text Index (http://www. opentext.com), 11f,12-13
Organism-based science sites, 200-202
Organization of American Historians (http://www.indiana.edu/ ~oah/index.html), 175
Organization of American States (http://www.oas.org/), 54
Organizations, physchology information provided by, 64

PAIRC–Planning and Architecture Internet Resource Center (http://www.arch.buffalo. edu/pairc), 148
Pat McClendon's Social Work Resources (http://users.aol. com/McClendon/socialwk. html), 71
Patent AIDS Database, 47-48
Patent Searching Tutorial, University of Texas, Austin (http:// www.lib.utexas.edu:80/ Libs/ENG/PTUT/og.html), 48
Patent sites, 45-48
Pedro's BioMolecular Research Tools (http://www.public. iastate.edu/~pedro/research_ tools.html), 198
PennWorld Tables (http://cansim. epas.utoronto.ca:5680/pwt/ pwt.html), 134
People for the American Way: About the Religious Right (http:// www.pfaw.org/aboutrr.htm), 122
People for the American Way: Religious Liberty Issues (http://www.pfaw.org/relig. htm), 122

Performing arts sites, 139-146
  dance, 143-144
  film/cinema, 144-145
  music, 140-143
  theater/drama, 145-146
Periodic Table of the Elements
  (http:// www.shef.ac.uk/uni/
  academic/A-C/chem/web-
  elements/web-elements-
  home. html), 208
Perry-Castaneda Library Map
  Collection (http://www.lib.
  utexas.edu/Libs/PCL/Map_
  collection/Map_collection.
  html), 52
Perseus Encyclopedia, Architecture
  Section (http:/www.
  perseus.tufts.edu/
  Secondary/Encyclopedia/
  encyc.subj.html#
  Architecture), 148
Peterson's Education and Career
  Center (http://www.
  petersons.com/), 59
Physical science sites, 203-213
Physics Around the World (http://
  www.physics.mcgill.ca/
  physics-services/physics_
  services.html), 209-210
Physics Lecture Demonstrations
  (http://www.mip.berkeley.
  edu/physics/physics.html),
  210
Physics sites, 209-211
Planned Parenthood Information
  Resources (http://www.
  ppfa.org/ppfa/resource.
  html), 75
PLANTS (http://plants.usda.gov/
  plants.qurymenu.html),
  200-201
Playbill Online (http://piano.symgrp.
  com/playbill), 145
Poetry sites, 157
Political information sites, 111-123

abortion, 119-120
affirmative action, 120
campaign(s), 114-116
campaign finance, 116
candidates, 114-116
election results, 114-116
environment, 120
firearms, 120-121
gay and lesbian issues, 121
immigration, 121
incumbent voting, 117-118
interest groups and issues, 118-119
labor, 121-122
meta-sites, 113
political news, 117
political parties, 114
religion, 122
welfare, 122-123
women's issues, 123
Political news sites, 117
Political parties sites, 114
PoliticsNow (http://www.
  politicsnow.com), 117
PoliticsNow: Campaign '96 (http://
  www.politicsnow.com/
  campaign/), 115-116
Poverty (Census Bureau; http://www.
  census.gov/ftp/pub/hhes/
  www/poverty.html), 131-132
Poverty, sites for, 74
Power Links Leisure, Sports, and
  Recreation page (http://
  www.abacom.com/innomagi/
  online/l_s_rec/l_s_rec.htm),
  189
PRARS (http://www.prars.com), 80
Preparing Your Child for College, 58
President (http://sunsite.unc.edu/
  lia/presidents/pres.html),
  176
Producerlink (http://www.
  producerlink.com/), 144
Professional organizations,
  psychology information
  provided by, 64

Profusion Search (http://www.
      designlab.ukans.edu/
      profusion/), 16-17
PsychArt (http://loki.sonoma.
      edu:80/psychology/psychart.
      html), 65
PsychNet (http://www.apa.org/), 64
Psychology Departments Around the
      World (http://psy.ucsd.edu/
      otherpsy.html), 64
Psychology sites, 63-67
      directories, 64-65
      mega-lists, 66-67
      organizations, 64
      reference tools, 65-66
PsychWeb (http://www.gasou.edu/
      psychweb/), 66
PsycSite (http://www.unipissing.
      ca/psyc/psycsite.htm),
      66-67

Queer Resources Directory (http://
      qrd.tcp.com/qrd/), 121
Queer Resources Directory (QRD;
      http://www.qrd.org/QRD/),
      107

Rainbow Query (http://www.glweb.
      com/RainbowQuery/
      Categories/Reference.html),
      106
Rap Directory (http://www.sci.kun.
      nl/thalia/rapdict/), 143
Recreation sites, 190
REESWeb: Russian and East
      European Studies (http://
      www.pitt.edu/~cjp/rees), 165
REESWeb: Russian and Eastern
      European Studies (http://
      www.pitt.edu/~cjp/rees.
      html), 54
ref@nlm.nih.gov, 197
Religion sites, 122

Relocation services, 29
Repositories of Primary Sources
      (http://www.uidaho.edu/
      special-collections/Other.
      Repositories.html), 162
Repositories of Primary Sources
      (http://www.uidaho.edu/
      special-collections/
      OtherRepositories.html),
      170-171
Republican Main Street (http://www.
      rnc.org), 114
Research in Education (RIE), 56
Resources for Economists on the
      Internet by William Goffe
      (gopher://wuecon.wustl.edu:
      10672/11/econfaq), 137
Resources for Economists on the
      Internet by William Goffe
      (hypertext version; http://
      econwpa.wustl.edu/
      EconFAQ/EconFAQ.html),
      137
Resources for Environmental Design
      Index (REDI; http://www.
      oikos.com/redi/index.html),
      150-151
Restaurant review sites, 185-186
Résumé Doctor (http://www.1mhv.
      net/~acorn/Acorn.html), 29
Resume services, 29
Review-rating services, 17-18
Revenue Canada (http://www.revcan.
      ca), 82
Right on the Web: The Right Links
      (http://www.rightweb.com/
      links.shtml), 118
Right to Know (http://www.ps.uga.
      edu/rtk/), 199
Right/conservative political issues
      site, 118
Riley, M., 27
Roger Ebert on Movies (http://www.
      suntimes.com/ebert/ebert.
      html), 184

Robot(s)
  defined, 8
  as search engine, 8
Robot-generated databases, 8-9

Sacramento Bee, 23
Salary Relocation Calculator
    (http://www.homefair.com/
    homefair/cmr/salcalc.html),
    29
San Jose Mercury News, 23
SavvySearch (http://www.cs.colstate.
    edu/~dreiling/smartform.
    html), 16
Scholarly Societies Project (http://
    www.lib.uwaterloo.ca/
    society/overview.html),
    175,205
Scholarly Societies Project: Webpages
    & Gophers of Scholarly
    Societies (http://www.lib.
    uwaterloo.ca/society/
    webpages.html), 195
School(s), hotlist directories on, 61
Science (http://www.sciencemag.
    org), 195
Science Online (http://www.
    sciencemag.org/science/),
    205
Screen It! Entertainment Reviews for
    Parents (http://www.
    screenit.com/movies/
    srch-mov.htm), 184-185
Screenwriters & Playwrights Home
    Page (http://www.teleport.
    com/~cdeemer/scrwriter.
    html), 145
Search engines, types of, 2
Search engines/robot-generated
    databases, 8-9
Select GPO Access (http://www.
    access.gpo.gov), 38,41
Selected Internet Resources in
    Women's Studies (http://
    www.npl.org/research/chss/

grd/resguides/women3.htm),
    108-109
Sexual Assault Information Page
    (http://www.cs.utk.edu/
    ~bartley/saInfoPage.html),
    75
Sexuality, sites for, 75
Shettleworth, E.G., Jr., 149
SI Online (Sports Illustrated; http://
    pathfinder.com/si/), 189
SilverPlatter, 6
Small Business Administration
    (SBA; http://www.
    sbaonline.sba.gov), 91-92
Social problem solution sites, 69-75
    gateway web sites, 70-71
    lifespan resources, 71-73
    special interest organizations,
    73-75
Social Security Administration
    (http://www.ssa.gov), 38
Social Work and Social Services
    Web Sites/George Warren
    Brown School of Social
    Work at Washington
    University in St. Louis
    (http://www.gwbssw.wustl.
    edu/%7Egwbhome/websites.
    html), 70-71
Social Work Links/University of
    Chicago (http://http.bsd.
    uchicago.edu/~r-tell/swlinks.
    html), 71
Society of Architectural Historians
    Web Site (http://www.
    upenn.edu/sah/aame/bioint.
    html), 149
Society of Architectural Historians
    Web Site (http://www.upenn.
    edu/sah/daah/daah1.html),
    150
Solstice (http://solstice.crest.org/),
    226
Space Telescope Science Institute
    (http://www.stsci.edu/

astroweb/astroweb-
    categories.html), 211
Spider, defined, 8
SPIRO (University of California
    Berkeley; http://www.mip.
    berkeley.edu/query_forms/
    browse_spiro_form.html),
    151
Sports sites, 187-190
    cream of the crop, 187-188
    media sites, 189
    networks, 189
    periodicals, 189
    professional organizations, 190
    recreation sites, 190
    sports indexes/links, 188-189
Sportsline USA (http://www.
    sportsline.com/), 188
Standard & Poors (http://www.
    stockinfo.standardpoor.
    com/idxinfo.htm), 81
State Web Pages on the Internet
    (Council of State
    Governments; http://www.
    csg.org/links/index.html),
    132
Starting Point™ Sports (http://www.
    stpt.com/cgi-bin/sports/
    sports.cgi), 188-189
Statistical Agencies on the Internet
    (International; http://www.
    census.gov/main/stat-int.
    html), 134
Statistical Agencies on the Internet
    (United States and non-
    United States; http://www.
    science.gmu.edu/csi779/
    drope/govstats.html), 134
Statistical Resources on the Web
    (http://www.lib.umich.edu/
    libhome/Documents.center/
    frames/statsfr.html), 129
Statistical web sites, 128-134
    collections of statistical sites, 129
    U.S. statistical data, 129-133

STAT-USA (http://www.stat-usa.
    gov), 87,94,131
Stock exchanges, 80-81
Stock indexes, 81
Stock quotes, 79
Stockmaster (http://www.
    stockmaster.com), 79
StreetEye search engine (http://
    streeteye.com), 7
Student Guide to Financial Aid, 56
Studies in Nonlinear Dynamics and
    Econometrics (http://
    mitpress.mit.edu/SNDE/
    WWW/journal/index.html),
    128
Subject directories, WWW-based,
    13-15
Summers, R., 134
SuperPages (http://yp.gte.net), 89
Sweet's Catalog File (http://www.
    sweets.com), 150
Switchboard (http://www.
    switchboard.com), 89

Tales of Wonder: Folk and Fairy
    Tales from Around the
    World (http://www.ece.
    ucdavis.edu/~darsie/tales.
    html), 158
Taxes, 82
Taxon Web Lift (http://www.ucmp.
    berkeley.edu/help/taxaform.
    html), 207
Teeter, T., 60-61
Telephone directories, 89-90
telnet://columbianet.columbia.edu,
    149
telnet://forsythetn.stanford.edu, 171
telnet://locis.loc.gov, 38,40
telnet://melvyl.ucop.edu, 149
telnet://victor.umd.edu, 151
Terrell, M.C., 102
The Abortion Rights Activist (http://
    www.cais.com/agm/main/
    index.html), 119-120

The All-Music Guide (http://205. 186.189.2/amg/music_root. html), 142

The Asian Community Online Network (ACON; http:// www.igc.apc.org/acon/), 102

The Atlanta Journal-Constitution, 23

The Boston Globe, 23

The Carols of Christmas (http:// www.osmond.net/chill/ christmas/carols.htm), 141

The Christian Science Monitor Archives (http://168.203. 8.8/plweb-cgi/iops1.pl), 117

The Christian Science Monitor Electronic Edition (http:// www.csmonitor.com), 117

The Corrections Connection (http:// www.corrections.com/index. html), 74

The Costume Page (http://members. aol.com/nebula5/costume. html), 144

The Digital Tradition Folk Song Database (http://www. deltablues.com/dbsearch. html), 141

The Eagle Forum (http://www.basenet. net/~eagle/eagle.html), 123

The Gregorian Chant Home Page (http://www.music.princeton. edu/chant_html/), 140-141

The Harry Fox Agency, Inc. (http:// www.nmpa.org/hfa.html), 142

The Internet Movie Database (http:// us.imdb.org), 184

The Internet Pilot to Physics (http:// www.tp.umu.se/TIPTOP/), 209

The Lendman Group (http://www. lendman.com/), 28

The Lied and Song Texts Page (http:// www.recmusic.org/lieder), 141

The Merck Manual of Diagnosis and Therapy (http://www.merck. com/!!rIkrg3k5NrIkrg3k5N/ pubs/ mmanual/), 219

The Music Publishers' Association (http://host.mpa.org/ *and* http://www.mpa.org/), 142

The New York Times, 23

The Nine Planets (http://seds.lpl. arizona.edu/nineplanets/ nineplanets/nineplanets. html), 211

The Old Farmer's Almanac (http:// www.almanac.com/index. html), 213

The Perseus Project (http://www. perseus.tufts.edu), 154

The Phyllis Schlafly Report, 123

The President (http://www. whitehouse.gov), 33-34

The Right Side of the Web (http:// www.clark.net/pub/jeffd/), 118

The Riley Guide (http://www. jobtrak.com/jobguide), 27

The Sports Network (http://www. sportsnetwork.com/), 188

The Ultimate Band List (http://www.ubl.com/), 142

The Ultimate Pro-Life Resource List (http://www.prolife.org/ ultimate/), 119-120

The Universal Black Pages (http:// www.ubp.com), 101-102

The Virtual Hospital (http://indy. radiology.uiowa.edu/ VirtualHospital.html), 221

The Virtual Library of Ecology, Biodiversity, and the Environment (http://conbio. rice.edu/vl/), 225

The Visible Human Project (http:// www.nlm.nih.gov/research/ visible/visible_human.html), 221-222

The Washington Post (http://www.
washingtonpost.com/), 117
The World Wide Web Virtual Library:
The Men's Issues Page
(http://info-sys.home.vix.
com/men), 107-108
Theater/drama sites, 145-146
Theatre Central (http://www.theatre-
central.com/), 145-146
Theatrical Terms (http://www.scsn.
net/users/ckeenan/dsunkle/
terms.html), 146
Thomas, R.B., 213
Thomas Register of American
Manufacturers, 6
Throop, D., 107
Tilenet (http://tile.net/lists/
history2.html), 174
Tile.Net Lists: Business (http://tile.
net/lists/business.html),
136
Time Life Gardening Library (http://
pathfinder.com/@@m52R*
PFR4gIAQCWD/vg/
TimeLife/), 201
TML: Thesaurus Musicarum
Latinarum (gopher://iubvm.
ucs.indiana.edu/11/tml),
140
Tokyo Stock Exchange (http://www.
tse.or.jp), 81
Top 5% (http://point.lycos.com/),
18
Top 10% Entertainmment Sites
(http://www.pebbs.com/
megabites/et.html), 186
Travel, international, sites for, 93-96
Treasury Bond Calculator (http://
www.ny.frb.org/pihome/
svg_bnds/sb_val.html),
82-83
Truth, S., 102
Tubman, H., 102
Turn Left: the Home of Liberalism
on the Web (http://www.

turnleft.com/liberal.html),
118-119
Turn Left–The Issues: Gun Issues
(http://www.turnleft.com/
issues.html#gun), 121
Turner, N., 102

UC Museum of Paleontology (http://
www.ucmp.berkeley.edu/),
207
UnCover database (http://www.carl.
org/uncover), 196
Unit of Measurement Converters
(http://www.eardc.swt.edu/
cgi-bin/ucon/ucon.pl *and*
http://www.mplik.ru/~sg/
transl/index.html), 202
United Nations (http://www.un.org/),
54
United States Federal Judiciary
(http://www.uscourts.gov/),
41
United States Geological Survey
(http://www.usgs.gov/),
206
United States History sites, 167-178
access to bibliographies, 171-172
archives and special collections,
170-171
biographical information,
175-177
directories, 174-175
finding book reviews, 172-173
gateways and guides to, 177-178
historical documents, 169-170
historical statistics, 173
listservs, 174
United States Patent and Trademark
Office (USPTO) Home
Page (http://www.uspto.
gov), 46
United States Statistical Data,
129-133
Universal Currency Converter (http://
www.xe.net/currency), 132

University(ies), hotlist directories on, 61

University of Arkansas at Little Rock College of Education ONLINE (http://www.ualr. edu/~coedept/index.html), 60-61

University of Colorado at Boulder (http://www.colorado.edu/ libraries/govpubs), 42

University of Idaho (http://drseuss. lib.uidaho.edu:80/govdoc/ otherdep.html), 42

University of Michigan (http://www. lib.umich.edu/libhome/ Documents.center/doclibs. html), 42

University of Michigan's Clearinghouse for Subject-Oriented Internet Resource Guides, Argus, 17

University pages, 2

U.S. Border Control (http://www. usbc.org/), 121

U.S. Business Advisor (http://www. business.gov), 91

U.S. Census Bureau (http://www. census.gov), 34

U.S. Census Bureau (http://www. census.gov/), 173

U.S. Copyright Office (http://lcweb. loc.gov/copyright/), 142

U.S. Department of Commerce, International Trade Administration NAFTA site (http://iepntl.itaiep.doc.gov/ nafta/nafta2.htm), 96

U.S. Department of Energy (http:// www.doe.gov/), 206

U.S. Department of Health and Human Services (HHS) (http://odphp2.osophs.dhhs. gov/consumer.htm), 70

U.S. Environmental Protection Agency (http://www.epa. gov/), 206,224

U.S. Gazetteer (http://www.census. gov/cgi-bin/gazetteer), 52

U.S. Government Printing Office (http://www.access.gpo.gov), 42

U.S. Patent Database, 46-47

U.S. Securities and Exchange Commission (http://www. sec.gov), 79

U.S. State Department Background Notes (http://www.state. gov/www/background_ notes/), 53

U.S. Treasury Department (http:// www.irs.ustreas.gov), 82

USA Today Sports Index (http:// www.usatoday.com/sports/ si.htm), 189

USDA Economics and Statistics (Cornell; http://usda. mannlib.cornell.edu/usda), 133

USDA Economics and Statistics System (http://usda. mannlib.cornell.edu/usda. html), 91

USDA Nutrient Database for Standard Reference, Release 11 (http://www.nal. usda.gov/fnic/foodcomp/ Data/SR11/), 198

USGS Geographic Names Information System (http:// www-nmd.usgs.gov/www/ gnis/), 52-53

VIBES (Virtual International Business and Economic Sources; http://www. uncc.edu/lis/library/ reference/intbus/vibehome. htm), 94

Victimization and crime, sites for, 74

Virtual government documents reference collection, 31-43

See also Government publications, virtual reference collection of
Voice of the Shuttle: Web Page for Humanities Research (http://humanitas.ucsb.edu/), 154
Vote Smart Web (http://www.vote-smart.org/), 116
Vote Smart Web (http://www.vote-smart.org/congress/congress.html#votes), 118

Walker, P., 92
Wall Street Research Net (http://www.wsrn.com), 78
Wanderer, defined, 8
WEATHER from CNN Interactive (http://www.cnn.com/WEATHER), 213
Weather sites, 212-213
WeatherNet (http://cirrus.sprl.umich.edu/wxnet/), 212
Web Finance (http://www.webfinance.net), 78
Web Investor's Dictionary (http://www.webinvestors.com), 78
Web Resources for Social Workers/ Colorado State University (http://www.colostate.edu/Depts/SocWork/webstuff.html), 71
Web Virtual Library: Architecture (http://www.clr.toronto.edu:1080/VIRTUALLIB/arch.html), 147-148
Webber, S., 94
WebPsych Partnership (http://www.cmhc.com/webpsych/), 66
Welcome to EnviroFacts (http://www.epa.gov/enviro/html/ef_home.html), 226
Welfare Reform and the General Welfare (http://libertynet.

org/~edcivic/welfref.html), 122-123
Welfare sites, 122-123
Westech Career Expo (http://www.careerexpo.com/pub/westech/), 28
Western European Specialists Section of the Association of College and Research Libraries (http://www.lib. virginia.edu/wess/index. html), 165
Women's issues sites, 123
Women's Studies Resources (http://www.aaln.org/vcl/electronics/etc/acad/womstud.html), 109
Women's studies sites, 108-109
WoPEc (http://netec.wustl.edu/~adnetec/WoPEc/WoPEc.html), 135
Working paper sites, 135-136
World Factbook, CIA (http://www.odci.gov/cia/publications/95fact/index.html), 53
World history sites, 161-166
    area studies, 164-165
    facts and figures, 163-164
    primary sources, 162-163
    starting points, 165-166
World History to 1500 (http://www.byuh.edu/coursework/hist201/), 166
World Lecture Hall (http://www.utexas.edu/world/lecture/index.html), 61, 200
World Wide Web (WWW), advertising revenue for, 6
World Wide Web (WWW) search tools. *See also specific type, e.g.,* AltaVista (http://www.altavista.com), 9-10,11f
    advertising sold by, 6
    characteristics of, 6-7
    comparisons of, 9-13, 11f
    consumer market served by, 6-7
    metasearch engines, 15-17

in reference services, 5-19
review/rating services, 17-18
search engines/robot-generated
    databases, 8-9
service changes in, 7
subject directories, 13-15
technological advances in, 7
types of, 7-9
    indexers, 8
    interface, 8-9
    robots, 8
World Wide Web Virtual Library
    Project (http://www.w3.
    org/pub/DataSources/
    bySubject/Overview. html),
    192
Worldclass Supersite (http://web.
    idirect.com/~tiger/supersit.
    htm), 86
Worldwide Books Online (http://
    www.worldwide.com),
    149-150
World-Wide Economics Departments,
    Faculties and Centres (non-
    United States; http://castle.
    uvic.ca/econ/depts.html),
    136
Wright, F.L., 149
World Economic Window (http://
    nmg.clever.net/wew/), 134
World Wide Web of Sports (http://
    www.tns.lcs.mit.edu/cgi-
    bin/sports), 188
WWW. *See* World Wide Web
WWW Virtual Library:
    Biotechnology, General/
    Products and Services
    (http://www.cato.com/
    interweb/cato/biotech/bio-
    prod.html), 194-195
WWW Virtual Library
    (Agriculture)–Associations
    and Organizations (http://
    ipm_www.ncsu.edu/cernag
    /associations.html), 195

WWW Virtual Library Electronic
    Journals List: Academic
    and Reviewed Journals
    (http://www.edoc.com/
    ejournal/), 195
WWW Virtual Library Environment
    (http://ecosys.drdr.virginia.
    edu/Environment.html),
    225
WWW Virtual Library on Gardening
    (http://www.gardenweb.
    com/vl/), 201
WWW Virtual Library–Agriculture
    (http://ipm_www.ncsu.edu/
    cernag/), 198
WWW Women's Sports Page (http://
    fiat.gslis.utexas.edu/~lewisa/
    womsprt.html), 188
WWW-pages of History Departments
    (http://grid.let.rug.nl/ahc/
    history.html), 174
WWW-VL Biosciences (http://golgi.
    harvard.edu/biopages.html),
    192

Yahoo!, 2
Yahoo! (http://www.yahoo.com),
    14-15,193
Yahoo!: Authors (http://www.yahoo.
    com/Arts/Humanities/
    Literature/Authors/), 157
Yahoo!: Government: Politics:
    Political Issues: Welfare
    Reform (http://www.yahoo.
    com/text/Government/
    Politics/Political_Issues/
    Welfare_Reform/), 123
Yahoo!: Mythology and Folklore
    (http://www.yahoo.com/
    Society_and_Culture/
    Mythology_and_Folklore/),
    158
Yahoo!: Poetry
    (http://www.yahoo.com/
    Arts/Humanities/Literature/

Genres/Poetry/), 157
Yahoo!: Society and Culture:
    Affirmative Action (http://
    www.yahoo.com/text/
    Society_and_Culture/
    Affirmative_Action/), 120
Yahoo! business site (http://biz.
    yahoo.com), 86
Yahoo Maps (http://www.yahoo.
    com/Science/Geography/
    Maps/), 52
Yahoo! recreation (http://www. yahoo.
    com/Recreation/), 190
Yahoo! Scoreboard (http://sports.
    yahoo.com/), 189
Yahoo! Searching the Web page of,
    search engines available
    through, 8
YAHOO! Social Work (http://www.
    yahoo.com/Social_Science/
    Social_Work/), 71
Yahoo! Society and Culture
    Environment and Nature
    directory (http://www.
    yahoo.com/society_and_
    culture/environment_and_
    nature/index.html), 226
Yahoo! Top: Entertainment: People
    (http://yahoo.com/
    Entertainment/People/), 182
Yahoo!: Politics (http://www.yahoo.
    com/Politics/), 113
YAHOO's! Poverty (http://www.
    yahoo.com/Society_and_
    Culture/Poverty/), 74
YAHOO's! Welfare Reform (http://
    www.yahoo.com/
    Government/Politics/
    Political_Issues/Welfare_
    Reform/), 74
Yamada Language Center (http://
    babel.uoregon.edu/yamada/
    guides.html), 156
Yanoff's List Environment (http://
    www.spectracom.com/islist/
index.html#
    ENVIRONMENT), 225
Yanoff's List Sports (http://www.
    spectracom.com/islist/
    inet3.html# SPORTS), 189
YellowNet (http://www.
    yellownet.com), 89
York, G., 129
Youth Indicators, 56

Zagat Dine (http://pathfinder.com/
    @@urxB8AUAUYa3cubH/
    travel/Zagat/Dine), 186

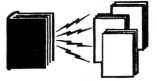

Haworth
DOCUMENT DELIVERY
SERVICE

This valuable service provides a single-article order form for any article from a Haworth journal.

- *Time Saving:* No running around from library to library to find a specific article.
- *Cost Effective:* All costs are kept down to a minimum.
- *Fast Delivery:* Choose from several options, including same-day FAX.
- *No Copyright Hassles:* You will be supplied by the original publisher.
- *Easy Payment:* Choose from several easy payment methods.

Open Accounts Welcome for ...
- Library Interlibrary Loan Departments
- Library Network/Consortia Wishing to Provide Single-Article Services
- Indexing/Abstracting Services with Single Article Provision Services
- Document Provision Brokers and Freelance Information Service Providers

---

MAIL or *FAX* THIS ENTIRE ORDER FORM TO:

Haworth Document Delivery Service
The Haworth Press, Inc.
10 Alice Street
Binghamton, NY 13904-1580

or **FAX:** 1-800-895-0582
or **CALL:** 1-800-342-9678
9am-5pm EST

PLEASE SEND ME PHOTOCOPIES OF THE FOLLOWING SINGLE ARTICLES:

1) Journal Title: _____
   Vol/Issue/Year: _____ Starting & Ending Pages: _____
   Article Title: _____

2) Journal Title: _____
   Vol/Issue/Year: _____ Starting & Ending Pages: _____
   Article Title: _____

3) Journal Title: _____
   Vol/Issue/Year: _____ Starting & Ending Pages: _____
   Article Title: _____

4) Journal Title: _____
   Vol/Issue/Year: _____ Starting & Ending Pages: _____
   Article Title: _____

(See other side for Costs and Payment Information)

COSTS: Please figure your cost to order quality copies of an article.

1. Set-up charge per article: $8.00
   ($8.00 × number of separate articles) _____

2. Photocopying charge for each article:
   1-10 pages: $1.00 _____

   11-19 pages: $3.00 _____

   20-29 pages: $5.00 _____

   30+ pages: $2.00/10 pages _____

3. Flexicover (optional): $2.00/article _____
4. Postage & Handling: US: $1.00 for the first article/
   $.50 each additional article _____

   Federal Express: $25.00 _____

   Outside US: $2.00 for first article/
   $.50 each additional article_____

5. Same-day FAX service: $.35 per page _____

GRAND TOTAL: _____

METHOD OF PAYMENT: (please check one)

❑ Check enclosed ❑ Please ship and bill. PO # _____
(sorry we can ship and bill to bookstores only! All others must pre-pay)

❑ Charge to my credit card: ❑ Visa; ❑ MasterCard; ❑ Discover;
❑ American Express;

Account Number:_____ Expiration date:_____

Signature: *X*_____

Name: _____ Institution: _____

Address: _____

_____

City: _____ State:_____ Zip:_____

Phone Number: _____ FAX Number: _____

MAIL or *FAX* THIS ENTIRE ORDER FORM TO:

Haworth Document Delivery Service	**or FAX:** 1-800-895-0582
The Haworth Press, Inc.	**or CALL:** 1-800-342-9678
10 Alice Street	9am-5pm EST)
Binghamton, NY 13904-1580	